M000250931

Top 50 Science Skills

for GED

SUCCESS

 McGraw Hill **Wright Group**

ROBERT MITCHELL

Photo credits: 10 © James L. Amos/CORBIS; **31** © 2003–2006 ShutterStock, Inc.; **67** © Albany Herald/CORBIS SYGMA; **73** © CORBIS; **106** © gettyimages; **158** courtesy of NASA; **158** © Bettmann/CORBIS

Executive Editor: Linda Kwil
Cover Design: Tracey Harris-Sainz
Interior Design: Linda Chandler

ISBN: 0-07-704475-4
ISBN: 0-07-704476-2 (with CD-ROM)

© 2007 by The McGraw-Hill Companies, Inc. All rights reserved. No part of this book may be reproduced, stored in a retrieval system, or transmitted in any form or by any means, electronic, mechanical, photocopying, recording, or otherwise, without prior permission of the publisher.

Send all inquiries to:
Wright Group/McGraw-Hill
130 E. Randolph Street, Suite 400
Chicago, IL 60601

9 HSO 13

Table of Contents

How to Use This Book

Test Overview

The GED Science Test contains 50 questions. Tested subjects are life science, physical sciences (physics and chemistry), earth science, and space science. The test questions measure your ability to apply critical thinking skills in each science subject. Many questions integrate science with the roles that individuals play in society: worker, consumer, family member, and citizen.

The breakdown of test questions is as follows:
Life science   45%
Physical science   35%
Earth and space science   20%

As much as 60 percent of the questions are presented with, and may be based on, visual text—graphs, tables, charts, and diagrams. The remaining questions are based on text passages—single questions standing alone, single questions based on one or more short paragraphs, or several questions that are each based on the same passage.

About *Top 50 Science Skills for GED Success*

Top 50 Science Skills for GED Success is a short, test-directed course in GED science preparation. The 50 skills chosen are those most representative of the type and difficulty level of skills tested on the GED Science Test. Each question in the Pretest addresses a particular skill. Guided instruction and follow-up questions for each skill are provided in the instruction section, pages 22–121.

Top 50 Science Skills for GED Success is divided into four main sections:

- *Pretest*—50 questions that check your understanding of core cognitive and contextual skills addressed on the GED Science Test. These skills are chosen from subject areas identified by the GED Testing Service.

- *Top 50 Skills Instruction*—Instruction and follow-up practice on the 50 skills most likely to be addressed on the GED Science Test. Additional practice questions increase your understanding and extend your knowledge.

- *Foundations in Science*—A review of the basic facts of science upon which modern science rests. Students new to the study of science, or students needing to review basic science facts, should begin this book by reviewing the Foundations of Science section, pages 140–159.

- *GED Posttest*—A model GED Posttest to check your readiness for the GED Test. Use the model to practice taking a GED test under test-like conditions.

Top 50 Science Skills for GED Success is designed to be both student- and instructor-friendly, organizing for you in 50 lessons a core of science skills identified by the GED Testing Service. Each two-page skill lesson addresses a single skill and provides follow-up practice. One or more lessons can be completed in a single study period.

Top 50 Science Skills for GED Success can be used in a variety of ways:

- student-directed self study
- one-on-one instruction
- group instruction

About the Pretest

This Pretest is an overview of 50 skills you are most likely to see addressed on the GED Science Test. The GED Test is based on the National Science Education Standards of the National Academy of Sciences. Questions come from the following themes of scientific inquiry:

- Unifying concepts and processes
- Science as inquiry
- Science and technology
- Science in personal and social perspectives
- History and nature of science

Within these themes of inquiry, the following traditional subject areas of science are covered:

- Life science
- Chemistry
- Physics
- Earth science
- Space science

For the actual GED Science Test, you will have 80 minutes to read the passages, graphs, and diagrams and answer 50 questions. However, this is not a timed test. In fact, you should take as much time as you need to answer each question. This Pretest is designed to help you identify specific skills and areas of scientific understanding in which you need more practice.

Answer every question on this Pretest. If you are not sure of an answer, eliminate the obviously wrong answers and choose the most likely choice. Then put a question mark by the item number to note that you are guessing. You may return to this question later if you wish. On the actual GED Test, an unanswered question is counted as incorrect, so making a good guess is an important skill to develop.

When you are finished, turn to the Answer Key on page 160 to check your answers. Then use the Pretest Evaluation Chart on pages 20–21 to figure out which skills to focus on in the instruction section of the book (pages 22–121).

After working through the instruction section, take the Posttest on pages 124–137. Your success on the Posttest will indicate your readiness to take the actual GED Science Test.

Pretest

Question 1 is based on the following passage.

(1) Imagine taking a microscope and looking at the edge of a piece of paper. (2) Using the world's most powerful microscope, you still could not see one atom. (3) Suppose, though, you could see them and count them. (4) You would find that it would take about one million atoms, placed side by side, to cross a distance equal to the thickness of a piece of paper. (5) Atoms are so small that, for most experiments, scientists must be content with studying very large numbers of them at the same time.

1 Which sentence is the best summary of the passage above?

(1) sentence 1
(2) sentence 2
(3) sentence 3
(4) sentence 4
(5) sentence 5

Question 2 refers to the following passage.

A robot is a great invention. Robots don't take breaks, and they don't get sick. They don't require a lunchroom or a smoking area. You don't need to give them health-care benefits. What's more, each robot can do the work of several employees, and the robot won't complain about working 24 hours each day.

2 What can you infer to be the author's attitude about robots?

(1) suspicious
(2) uncertain
(3) bored
(4) supportive
(5) frightened

Question 3 is based on the following passage.

A general principle about charged particles is the following: Like charges repel each other; unlike charges attract each other.

 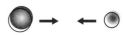

Like charges repel.   Unlike charges attract.

3 Suppose two identical negatively charged spheres are suspended by strings from support stands. Which drawing below illustrates how the charged spheres will react when the stands are moved close together?

①

②

③

④

⑤

Questions 4 and 5 are based on the following passage.

When a squirrel hibernates, its bodily functions slow down. At the same time, the blood flow to the squirrel's brain almost ceases—a condition that leads immediately to a stroke in humans. Without a continual supply of blood, human brain cells break down and die. This condition can lead to disability or even death. The question is, why don't the brain cells of squirrels die during hibernation?

A clue may be found in the human brain, where a lack of blood causes brain cells to lose potassium and to gain calcium. Cells affected in this way die. By studying changes in potassium and calcium levels in a hibernating squirrel's brain, scientists hope to discover what protects the squirrel. The answer may someday enable doctors to help prevent strokes in some patients and to help stroke victims recover more fully.

❹ Which hypothesis is most likely correct and is best supported by information in the passage?

① During hibernation, squirrels do not suffer strokes because they are able to quickly replace dead brain cells.
② During hibernation, a squirrel's brain safely regulates its cells' levels of potassium and calcium.
③ During hibernation, a squirrel's brain cells break down but the squirrel is not harmed.
④ The brain cells of a squirrel do not contain potassium or calcium.
⑤ Any dead brain cell can be brought back to life with an injection of potassium.

❺ According to the passage, which of the following can cause a stroke in humans?

① a restricted blood flow to the brain
② a diet overly rich in calcium
③ sleeping more than eight hours each day
④ permanent disability or death
⑤ a diet that does not contain potassium

Questions 6 are 7 based on the following passage and illustration.

A container is divided into two parts by a semi-permeable membrane—a barrier that some molecules can pass through but others cannot. Pure water is placed on the left side of the membrane. An equal level of liquid food coloring is placed on the right side.

The experiment demonstrates osmosis—the movement of molecules across a semi-permeable membrane from a region of higher concentration to one of lower concentration.

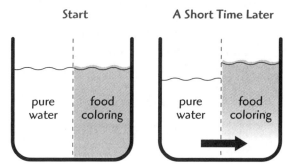

❻ What is an unstated assumption that must be true if the experiment is to show results?

① Neither water nor food-coloring molecules are able to pass through the membrane.
② Either water or food-coloring molecules, or both, can pass through the membrane.
③ Water is denser than food coloring.
④ Water is less dense than food coloring.
⑤ The water and the food coloring are at the same temperature.

❼ What is a reasonable conclusion that can be drawn from the results of this experiment?

① Molecules of water are closer together than molecules of food coloring.
② Molecules of water cannot easily, if at all, pass through the membrane.
③ Molecules of food coloring cannot easily, if at all, pass through the membrane.
④ Molecules of food coloring can easily pass through the membrane.
⑤ Molecules of food coloring do not attempt to pass through the membrane.

Question 8 is based on the following passage.

Competition for food often determines where an animal can live in an ecosystem. When two different species of animals have the same sources of food, each species may have to find its own region in the ecosystem where it has sole access to its particular food supply.

8 Which information is most important to know in order to decide whether owls and hawks can easily live side by side in the same part of an ecosystem?

  ① whether owls and hawks use the same hunting methods
  ② whether owls and hawks eat the same amount of food each day
  ③ whether owls and hawks have the same life span
  ④ whether owls and hawks hunt the same prey
  ⑤ whether owls and hawks feed at the same time of day

Question 9 is based on the passage below.

Between the time of the famous Greek philosopher Aristotle (384–322 B.C.) and the period in history known as the Renaissance (the fifteenth, sixteenth, and seventeenth centuries), very little progress was made in scientific understanding. This changed during the Renaissance with the discoveries that Earth was not flat and was not the center of the universe. In fact, Earth was realized to be an object possibly similar to other objects in the night sky. Many of the discoveries during this time period were rejected by political leaders because the discoveries disagreed with church teachings.

9 What values did discoveries during the Renaissance bring into conflict with science?

  ① economic values
  ② health values
  ③ family values
  ④ religious values
  ⑤ occupational values

Question 10 refers to the following passage and illustration.

The earliest known writings about levers were provided by Archimedes (287–212 B.C.), a Greek mathematician. Archimedes said, "Give me the place to stand, and I shall move the Earth!"

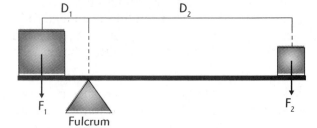

The principle of the lever says that in the balanced lever above: $F_1 \times D_1 = F_2 \times D_2$.

The product of the distance times the force on the left side of the fulcrum is equal to the product of the distance times the force on the right side of the fulcrum.

10 In the lever pictured above, suppose weight F_1 is 50 pounds and weight F_2 is 10 pounds. If distance D_1 is 10 inches, what is distance D_2?

  ① 20 inches
  ② 35 inches
  ③ 50 inches
  ④ 75 inches
  ⑤ 100 inches

Question 11 is based on the following diagram and passage.

THE T4 PHAGE VIRUS

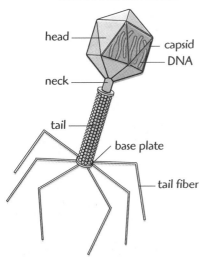

A virus is an infectious agent that can be found in all living things. A virus is not a cell, does not have the properties of a cell, and cannot live if left on its own. A virus exists only inside a living cell. A virus does not have a nucleus or a cell membrane. It consists only of genetic material surrounded by a protective coating of protein. Viruses tend to be very small, ranging from 0.05 to 0.1 microns. This is 20,000 to 100,000 times smaller than a millimeter.

A virus reproduces itself by invading a living cell. The virus then takes control of the cell and uses it to produce more of the virus. In the process, the normal cell may be destroyed. Some diseases caused by viruses are the common cold, chicken pox, mumps, measles, hoof-and-mouth disease (in livestock), some types of cancers, and AIDS.

⓫ For what reason does a virus invade a cell?

  ① to destroy the cell
  ② to become part of the cell
  ③ to absorb energy
  ④ to change into a cell
  ⑤ to reproduce

Question 12 is based on the following diagram.

HOW PARENTS PASS ON SICKLE-CELL ANEMIA

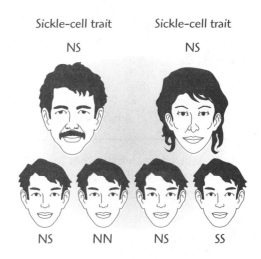

NS = sickle-cell trait
NN = normal blood
SS = sickle-cell disease

⓬ The diagram shows the gene combinations of a child who could be born to parents who each have the sickle-cell trait *(NS)*. Each parent has one normal blood gene *N* and one sickle-cell gene *S*. Any child of this couple will randomly inherit one gene from each parent.

What is the chance that a child of this couple will have an *SS* gene combination, thus suffering from the disease of sickle-cell anemia?

  ① 0 percent (no chance)
  ② 25 percent (one chance in four)
  ③ 50 percent (two chances in four)
  ④ 75 percent (three chances in four)
  ⑤ 100 percent (certain)

Question 13 is based on the following drawing.

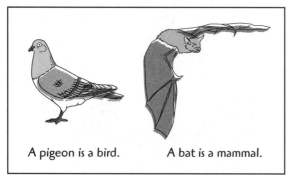

A pigeon is a bird.   A bat is a mammal.

13 What is the main characteristic that leads to the classification of one of the animals above as a bird and one as a mammal?

① method of movement
② number of limbs
③ size of newborn
④ number of offspring
⑤ method of birth

Question 14 is based on the following passage.

Convergent evolution occurs when unrelated organisms evolve similar traits or structures. An example of convergent evolution is the development of wings on unrelated species. Bees (an insect), hawks (a bird), and bats (a mammal) all have wings. All three types of wings are used for flying, but each animal evolved independently and the three animals are not related.

14 Which of the following is an example of convergent evolution?

① the tail of a dog and the tail of a cow
② the arms of a human and the arms of an ape
③ the legs of a spider and the legs of a cow
④ the horns of a cow and the horns of a goat
⑤ the tail of a shark and the tail glands of a catfish

Question 15 is based on the following drawing.

BEAK STRUCTURES OF NORTH AMERICAN BIRDS

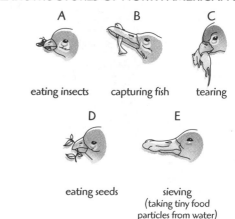

A   B   C
eating insects   capturing fish   tearing

D   E
eating seeds   sieving
(taking tiny food particles from water)

15 Which drawing shows the beak structure found on birds that are *least* dependent on keen eyesight for food gathering?

① A
② B
③ C
④ D
⑤ E

Question 16 is based on the following passage.

In a learning-theory experiment, one group of octopuses was trained to attack a red ball. A second group was trained to attack a white ball. Meanwhile, two groups of untrained octopuses watched: one group watched the red-ball tank; the other group watched the white-ball tank.

Later, both red and white balls were placed in the tanks with the untrained octopuses. A surprising thing was observed: each untrained octopus attacked only the color ball that was attacked by the group it had watched.

Although octopuses have the largest brain of any invertebrate, this result astounded many scientists. This social-learning skill had been considered to be far beyond the ability of an octopus.

16 In hearing about this experiment, one scientist said the following:

> The learning ability of an octopus very likely arose from its need to learn from other octopuses at an early age, because the parents of an octopus die soon after its birth.

How is this scientist's statement best classified?

① a proposed experiment
② an experimental finding
③ a hypothesis
④ a prediction
⑤ a scientific fact

Question 17 is based on the following graph.

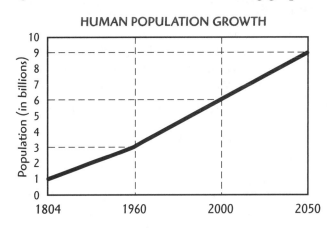

17 How is the world's population estimated to change between 1960 and 2050?

① It will stay about the same.
② It will increase by half.
③ It will double.
④ It will triple.
⑤ It will quadruple.

Question 18 is based on the following passage.

Products that can be recycled include glass, paper products, aluminum cans, plastic containers, car oil, and various metals. Many cities have recycling services for their residents, and recycled products are picked up in front of residential homes.

18 What is the main purpose of recycling?

① to eliminate the need for garbage service
② to convert waste into reusable products
③ to save money on the purchase of new products
④ to create jobs for the unemployed
⑤ to convert usable products into trash that is nonpolluting

Question 19 is based on the following passage and graph.

In a predator-prey relationship, one animal (a predator) kills and eats another animal (the prey). In every ecosystem, the population of each predator and prey varies in a cyclical way.

HAWK AND MICE POPULATIONS

19 At time t_1, the mice population is about to start decreasing. What is the most likely cause for this decrease?

(1) The growing hawk population is increasingly killing more mice.
(2) The hawk population has contracted a disease and is dying off.
(3) The ecosystem has become polluted and both populations are in decline.
(4) Mice food sources are decreasing.
(5) The decreasing hawk population is killing fewer mice.

Question 20 is based on the following passage.

The Gaia hypothesis, proposed in the 1970s by British scientist James Lovelock, proposes that Earth behaves as a single living organism. According to this theory, Earth regulates its own temperature, provides itself with resources needed for life, disposes of its own wastes, and fights off disease.

20 According to the Gaia hypothesis, which of the following would most likely bring greatest long-term harm to Earth?

(1) lightning-caused forest fires
(2) severe earthquakes along fault lines
(3) collision with a large asteroid
(4) volcanic eruptions
(5) a naturally occurring ice age

Question 21 is based on the following passage.

Cholesterol is a wax-like substance found in human blood. In small amounts, cholesterol is important to good health. The human body uses it to help produce hormones and bile acids that aid in digestion. However, excess cholesterol can cause clogging of blood arteries, a condition that can interfere with proper blood flow and may lead to death.

Humans increase their cholesterol level in two ways: eating foods rich in cholesterol and eating foods that contain saturated fats—foods such as fatty beef, pork, and chicken. Cholesterol is not found in plant products.

To lower cholesterol level, doctors recommend a diet rich in fruits, vegetables, and grain products. In general, a healthier diet is achieved by reducing consumption of fatty red meat and increasing consumption of other protein sources such as fish and beans.

21 Which of the following can you infer to be true from information given in the passage?

(1) Even a small amount of cholesterol in the human body is unhealthy.
(2) Excess cholesterol in the human body can lead to heart disease.
(3) Plants that have a high oil content, such as olives, contain cholesterol.
(4) Family medical history is very much related to an individual's cholesterol level.
(5) Cholesterol problems occur only in humans and not in other animals.

Question 22 is based on the following passage.

AIDS (Acquired Immune Deficiency Syndrome) is a disease of the body's immune system—the system that enables the body to destroy germs that cause infections and diseases.

The first symptoms of AIDS may be weight loss, swollen lymph nodes, body weakness, persistent cough, and chronic yeast infections of the mouth or genital areas. Other symptoms may include pneumonia or types of cancer.

AIDS is caused by a virus known as HIV, the Human Immunodeficiency Virus. Once infected with HIV, a person may feel fine and show no symptoms of AIDS for years. Even though an HIV-infected person looks healthy, he or she is infectious and can spread the virus to other people. The HIV virus spreads from the blood or sexual fluids of an infected person to the blood of the uninfected.

AIDS is usually spread in one of three ways:

- by having unprotected sex with an infected person
- by sharing a hypodermic needle with an infected drug user
- from an infected mother to the fetus during pregnancy, or to the baby during delivery or breast-feeding

22 Which of the following is the *least* helpful way that an individual can help in the fight against AIDS?

1. Avoid contact with needles used by infected drug users.
2. Tell children about AIDS after they reach the age of sixteen.
3. Engage only in safe sex with carefully chosen partners.
4. Inform any at-risk friends about the dangers of AIDS.
5. Support community groups dedicated to help stopping the spread of AIDS.

23 What potential natural disaster can be triggered by an earthquake that occurs on the ocean bottom?

1. volcano
2. hurricane
3. global warming
4. tsunami
5. forest fire

Question 24 is based on the following passage.

Three Mile Island in Pennsylvania is the location of a nuclear power plant that on March 28, 1979, had a partial core meltdown—the overheating and melting of the core of a nuclear reactor. The accident occurred over a five-day period, with government officials frantically trying to decide whether a complete evacuation of nearby communities was called for. The fear was that radioactive gas would escape into the air and that radioactive waste might find its way to groundwater.

Luckily, the reactor was finally brought under control, and although no injuries or deaths were reported, the dangers of nuclear power plants remain foremost in many people's minds.

24 Which of the following was most likely true when nuclear power was first developed?

1. Scientists believed that nuclear power plants were safe and that disasters such as a core meltdown could be prevented.
2. Scientists believed that the public would never discover the dangers posed by radioactive waste.
3. Scientists did not know that a core meltdown in a nuclear power plant was even possible.
4. Scientists did not know that nuclear power plants would create radioactive waste.
5. Scientists did not know that radioactive waste was terribly toxic to humans.

Question 25 is based on the following drawing.

25. What do many people find offensive or, at least, uncomfortable about the drawings above?

① the implication that humans are inferior to a lower species similar to apes
② the implication that humans and apes have the same level of intelligence
③ the implication that humans evolved from a lower species
④ the implication that apes evolved from humans
⑤ the implication that humans and apes are the same species

Question 26 is based on the following photograph.

26. What name is given to the object shown above?

① species
② fossil
③ mutation
④ organism
⑤ population

Questions 27 and 28 are based on the following drawing and passage.

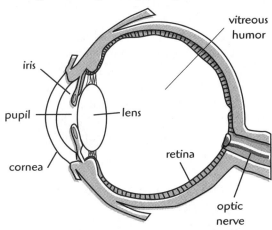

A cataract is a medical condition in which the lens of the eye becomes cloudy, resulting in very blurred and cloudy vision. (The lens focuses light on the retina and provides a sharp image.) Cataracts can result from diseases such as diabetes, can occur as a result of eye injury, and often occur in older people.

As far back as Roman times in the first few centuries, a type of cataract surgery called couching was performed. The intent of this surgery was to push the lens down out of the way and out of alignment with the pupil.

Today the most effective treatment for cataracts is to remove the eye lens and replace it with a plastic lens which remains permanently in the eye. Modern cataract surgery is relatively simple, pain free, and quick. Patients are able to go home soon after surgery.

27 What is the modern treatment for cataracts?

   ① lens repair
   ② removal of the eye
   ③ removal of pupil
   ④ removal of cloudy substances
   ⑤ lens replacement

28 In the couching procedure performed in ancient times, what was most likely the best result that could be hoped for?

   ① perfect vision
   ② balanced vision in both eyes
   ③ a better image from improved focusing
   ④ non-cloudy vision, but poorer focusing
   ⑤ improved focusing, but very cloudy vision

Question 29 is based on the following passage and bar graph.

Density is defined as the amount of matter per unit of volume. If two substances have the same volume, the substance with the higher density has more matter and is heavier. The graph below shows the density in grams per cubic centimeter of water and of ice.

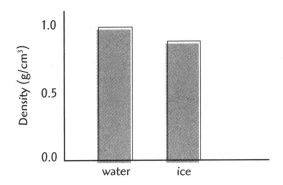

DENSITY OF WATER AND ICE

29 Which of the following statements can you infer to be true?

   ① On average, H_2O molecules are the same distance apart in water and in ice.
   ② On average, H_2O molecules are farther apart in water than in ice.
   ③ On average, H_2O molecules are farther apart in ice than in water.
   ④ On average, H_2O molecules are closer together in water vapor than in water.
   ⑤ On average, H_2O molecules are closer together in water vapor than in ice.

Questions 30, 31, and 32 are based on the following passage and illustration.

The proper balance of carbon dioxide and oxygen gases in the atmosphere is needed for life to be possible on Earth. The carbon-oxygen cycle relies on two processes: respiration and photosynthesis.

Respiration is the scientific word for breathing—the process in which animals inhale oxygen from the atmosphere and exhale carbon dioxide to the atmosphere. During respiration, cells in an animal use oxygen to break down sugar to release energy. Carbon dioxide gas is a byproduct.

Photosynthesis is the process in which plants take in carbon dioxide from the atmosphere. During photosynthesis, plant cells using sunlight as an energy source combine carbon dioxide gas and water to produce sugar. Oxygen gas is given off as a byproduct.

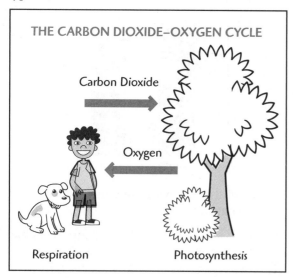

THE CARBON DIOXIDE–OXYGEN CYCLE

Carbon Dioxide

Oxygen

Respiration   Photosynthesis

30 Which of the following is a hypothesis?

① The observed increase in atmospheric carbon dioxide may be directly related to the destruction of tropical rain forests.
② An animal uses more oxygen while exercising than while at rest.
③ Plants produce sugar which is used as a source of energy in animals.
④ Photosynthesis takes place only in plants.
⑤ Carbon dioxide gas is a natural byproduct of breathing.

31 Which kind of change occurs in the process of photosynthesis?

① physical change because energy is absorbed during the reaction
② physical change because new substances are formed
③ chemical change because energy is absorbed during the reaction
④ chemical change because new substances are formed
⑤ neither chemical nor physical change

32 What are the sources of energy that enable respiration and photosynthesis to take place?

① The source of energy for respiration is sunlight; the source of energy for photosynthesis is chemical energy from food.
② The source of energy for respiration is chemical energy from food; the source of energy for photosynthesis is sunlight.
③ The source of energy for both respiration and photosynthesis is sunlight.
④ The source of energy for respiration is carbon dioxide gas; the source of energy for photosynthesis is carbon dioxide gas.
⑤ The source of energy for respiration is oxygen gas; the source of energy for photosynthesis is carbon dioxide gas.

Question 33 is based on the following passage.

The bubbly effect of a carbonated beverage occurs because of the presence of carbon dioxide gas dissolved in water, along with flavor additives and sweeteners.

Suppose an open bottle of carbonated cola sits in a refrigerator for two hours. During this same time, a second open bottle of carbonated soda sits on a countertop at room temperature. After the two hours, the warm cola tastes flat, but the cold soda still has a bubbly taste.

33 Which of the following best explains the difference in taste of the two bottles?

1. Changing the temperature does not affect the amount of carbon dioxide gas that a liquid can hold.
2. The warm cola was exposed to fresh air, but the cold cola was not.
3. Dissolved carbon dioxide gas escapes more quickly from a bottle of cola when it is shaken than when it is warmed.
4. Lowering the temperature decreases the amount of carbon dioxide gas that a liquid can hold.
5. Raising the temperature decreases the amount of carbon dioxide gas that a liquid can hold.

34 What element in a meteorite found on Earth would be the best clue that life may also exist, or has previously existed, on another planet besides Earth?

1. gold
2. helium
3. carbon
4. copper
5. silicon

Questions 35 and 36 are based on the following passage.

Mercury is the most common of only four metals that are liquid at room temperature. Today, mercury is used mostly in the production of industrial chemicals or in certain electronic applications. In previous decades mercury was commonly used in thermometers and in dental fillings. Because mercury was discovered to be toxic to human health, its use in thermometers and dental work has been stopped.

In humans, mercury attacks the central nervous system and the endocrine system. High exposure over long periods of time may result in brain damage and ultimately death. Mercury can also be a major health risk to an unborn fetus. Because of this danger, pregnant women are advised to avoid any contact with chemicals containing mercury.

During the nineteenth century, felt hatmakers rubbed mercury on the felt of hats to improve their luster. Unfortunately, many hatters suffered from mercury poisoning, and many ended up with severe brain damage. The phrase "mad as a hatter" is thought to relate to this condition of early hatters.

35 What is the best company policy regarding women in the workplace?

1. Pregnant women should not be allowed to work around dangerous chemicals.
2. Pregnant women should be warned about the risks of dangerous chemicals.
3. Pregnant women should be given unpaid leave during their pregnancies.
4. Women should not be allowed to work in companies that use chemicals.
5. No special company policy should be enacted regarding pregnant women.

36 What is the most likely origin of the phrase "mad as a hatter"?

1. a character in Alice in Wonderland
2. a type of hat worn in the nineteenth century
3. felt hunters of the nineteenth century
4. nineteenth century felt hatmakers
5. the effect that mercury has on felt

Question 37 refers to the following passage and illustration.

A general principle in physics is that a force is required to keep an object moving in a circle. The force that keeps that object in its circular path is called centripetal force. For example, a ball whirled at the end of a string experiences a centripetal force provided by the string. The person whirling the ball feels this force as a pulling force by the string on his or her hand. Notice that the centripetal force felt by the moving object is always an inward force, directed toward the center of the circle around which the object is moving.

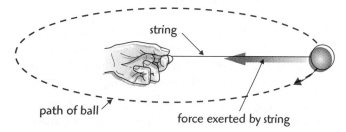

Centripetal force exerted by the string keeps the ball moving in a circular path.

37 Which of the following is the best example of centripetal force?

① a baseball thrown by a pitcher
② an airplane flying at 34,000 feet
③ the force of friction felt by a car
④ a skydiver at terminal velocity
⑤ the Moon orbiting Earth

38 What is the source of energy that keeps a whirling ball moving in a circle?

① Earth's gravitational field
② the air through which the ball moves
③ the string connecting the ball with the person doing the whirling
④ the person doing the whirling
⑤ the movement of the ball

Questions 39 and 40 refer to the following passage, illustration, and graph.

A block slides without friction down a slick ramp. The graph shows the values of both the gravitational potential energy (potential energy that depends only on the height of the block above the ground) and the kinetic energy (energy of motion) as it slides.

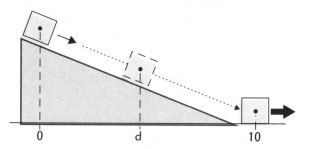

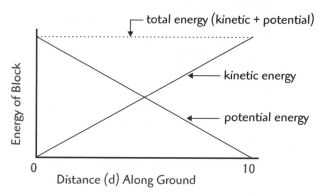

39 Which statement about the block is true?

① On the graph at the point where $d=10$, exactly half of the block's energy is kinetic energy.
② On the graph at the point where $d=0$, the block's energy is all potential energy.
③ Only half of the block's original potential energy is changed to kinetic energy.
④ On the graph at the point where $d=0$, the block's energy is all kinetic energy.
⑤ The maximum value of the block's kinetic energy is greater than the maximum value of the block's potential energy.

40 What remains constant as the block moves down the ramp?

　① the height of the block above the ground
　② the total kinetic energy of the block
　③ the total potential energy of the block
　④ the sum of the block's potential energy and kinetic energy
　⑤ the difference between the block's potential energy and kinetic energy

41 Which of the following goals depends more on developing the technology than learning new science?

　① developing a better theory about how Earth formed
　② understanding the role of genes in inherited diseases
　③ learning how much of behavior is inherited and how much is learned
　④ understanding how to cure cancer
　⑤ sending astronauts to Mars

Question 42 refers to the following passage.

In 1687, the English scientist Isaac Newton published his law of universal gravitation. According to this law, every two bodies in the universe attract because of gravitational force. The gravitational force increases as the mass of the objects increases, and decreases as the distance between the objects increases.

42 At the distances shown, between which two objects is the force of gravity greatest?

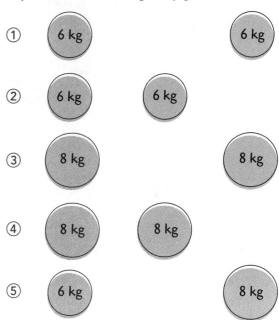

Questions 43, 44, and 45 refer to the following diagram and passage.

OCEAN FLOOR

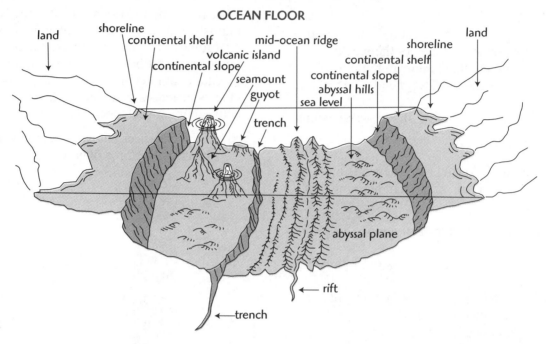

The Mid-Atlantic Ridge is a long underwater mountain range that sits about halfway between the continents that lie on either side of it.

Scientists believe that the sea floor is spreading outward along this ridge. The spreading seems to be caused by the continual flow of magma (molten rock) from cracks in Earth's crust and from eruptions in volcanoes along this mountain chain. Because of the sea floor spreading, North and South America are slowly moving farther from Europe and Africa.

43 What does the existence of the Mid-Atlantic Ridge tell us about the structure of Earth?

① The molten liquid interior is not only below continents, it is also below oceans.
② Volcanoes form only on mountains on continents.
③ Underwater volcanoes are unlike volcanoes found on land.
④ Underwater volcanoes do not spew magma from cracks in Earth's crust.
⑤ Earth's crust is thicker below oceans than it is below continents.

44 What is the best evidence that the sea floor spreading occurs at about the same rate on both sides of the Mid-Atlantic Ridge?

① The shape of South America is similar to the shape of Africa.
② The sea floor to the left of the ridge contains the same minerals as the sea floor to the right.
③ The continents to the left of the ridge are about the same distance from the ridge as the continents to the right.
④ The ridge is the same general shape as the shorelines on each side of it.
⑤ Many types of minerals found in South America are also found in Africa.

45 What is the source of energy that is causing the sea floor to spread?

① water wave energy from the ocean
② heat energy from Earth's interior
③ chemical energy released during reactions near the ocean floor
④ solar energy absorbed in ocean water
⑤ heat energy contained in ocean water

Question 46 refers to the passage and illustration below.

The greenhouse effect is actually two effects considered together: the warming of Earth by sunlight, and the insulating effect of clouds and atmospheric gases such as carbon dioxide. The greenhouse effect got its name from heating that takes place inside a nursery greenhouse.

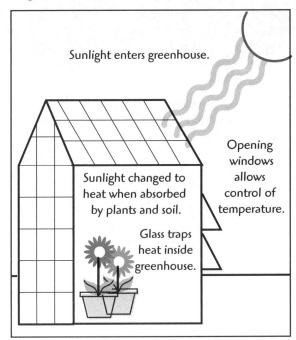

Sunlight enters greenhouse.

Opening windows allows control of temperature.

Sunlight changed to heat when absorbed by plants and soil.

Glass traps heat inside greenhouse.

46 Which of the following is most similar to the heating that occurs within a greenhouse?

① warming yourself by a fire
② keeping warm on a cold day by wearing a wool sweater and a jacket
③ getting suntanned on a beach on a warm, sunny day
④ warming yourself in a hot tub
⑤ sitting inside a car on a sunny day with the windows closed

47 What is the best visible evidence that suggests that the continents of North and South America once sat next to the continents of Europe and Africa?

① the fact that North America has more land area than South America
② the fact that Africa sits farther north than South America
③ the fact that the coastlines of the continents are like the edges of separated pieces of a jigsaw puzzle
④ the fact that the Atlantic Ocean runs north and south
⑤ the fact that both South America and Africa get very narrow at their southern tips

Question 48 refers to the passage below.

At the beginning of its life cycle, a star is a large, cool, contracting cloud of gas. As the cloud contracts due to gravity, the temperature of the cloud rises. The contraction continues as the temperature increases to several million degrees Fahrenheit. At this temperature, nuclear reactions begin taking place. These reactions—the fusion of hydrogen atoms to form helium atoms—release a tremendous amount of additional heat and light. The star continues to exist until its supply of hydrogen gas is gone.

48 What is the main source of energy in a star in the middle of its life cycle?

  ① the fusion of hydrogen to form helium
  ② the fusion of helium to form hydrogen
  ③ the change of light energy to heat
  ④ the change of heat energy to light
  ⑤ the contraction of gravitational energy

Question 49 refers to the illustration below.

THE BIG DIPPER

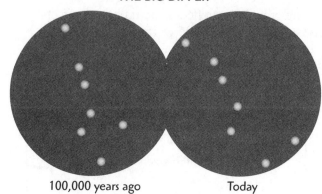

100,000 years ago   Today

49 The group of stars (constellation) known as the Big Dipper is shown above. What can you infer from this illustration?

  ① The distance between the Sun and Earth slowly increases over time.
  ② The universe is expanding at an ever-increasing rate.
  ③ This group of stars is not in the same galaxy as Earth.
  ④ Stars slowly move relative to one another over time.
  ⑤ Two different groups of stars are shown in the illustration.

Question 50 refers to the following passage.

Pythagoras, a sixth-century B.C. Greek mathematician, believed that the secrets of the universe are revealed by numbers. Pythagoras based this conclusion on a discovery about musical harmony.

Suppose you take two strings whose lengths are in the ratio of two small whole numbers, say 2:3. You can do this by choosing one string two feet long and another string three feet long. If you tightly stretch and then pluck the strings, you will find that the two sounds are harmonious—pleasant to hear at the same time.

Pythagoras concluded that whole number ratios, such as 2:3, have much to do with the way the world is structured. This conclusion led Pythagoras to believe that all celestial bodies are separated from one another by distances that are in harmonic ratios—ratios of lengths that produce pleasing sounds in stretched strings. He also believed that the movement of celestial bodies makes a harmonious sound that he called the "music of the spheres."

50 What insight was shown by Pythagoras, even though his conclusion about the music of the spheres was not correct?

(1) Celestial bodies move.
(2) Mathematics is important in science.
(3) Moving celestial bodies make sounds.
(4) Vibrating strings make sounds.
(5) Musical harmony is pleasant to hear.

Pretest Evaluation Chart

After you complete the Pretest, check your answers with the answers in the Answer Key on page 160. Then use this chart to figure out which skills you need to focus on in the instruction section of the book. In column 1, circle the number of each question you missed. The second and fourth columns tell you the name of the skill and its page number in the instruction section of this book. Focus your preparation on these skills. After you complete your study of each skill, put a check in the final column.

Question Number	Skill Name	Skill	Pages	Completed ✔
1	Summarize the Main Idea	1	22–23	
2	Identify Implications or Inferences	2	24–25	
3	Apply Scientific Concepts	3	26–27	
4	Distinguish Facts from Hypotheses or Opinions	4	28–29	
5	Identify Cause and Effect	5	30–31	
6	Recognize Unstated Assumptions	6	32–33	
7	Draw a Conclusion from Supporting Evidence	7	34–35	
8	Evaluate Scientific Evidence	8	36–37	
9	Understand the Influence of Personal Values	9	38–39	
10	Understand Inductive and Deductive Reasoning	10	40–41	
11	Cellular Basis of Life	11	42–43	
12	Inheritable Traits in Organisms	12	44–45	
13	Classification of Species	13	46–47	
14	Related Scientific Characteristics	14	48–49	
15	Adaptive Structure of Organisms	15	50–51	
16	Adaptive Behavior of Organisms	16	52–53	
17	Issues Concerning Population Growth	17	54–55	
18	Care of Natural Resources	18	56–57	
19	Organisms Living Together	19	58–59	
20	Care of the Environment	20	60–61	
21	Personal Health	21	62–63	
22	Community Health	22	64–65	
23	Natural Disasters	23	66–67	
24	Human–Created Hazards	24	68–69	
25	Human Aspects of Science	25	70–71	
26	Traces of Ancient Life	26	72–73	
27	Advances in Medicine	27	74–75	
28	Historical Perspectives in Life Science	28	76–77	

Question Number	Skill Name	Skill	Pages	Completed ✔
29	Phases of Matter	29	78–79	
30	Chemistry of Life	30	80–81	
31	Physical and Chemical Changes	31	82–83	
32	Energy Flow in Chemical Reactions	32	84–85	
33	Mixture of Elements	33	86–87	
34	Chemistry and the Origin of Life	34	88–89	
35	Chemistry and Human Health	35	90–91	
36	Historical Perspectives in Chemistry	36	92–93	
37	Motion and Forces	37	94–95	
38	Interaction of Energy with Matter	38	96–97	
39	Conservation of Energy	39	98–99	
40	Change and Constancy in Nature	40	100–101	
41	Differences Between Technology and Science	41	102–103	
42	Historical Perspectives in Physics	42	104–105	
43	Origin of Earth	43	106–107	
44	The Evolving Earth	44	108–109	
45	Geochemical Cycles and Earth's Energy	45	110–111	
46	The Greenhouse Effect and Global Warming	46	112–113	
47	Historical Perspectives in Earth Science	47	114–115	
48	Celestial Objects in the Universe	48	116–117	
49	The Evolving Universe	49	118–119	
50	Historical Perspectives in Space Science	50	120–121	

Summarize the Main Idea

To **summarize the main idea** is to briefly express the key point being made in a passage (a reading selection) or the main points addressed by a graphic.

- A passage may contain one or more paragraphs. To summarize a passage, you can quote the most important phrases or sentences, or you can restate the key thought in your own words.
- A graphic may contain one or more graphs, maps, or diagrams. To summarize a graphic, use your own words to state any key points addressed by the graphic.

In a passage, the main idea may be expressed in a single sentence—often the first sentence or the final sentence. In some passages the main idea is not stated as a single sentence, but must be summarized from all the information given.

In the following paragraph, no one sentence summarizes all the information given. How can you summarize this paragraph in a single sentence?

Ecology is the study of organisms and the relationship of these organisms to their environment. An environment is made up of all living and nonliving things that affect an organism's life in some way. Ecology is divided into many branches. Among these are behavioral ecology, population ecology, community ecology, ecosystem ecology, and global ecology. Each branch can be further divided into animal and plant ecology.

A good summary sentence is "Ecology, the study of organisms and their environment, is divided into many branches."

Reading Selection

During pollination in seed plants, pollen grains from the stamen (male organ of a flower) are transferred to the carpel (female part of a flower). Many plants self-pollinate. In these plants, pollen moves from the male part of a flower to the female part of the same flower or to the female part of another flower on the same plant. Many plants cross-pollinate. In these plants, pollen originates on one plant and is delivered to the female part of a second plant. For all seed plants, pollination is the most important step in the reproductive cycle.

❶ Use your own words or words from the selection to summarize the reading selection.

_____

_____

❷ Define each term below, used as supporting details in the reading selection.

self-pollinate _____

cross-pollinate _____

GED Practice

Question 1 is based on the following passage.

(1) Ocean waves often break up land masses near the water. (2) These waves move the broken dirt and rock down the shore. (3) Beaches form when waves move dirt and rocks toward the shore. (4) Cliffs form when waves move rock fragments away from the shore. (5) The action of ocean waves can change the shape of an entire shoreline.

❶ Which sentence is the main idea of the passage above?

  ① sentence 1
  ② sentence 2
  ③ sentence 3
  ④ sentence 4
  ⑤ sentence 5

Question 2 is based on the diagram below.

❷ Which statement best summarizes the key point made in the diagram?

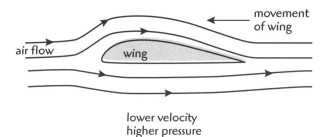

higher velocity
lower pressure

movement of wing

air flow   wing

lower velocity
higher pressure

  ① Wing lift results from high pressure air on the front edge of the wing.
  ② Wing lift results from high pressure air on the back edge of the wing.
  ③ Wing lift results from high pressure air on the top of the wing.
  ④ Wing lift results from high pressure air on the bottom of the wing.
  ⑤ Air pressure is equal on all sides of a wing.

Question 3 is based on the passage below.

The process of digestion begins with your first bite of food. Digestion takes place in the mouth, stomach, and intestines. During digestion, food is broken down into small molecules that pass into the bloodstream. The process of absorption comes next. During absorption, food molecules, now in the blood, pass into cells. In the next process, assimilation, cells use the food molecules as a source of energy and for body growth and maintenance.

❸ Which statement best summarizes the passage?

  ① Digestion is the main process the body goes through during eating.
  ② Food nourishment takes place in three equally important steps.
  ③ The blood is an important carrier of food substances to body cells.
  ④ Without blood, a person could not use food for nourishment.
  ⑤ Food molecules provide both energy and nutrients to cells.

Question 4 is based on the table below.

Sodium (Na)	10.60
Magnesium (Mg)	1.27
Calcium (Ca)	0.40
Potassium (K)	0.38
Strontium (Sr)	0.01

❹ According to the table, which two metals are most abundant in seawater?

  ① potassium and strontium
  ② calcium and sodium
  ③ sodium and magnesium
  ④ hydrogen and oxygen
  ⑤ silicon and sodium

Identify Implications or Inferences

To imply is to suggest. An **implication** is a point of view, an idea, or a fact that a writer or speaker suggests to you. For example, someone may write, "Doctors prescribe too many pills for children. I suspect that doctors are paid by drug companies for prescribing their pills!" This writer implies that some doctors put interest in money ahead of interest in patients.

To infer is to guess at what is not stated directly. An **inference** is a point of view, an idea, or a fact that you arrive at because of what you read, hear, or see. Quite often, you infer what another person implies. For example, you can infer that the person mentioned in the previous paragraph doesn't have high regard for the financial motivation of doctors.

For an example of both implication and inference, read the following paragraph.

> Gas prices and heating oil prices have risen too high! We need to decrease our dependence on oil, both foreign and domestic. It is time to develop alternative ways to power automobiles and to heat our homes. If we wait until the earth runs out of oil before we act, we will be very sorry. The time to act is now!

The writer of this paragraph implies two things: 1) Earth's supply of oil is very limited and is close to running out, and 2) Alternative ways can be found to power automobiles and heat our homes.

From this example, you can infer two things: 1) This writer is upset about high gasoline and heating oil prices, and 2) This writer believes it is important to find other sources of energy.

Reading Selection

In a process called bioremediation, bacteria or other microorganisms are used to remove some types of polluting substances from air, water, and soil. Bioremediation works best on organic compounds—carbon-based substances such as gasoline and cleaning solutions. Bioremediation was used to help clean up Alaskan beaches contaminated with oil from the damaged oil tanker *Exxon Valdez*. Also, bioremediation is used in tanks or lagoons to help clean some types of industrial wastes—wastes often illegally dumped and left.

❶ What does the writer imply about the environmental value of bioremediation?

_____

❷ What type of compound can you infer that oil is? _____

❸ What can you infer about the difference between an organic compound and an inorganic compound—a compound that is not an organic compound?

_____

_____

GED Practice

Questions 1 and 2 refer to the following passage.

During the 1950s and 1960s the peregrine falcon almost became extinct in the wild. Then, in the 1970s, after the pesticide DDT was banned from agricultural use, the falcon population slowly began to increase. Repopulation was helped by environmentalists who released into the wilderness peregrine falcons that had been hatched in captivity.

1 What is implied to be the cause of the near extinction of the peregrine falcon?

   ① an increase in predators
   ② a decrease in food supply
   ③ DDT poisoning
   ④ the decreased use of DDT
   ⑤ falcon hunting

2 What can you infer from the passage?

   ① DDT may cause harm to many species of animals.
   ② DDT is harmful only to falcons.
   ③ DDT is harmful only to insects for which the pesticide is used.
   ④ DDT is most effective when used as directed.
   ⑤ DDT is not itself hazardous to either animals or plants.

Question 3 refers to the following formula.

$$AgBr \xrightarrow{\text{light}} Ag + Br$$

silver bromide   silver   bromine

3 What can you infer from the chemical reaction formula shown above?

   ① Energy is required to split a silver bromide molecule.
   ② Energy is required to join a silver atom with a bromine atom.
   ③ Silver bromide is radioactive.
   ④ Silver is a solid; bromine is a gas.
   ⑤ Silver is heavier than bromine.

Questions 4 and 5 refer to the following advertisement.

Orin's Solar Panels bring solar energy into your home. Save money on electric bills and be good to the environment. Orin's Solar Panels are guaranteed for 30 years. Buy Orin's and buy peace of mind.

4 What does the writer imply about Orin's Solar Panels?

   ① Solar panels cannot be used in your town throughout the whole year.
   ② Orin's panels are the best-quality panels that money can buy.
   ③ Solar panels are expensive to purchase.
   ④ Orin's panels are the lowest-priced solar panels on the market.
   ⑤ Solar panels may not provide for all of your electricity needs.

5 What does the writer want you to infer about the use of solar panels?

   ① high installation fees
   ② efficiency dependent on sunshine
   ③ environmentally dangerous
   ④ environmentally friendly
   ⑤ high maintenance costs

Question 6 refers to the following sign.

In Case of Fire Use EXITS at Front of Theater

6 Which of the following can you infer from reading this sign?

   ① The theater has had a fire before.
   ② The theater does not have exit doors.
   ③ Exit doors are located at the rear of the theater.
   ④ Exit doors are locked during times the theater is open.
   ⑤ Exit doors are not locked during times the theater is open.

Apply Scientific Concepts

On the GED Science Test, you will be asked to apply **scientific concepts** to new situations. This is a measure of two abilities: applying given concepts in a new context and applying prior knowledge in a new context.

Many principles in science apply to different situations. One important principle is the theory of universal gravitation. According to this theory, every two objects in the universe feel a force of gravitational attraction. This force of attraction is greater for objects of greater mass.

How does the theory of universal gravitation help explain the following discovery?

> While on the moon, astronauts noticed that they could jump much higher than when jumping back home on Earth.

The experience of the astronauts is explained by applying the theory of universal gravitation to the moon. The astronauts were able to jump so high because they weighed less on the moon! They weighed less because the mass of the moon is much less than the mass of Earth; the diameter of the moon is less than one-third the diameter of Earth. The astronauts were held to the surface of the smaller moon by much less force than they are held to the surface of the larger Earth. A 200-pound astronaut on Earth would weigh about 33 pounds on the moon.

Reading Selection

Among scientists there is an ongoing debate known as the nature-versus-nurture controversy. The debate centers around two competing ideas:
1) Human personalities are mainly a result of biological heritage. In other words, each of us inherits our personality traits from our parents, much as we inherit our physical characteristics. This is the nature argument.
2) Human personalities are mainly a result of culture, the way we are raised and educated. This is the nurture argument.

Scientists, in general, agree that both biological heritage and culture influence personality. However, there is disagreement between which is more important, nature or nurture.

❶ After each characteristic, write *nature* or *nurture* or *both*.
- Write *nature* if you think that the characteristic is mainly inherited.
- Write *nurture* if you think the characteristic is learned from one's culture.
- Write *both* if you think both nature and nurture are important influences.

① natural hair color _____
② dyed hair color _____
③ choice of clothes _____
④ length of fingers _____
⑤ sense of humor _____
⑥ interest in school _____
⑦ body height _____
⑧ body weight _____
⑨ running speed _____
⑩ ability to play piano _____

GED Practice

Questions 1 and 2 refer to the following passage.

Energy can be changed from one form to another without any energy being lost in the process. For example, a light bulb changes electrical energy into both light energy and heat energy. Heat is due to the inefficiency of the bulb. A totally efficient bulb would produce light but not heat.

1 What kind of energy change takes place when a candle burns?

① Light is changed to chemical energy.
② Heat is changed to light.
③ Light and heat are changed to chemical energy.
④ Chemical energy is changed to light and heat.
⑤ Gravitational energy is changed to light and heat.

2 Which of the following best describes the properties of an efficient electric oven?

① runs on 120-volt power
② contains an automatic timer
③ provides both heat and light
④ provides light but very little heat
⑤ provides heat but very little light

Question 3 refers to the following passage.

In every ecosystem, organisms compete for limited food resources. Competition occurs between members of the same species and between different species. Competition is especially severe when limited resources are available.

3 Which pair of animals is *least* likely to compete for food sources?

① a tuna and a mackerel
② a wolf and a frog
③ an eagle and a hawk
④ a lion and a hyena
⑤ two crocodiles

Question 4 refers to the following drawing.

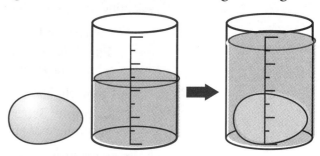

4 An egg is placed inside a jar that contains water. The jar has the shape of a cylinder. What property of the egg can be measured using this procedure? Assume you can measure the diameter of the jar and the height of the water.

① the egg's length
② the egg's weight
③ the egg's volume
④ the egg's surface area
⑤ the egg's color

Question 5 refers to the following drawing.

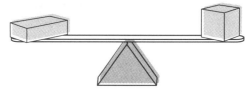

5 Two bricks are placed on the balance shown above. What property of the bricks can the balance be used to compare?

① the weight of the bricks
② the temperature of the bricks
③ the length of the bricks
④ the volume of the bricks
⑤ the surface area of the bricks

4

Distinguish Facts from Hypotheses or Opinions

In the search for understanding, scientists must carefully distinguish between scientific facts, hypotheses, and opinions.

- A **scientific fact** is a conclusion based on evidence that scientists agree on.
  Example: Fossil evidence indicates that saber-toothed tigers once lived in what is now the United States.

- A **hypothesis** is a tentative explanation based on insufficient evidence.
  Example: Saber-toothed tigers became extinct because of the sudden occurrence of an ice age.

- An **opinion** is a personal belief that is based on a person's own experiences or values.
  Example: The study of saber-toothed tigers is a waste of taxpayers' money.

Science cannot prove or disprove personal opinions. Science can only address those questions for which scientific evidence can be obtained.

Reading Selection

Scientists have discovered that a surprising similarity exists between many organisms at the embryonic stage—the earliest stage of development. For example, the embryos of a fish, a bird, and a human look surprisingly similar. Only an expert can tell them apart. Many scientists explain the embryonic similarity as being a sign of common biological ancestry. Biologists have also discovered that the DNA of human beings is very similar to the DNA of many other animals, including mice and chimpanzees. Biologists suggest that similarity in DNA also may indicate common biological ancestors. These findings are considered controversial by many religious leaders. These leaders believe that human beings do not share a common biological ancestor with other animals.

1 Write a scientific fact that is mentioned in the reading selection.

_____

_____

2 Write a hypothesis that is mentioned in the reading selection.

_____

_____

3 Write an opinion that is mentioned in the reading selection.

_____

_____

GED Practice

Question 1 is based on the drawing below.

COMPARISON OF HUMAN AND BABOON JAWS

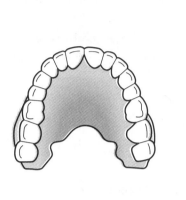 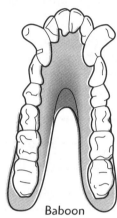

Human   Baboon

❶ Which of the following statements is best classified as a hypothesis?

  ① Humans and baboons have the same number of teeth.
  ② Both humans and baboons have teeth used for grinding food.
  ③ Both humans and baboons have teeth used for cutting food.
  ④ The baboon jaw is characteristic of an animal with low intelligence.
  ⑤ The differences between human and baboon jaws evolved because of differences in diet.

❷ Which of the following is an opinion that can neither be proved nor disproved with evidence?

  ① Stress is a state of mental or emotional strain and tension.
  ② Stress decreases the immune system's ability to fight disease.
  ③ Severe work stress is normal and improves work performance.
  ④ Chronic stress is defined as long-lasting severe stress.
  ⑤ Stress can have both physical and psychological effects on the human body.

Questions 3, 4, and 5 are based on the passage below.

Fossil evidence strongly indicates that dinosaurs became extinct about 70 million years ago. Scientists have proposed that the extinction resulted from a sudden ice age. The ice age, which destroyed the dinosaurs' food supply, could have been caused by an asteroid crashing into Earth and clouding the atmosphere with dirt. Other scientists say that we will never know how dinosaurs became extinct.

❸ How do you classify the idea that dinosaur extinction resulted from an asteroid striking Earth?

  ① scientific falsehood
  ② scientific fact
  ③ hypothesis
  ④ opinion
  ⑤ not a serious proposal

❹ How is the first sentence of the passage best classified?

  ① scientific falsehood
  ② scientific fact
  ③ hypothesis
  ④ opinion
  ⑤ not a serious proposal

❺ How is the final sentence of the passage best classified?

  ① scientific falsehood
  ② scientific fact
  ③ hypothesis
  ④ opinion
  ⑤ not a serious proposal

❻ Classify the following statement:

The change in weather patterns at the beginning of the twenty-first century may be the result of global warming.

  ① scientific falsehood
  ② scientific fact
  ③ hypothesis
  ④ opinion
  ⑤ not a serious proposal

Identify Cause and Effect

In a cause-and-effect relationship there is an event (the **effect**) that occurs as a result of a prior event (the **cause**). Many times, one cause leads to an effect that then itself becomes the cause of a second effect, and so on. This is called a cause-and-effect chain.

> **Example:** A child falls, injures her arm, and then cries. Her mother comes outside to see why her child is crying. There is a chain of causes and effects.

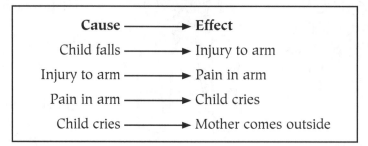

Cause ———————→ Effect

Child falls ———————→ Injury to arm

Injury to arm ———————→ Pain in arm

Pain in arm ———————→ Child cries

Child cries ———————→ Mother comes outside

Reading Selection

Stress or fright happens to everyone. People may react suddenly to surprise or shocking news; some people may react to seeing a snake or to looking over the edge of a cliff. During times of stress or fright, the adrenal glands flood the bloodstream with two hormones: adrenaline and noradrenaline. These hormones give you extra strength and endurance for dealing with the perceived threat. During this time, these hormones may also cause you to experience some or all of the following changes:

- Your heart beats faster.
- Your eyes dilate.
- Your liver releases stored sugar, increasing muscle energy.
- Your digestive processes slow down.
- The blood vessels near the surface of your skin contract, slowing the bleeding of any surface wounds and causing a greater flow of blood to the muscles, brain, and heart.
- The bronchial tubes in your lungs dilate, increasing the rate at which you are able to absorb oxygen.

❶ Name three possible causes of stress or fright reaction.

_____, _____, _____

❷ What is the first thing that happens in the human body as a result of stress or fright? _____

❸ Name one effect that follows from each of the following causes:

① The bronchial tubes in your lungs dilate. _____

② Your liver releases stored sugar. _____

③ The blood vessels near the surface of your skin contract. _____

GED Practice

Questions 1 and 2 refer to the following paragraph.

Scientists believe that global warming—the slow increase in Earth's atmospheric temperature—is occurring now. They think that this warming may be partially caused by slow increases in atmospheric carbon dioxide gas and atmospheric pollutants. Deforestation (the destruction of forests) leads to an increase of carbon dioxide gas because trees and other plants are not available to remove this gas from the atmosphere. The burning of fossil fuels directly adds pollutants (burn products) to the atmosphere.

1 Which of the following is believed to contribute to global warming?

(1) hydroelectric power plants
(2) coal-burning power plants
(3) nuclear power plants
(4) old-growth forests
(5) rain forests

2 Which action would be *least* likely to help reduce global warming?

(1) increase gas mileage in cars
(2) increase use of solar power
(3) replant burned forests
(4) build more fossil fuel power plants
(5) reduce fossil fuel power usage

Question 3 refers to the following paragraph.

Oil is a lubricant that reduces friction between moving parts in a machine. Friction leads to excessive heat and wear and tear on metal surfaces in contact. Friction can seriously damage fast-moving metal surfaces.

3 What would likely happen if a car engine is run while out of oil?

(1) increased speed of car
(2) increased gas mileage
(3) mechanical breakdown of electrical system
(4) overheating of brakes
(5) mechanical breakdown of engine

Question 4 refers to the drawing below.

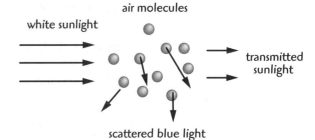

WHY THE SKY IS BLUE

air molecules

white sunlight

transmitted sunlight

scattered blue light

4 Why is the sky blue in color?

(1) Sunlight has more blue light than any other color.
(2) Gas molecules in air scatter blue light more than any other color.
(3) Gas molecules in air absorb blue light more than any other color.
(4) The ocean color causes the sky to appear blue.
(5) Blue is the color of outer space.

Question 5 is based on the following information.

Mushroom-shaped rocks are often found in windy deserts.

5 What is the most likely cause of mushroom-shaped rocks?

(1) erosion from the impact of wind-blown sand
(2) erosion from rain hitting the rock from above
(3) lightning strikes hitting the desert
(4) earthquake movement of surrounding land
(5) clawing and digging of desert animals

Recognize Unstated Assumptions

When you make an **assumption**, you think something is true without checking to see that it is true.

Read the paragraph below.

> Shanda is reading in her room. All of a sudden, the ceiling light goes out. Shanda replaces the bulb with a new one. To her surprise, the new bulb does not work either. Shanda now wonders why the new bulb doesn't work.

What assumption did Shanda make? Without thinking much about it, Shanda did what most of us would do. She assumed the problem was the bulb. As it turned out, a storm had caused a power outage to her home. The bulb was fine. After a few minutes the problem was repaired by the power company and Shanda's light came back on. Shanda had made an assumption based on experience, even though that assumption turned out to be incorrect.

A writer often makes an **unstated assumption**. A writer often assumes that his or her readers believe something to be true. In many cases, readers may have very different opinions than a writer.

What two unstated assumptions are made by the writer of the following sentence?

> When life is discovered on another planet, its form will be much different from any of the life forms presently on Earth.

The writer assumes two things.

- Life does exist on other planets.
- We on Earth will discover and learn about these alien life forms.

A writer (or speaker) often makes unstated assumptions to try to influence others. This technique is often used by salespeople and politicians.

Reading Selection

The question of where life first formed in the universe is an important one to answer. Did life first start on Earth or on Mars? If it started on Mars, how was Earth seeded with this life? Were simple life forms brought to Earth by an asteroid that first struck Mars and then struck Earth? During the next few decades, one goal must be to land humans on Mars. We must determine where life began and if life still exists on Mars.

❶ What unstated assumption is the author of the reading selection making about the value of manned space vehicles compared to unmanned space vehicles?

_____

❷ What unstated assumption is the author making about life on Mars?

_____

Question 1 refers to the passage below.

To make ice as quickly as possible, Tanya first ran the tap water until it was as cold as it would get. She then placed the tray full of this cold tap water into the freezer.

1 What unstated assumption is Tanya making?

① Cold water will freeze more quickly than warm water.

② Cold water freezes at the same rate as the warm water.

③ Cold water will not freeze in a freezer.

④ Warm water will freeze more quickly than cold water.

⑤ Warm water will not freeze in a freezer.

2 Which statement is an unstated assumption of those who favor the building of nuclear power plants?

① The demand for electrical energy will decrease in the future.

② Scientists see no danger in radioactive nuclear waste.

③ Scientists will find a safe way to store or dispose of radioactive nuclear waste.

④ Nuclear power plants do not produce dangerous waste.

⑤ There is a shortage of nuclear power scientists.

3 What unstated assumption is made by a woman who goes on a 1,200-calorie-per-day diet?

① Weight loss is directly related to the calorie content of food.

② Weight loss has nothing to do with the calorie content of food.

③ Calories are the measure of how much food weighs.

④ Calories have something to do with the cost of food.

⑤ Calories are related to the nutritional value of food.

Question 4 refers to the cartoon below.

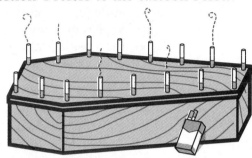

4 What unstated assumption is made by the cartoonist?

① Readers will realize that cigarettes are not really used as coffin nails.

② Readers will link the coffin with cigarette expense.

③ Readers will link the coffin and cigarettes with health danger.

④ Readers will conclude that cigarettes are more harmful to human health than cigars.

⑤ Readers will conclude that cigarette smoking is a difficult habit to break.

Question 5 refers to the following advertisement.

Most Powerful Engine in its Class

5 What unstated assumption is the ad designer making?

① Car buyers are impressed by the exterior design of a car.

② Car buyers are impressed by the interior space in a car.

③ Car buyers are not impressed by a powerful engine.

④ Car buyers are impressed by fuel economy.

⑤ Car buyers are impressed by a powerful engine.

7

Draw a Conclusion from Supporting Evidence

A **conclusion** is a logical opinion formed after considering the known facts or evidence. A conclusion often can be stated as a generalization—something that applies in many situations. Understanding science often involves being able to form the most logical conclusion from **supporting evidence**. (Forming a conclusion is often called drawing a conclusion.)

What is a logical conclusion you can draw from the following paragraph?

> Fossils are hardened remains or traces of any plant or animal that lived in historical times. Many fossils have been found in the layers of sedimentary rock that make up the cliff faces of the Grand Canyon. The 200-million-year-old rocks contain mainly fossils of reptiles; the 400-million-year-old rocks contain mainly fossils of fishlike animals; and even older rocks contain only fossils of worms.

One logical conclusion that can be stated as a generalization is the following: A geological time period is characterized by certain types of life forms.

The evidence indicates that this is true for the Grand Canyon. Logic (reasoning) tells you that this generalization is likely to be true for all other parts of Earth.

Reading Selection

As social insects, each ant plays a role in the existence of the colony. The single queen ant lays eggs to ensure the colony's survival. From the fertilized eggs come a large number of female ants and a much smaller number of winged males. The female ants are workers whose job is to find food and to protect the colony. These female workers are not able to become pregnant and carry eggs. The job of the winged males is to mate with the queen, after which they die. Many types of bees exhibit the same features as ants.

Human beings are also social animals. Apply what you know about human beings to draw conclusions that answer the following questions.

❶ How does the role of human males differ from the role of male social insects?

_____

_____

❷ How does the role of human females differ from the role of female social insects?

_____

_____

GED Practice

Questions 1 and 2 refer to the following passage.

For a substance to burn in air, oxygen gas must be present. Without oxygen, a flame will go out. For example, as part of an experiment, Jamie placed a candle in a small jar, lit the candle, and then sealed the jar by placing a lid on it. The candle burned for 24 seconds and then went out.

1 Which phrase best describes a property of a sealed jar?

   ① contains no oxygen
   ② contains only oxygen
   ③ contains infinite oxygen
   ④ contains limited oxygen
   ⑤ contains no nitrogen

2 What is a logical conclusion that can be drawn from this experiment?

   ① In a larger jar, the candle would burn for more than 24 seconds.
   ② In a smaller jar, the candle would burn for more than 24 seconds.
   ③ In this jar, a larger candle would burn for more than 24 seconds.
   ④ In this jar, a shorter candle would burn for more than 24 seconds.
   ⑤ A candle is unable to burn for a long time in either an open or closed jar.

Question 3 refers to the following passage.

Kerry had several fillings in her teeth before she was six years old. The dentist said that many of these fillings might have been prevented if Kerry had brushed her teeth daily after meals.

3 What conclusion can you draw from information given by the dentist?

   ① Tooth decay occurs in all children.
   ② Tooth decay occurs only in children.
   ③ Brushing prevents all tooth decay.
   ④ Candy is the main cause of tooth decay in children.
   ⑤ Food particles left in the mouth can lead to tooth decay.

Question 4 refers to the following drawing.

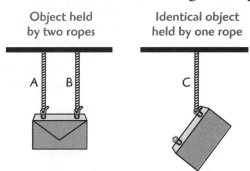

Object held by two ropes — Identical object held by one rope

4 Which phrase describes the weight held by rope C compared to the weight held by rope A?

   ① one fourth as much
   ② one half as much
   ③ an equal amount
   ④ twice as much
   ⑤ four times as much

Question 5 refers to the following drawing.

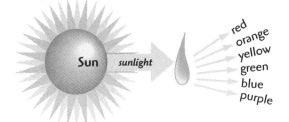

Sun — sunlight — red orange yellow green blue purple

5 What property of sunlight is shown in the illustration above?

   ① Sunlight creates raindrops.
   ② Sunlight contains many colors.
   ③ Sunlight cannot pass through water.
   ④ Sunlight warms raindrops.
   ⑤ A raindrop contains many colors.

6 With a map oriented as shown by the map compass at right, which direction is indicated by the dotted arrow?

   ① northwest
   ② northeast
   ③ southeast
   ④ southwest
   ⑤ westeast

Evaluate Scientific Evidence

On the GED Science Test, some questions measure your ability to make judgments about information that is presented to you. You must evaluate new evidence and any previously known facts before drawing a conclusion.

In some situations, you may need to determine what additional information must first be obtained before you can draw a conclusion. Sometimes you simply do not have enough information to draw any conclusion.

Evidence and other facts are divided into two types:

- *Relevant information* includes any facts or evidence that directly supports a conclusion.
- *Irrelevant information* includes any facts or evidence that *does not* directly support a conclusion.

What additional information would help you decide either to agree or disagree with the spokesperson mentioned in the following paragraph?

According to a spokesperson for a nutritional supplements company, "There is no medical evidence that Big Muscle Supplements cause ill health. In fact, we have actually found that these supplements will help you reach your ideal weight and health."

Before agreeing or disagreeing, you would certainly want to know if Big Muscle Supplements have been tested by health-care experts. What information is available from the FDA (Food and Drug Administration)? What tests have been performed by the company itself?

Reading Selection

A tide is the alternate rising and falling of the surface of the ocean. At any point along a coast, a rising tide occurs at a regular interval, followed by a falling tide. A rising tide is called a flood tide, and a falling tide is called an ebb tide. Each high tide (the high point of a flood tide) is followed several hours later by a low tide (the low point of an ebb tide); each low tide is followed several hours later by a high tide. Oceanographers often keep tide tables to indicate the time when every high and low tide will occur on each day of the month.

❶ Suppose a high tide occurs in a bay near your town every twelve hours, followed by a low tide six hours later. What must you know in order to tell the time of the next high tide?

_____

❷ What information would enable you to know what type of tide—flood or ebb— will be occurring tomorrow at noon?

_____

GED Practice

Question 1 refers to the following passage.

Scientists know that the level of pollutants in food increases as you move up the food chain. Foods that contain the least amount of pollutants are root vegetables, followed by grains, fruits, and leafy vegetables. Foods that contain the most pollutants are red meat, fish, poultry, and dairy products.

1 Which fact supports the claim that a healthful diet should be rich in fruits and vegetables and poor in meat?

(1) Growing foods organically reduces levels of pollutants.
(2) Many pollutants in food are destroyed by cooking.
(3) Many pollutants in food cause no known harmful effects.
(4) Shellfish contain higher levels of pollutants than other types of fish.
(5) Many pollutants in food increase risks of cancer and other diseases.

2 Assume that both light and sound are created at the same place and time when lightning occurs. From which fact below can you conclude that light travels faster than sound?

(1) The sound of thunder decreases as you move farther from the storm.
(2) You see a lightning flash before you hear thunder.
(3) The speed of sound is about 1,100 feet per second.
(4) Light and sound are forms of energy.
(5) Both light and sound travel through air and water.

3 Which fact is most relevant to a police officer trying to determine whether a driver is drunk?

(1) The driver is a known alcoholic.
(2) The driver has been picked up for drunk driving before.
(3) The driver's blood-alcohol level is above the legal limit.
(4) The driver has consumed two drinks.
(5) The driver's car has no brake light.

Question 4 refers to the following drawing.

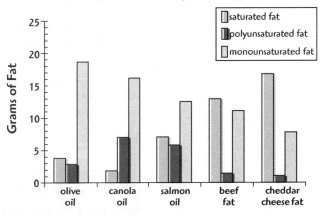

FAT CONTENT FOR SELECTED PRODUCTS
(present in one 25-gram serving)

4 What do you need to know to determine which type of listed food product is most nutritious?

(1) the cost of each food product
(2) the presence of each type of fat in other commonly eaten foods
(3) the availability of each food product
(4) the risks and benefits of each of the three types of fat
(5) the total number of calories allowed each day on a person's diet

Question 5 refers to the following drawing.

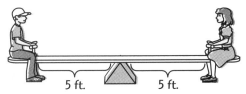

5 ft.   5 ft.

5 Assume that the teeter-totter is moving. What do you need to know in order to predict whether the teeter-totter will balance when the children stop it?

(1) the sum of the weights of the two children
(2) the height of each child
(3) the weight of each child
(4) the age of each child
(5) the weight of the teeter-totter

Understand the Influence of Personal Values

A **value** is a belief that a person thinks is very important. Values help people make decisions about their lives, such as how they vote. People express values in conversations, in letters written to newspapers, and in donations of money or time to organizations.

Sometimes a conflict between values occurs. This may happen when a personal belief is in conflict with discoveries in science. An example occurred centuries ago when astronomers discovered that Earth revolved around the Sun, placing the Sun at the center of the solar system. Religious teaching at the time said that the Sun revolved around Earth, placing Earth at the center of the solar system. Sometimes, as in this case, widely held beliefs slowly changed to agree with new discoveries.

A conflict between values often forces a person to choose one value over another.

> Reggie is nineteen and has a job at a factory. The men he works with all chew tobacco. To "feel like the other men," Reggie started to chew tobacco about three weeks ago. Last night, for the first time, Reggie heard medical evidence indicating that chewing tobacco can cause cancer of the mouth. Because of concern for his own health, Reggie finds himself having to make an uncomfortable choice.

Reggie is in a common situation. He is faced with choosing between the value he places on his health and the value he places on being like the other men at work.

Reading Selection

Kimi's religious beliefs say that she is not allowed to have a medical operation. Recently Kimi found out that she needs an operation if she wants to give birth to a child. She is not yet pregnant, but having a child is Kimi's lifelong dream.

1 What values are in conflict within Kimi?

_____

_____

2 Whom could Kimi speak with to help her make a decision?

_____

_____

3 Sean is working for a company that wants him to work on military weapon research. Sean does not believe in war and does not want to work on weapons. What values are in conflict in Sean?

_____

GED Practice

Question 1 is based on the passage below.

Commercially prepared foods contain several types of food additives. Preservatives retard food spoilage, artificial flavoring improves the taste of many foods, and artificial coloring improves the appearance.

In recent years, medical researchers have discovered that food additives, eaten in great quantities, may cause cancer. The long-term effect of the small amounts of additives typically found in commercial foods is not known.

1 What value is likely to be brought into conflict with our frequent use of commercially prepared foods?

   ① economic values
   ② religious values
   ③ work values
   ④ health values
   ⑤ personal choice values

2 Ellen values conservation of natural resources. Which source of home-heating energy would Ellen *least* likely be interested in?

   ① solar energy
   ② wind energy
   ③ flowing water energy
   ④ hot springs energy
   ⑤ furnace oil energy

3 Scientists have discovered that human beings and chimpanzees have many genetic similarities. What values may conflict with this scientific discovery?

   ① economic values
   ② religious values
   ③ personal health values
   ④ work values
   ⑤ personal freedom values

Questions 4 and 5 are based on the drawing below.

4 What is the attitude of the author of this cartoon about cell phones?

   ① Cell phones are fun to use.
   ② Cell phones can be used anywhere.
   ③ Cell phones can be annoying.
   ④ Cell phones are easy to carry.
   ⑤ Cell phones are not expensive.

5 What value is most important to the author of this cartoon?

   ① courtesy toward others
   ② the right of free speech
   ③ personal health concerns
   ④ quality of environment
   ⑤ freedom of religion

Question 6 refers to the following drawing.

6 What value does this cartoon show?

   ① courtesy toward others
   ② the right of free speech
   ③ quality of environment
   ④ personal health concerns
   ⑤ freedom of religion

Understand Inductive and Deductive Reasoning

Inductive reasoning involves making a generalization (general principle) based on one or a few specific examples. This generalization can then be applied in similar situations.

> **Specific Example:** When dropped side by side, a basketball and a baseball fall to the ground at the same rate. Both hit the ground at the same time.
>
> **Stating a Generalization:** All objects drop at the same rate in Earth's gravitational field.

Deductive reasoning means using a generalization to draw a conclusion about a new application. Scientists use deductive reasoning to apply general rules to specific examples.

> **Generalization:** As a general rule, objects expand when heated and contract when cooled.
>
> **Apply to Specific Example:** A metal screen door that fits snuggly during winter tends to stick during summer because the door expands during warmer months.

Reading Selection

Camouflage is a widely seen method in nature by which an organism blends into its background environment. An organism may exhibit both the color and shape characteristics of its surroundings. Camouflage is a form of deception that plays two roles in nature:

- First, camouflage helps ensure an organism's survival, making it more difficult for a predator to see it.
- Second, camouflage helps a predator remain unseen while it sneaks up on prey.

❶ In your own words, write a generalization based on the reading selection.

_____

❷ For what reason may a fish be dark-colored on its top side and light-colored on its bottom side?

_____

_____

❸ A polar bear lives on the snow-covered ice of the Arctic. What color would you expect a polar bear to be? What survival advantage does this color give the polar bear?

_____

GED Practice

Questions 1 and 2 are based on the following passage.

Homeostasis is an organism's tendency to maintain constant internal conditions. An organism does this by compensating for changes in its environment. For example, in response to rising outdoor temperature, the human body tends to cool itself by sweating, thus maintaining a constant internal temperature.

1 Which phrase best describes the generalization given in the passage?

  ① changing the external environment
  ② cooling one's body temperature
  ③ maintaining constant external conditions
  ④ maintaining constant internal conditions
  ⑤ increasing outdoor temperature

2 Which of the following is an example of homeostasis in humans?

  ① weight gain caused by excessive eating
  ② memory loss accompanying aging
  ③ heart rate increase during exercise
  ④ headache caused by exposure to annoying noise
  ⑤ body odor due to infrequent bathing

Question 3 is based on the passage below.

In physics, work is defined as a process in which force is applied to an object, with the result that the object moves. An object that does not move does not have work performed on it.

3 Which of the following activities would a physicist classify as work?

  ① watching the nightly news on TV
  ② mentally dividing 120 by 4
  ③ attempting to lift a rock that will not budge
  ④ singing a song in your head
  ⑤ throwing a football

Questions 4, 5, and 6 are based on the graph below.

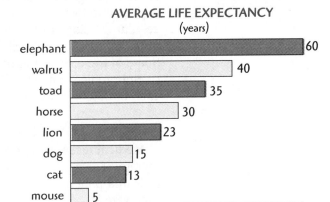

AVERAGE LIFE EXPECTANCY
(years)

- elephant 60
- walrus 40
- toad 35
- horse 30
- lion 23
- dog 15
- cat 13
- mouse 5

4 What general rule is most consistent with information given on the graph?

  ① Smaller animals have a longer life expectancy than larger animals.
  ② Larger animals have a longer life expectancy than smaller animals.
  ③ Life expectancy is not related to the size of an animal.
  ④ Smaller animals tend to be healthier than larger animals.
  ⑤ Larger animals tend to be healthier than smaller animals.

5 According to the graph, which animal is an exception to the general trend?

  ① walrus
  ② dog
  ③ horse
  ④ toad
  ⑤ mouse

6 Basing your answer on the graph, estimate the average life expectancy of a squirrel.

  ① about 8 years
  ② about 16 years
  ③ about 21 years
  ④ about 27 years
  ⑤ about 32 years

11

Cellular Basis of Life

Background Information

Human beings start life as a single fertilized cell called a zygote. This single cell divides into two cells, each of which then divide into two more cells. This type of cellular division continues as the zygote develops. At the point where there are about 50 to 150 total cells, the zygote has reached a stage called the blastocyst. Some of the cells of the blastocyst are special cells called blastocyst stem cells, or embryonic stem cells. Each blastocyst stem cell has the ability to change into each of 200 or more cell types that are in a human being.

Reading Selection

Medical researchers hope someday to use blastocyst stem cells in medical therapy. The goal is to discover a way in which to use stem cells to replace injured cells in a patient. By doing so, scientists hope to restore to the patient functions that were lost when the original cells were damaged.

One use of stem cells that is particularly promising is to aid people who have suffered paralysis from a spinal cord injury. The hope is to replace damaged spinal cord nerve cells with healthy nerve cells that can repair the damaged area. Research is presently focusing on the first step: teaching blastocyst stem cells to change step by step into neural stem cells—cells that have the ability to change into different kinds of nerve cells. The neural stem cells can then be encouraged to become spinal neuron cells—the nerve cells needed to repair a damaged spinal cord. If successful, scientists then hope to inject newly created spinal neuron cells into the damaged spinal cord region of patients. The hope is that the transferred cells will repair the spinal cord injury and reduce or eliminate the paralysis.

❶ Briefly describe what is meant by the word *zygote*.

_____

❷ What special properties does a blastocyst stem cell have?

_____

_____

❸ Briefly describe what a neural stem cell is.

_____

_____

❹ In the future, what kind of injuries may be helped by using blastocyst stem cells to create neural stem cells?

_____

GED Practice

Questions 1 and 2 are based on the following passage.

A nerve cell, called a neuron, consists of a cell body, a nucleus, a long fiber called an axon, and a large number of branching fibers called dendrites. When a message (nerve impulse) travels from one neuron to another, that message is sent through the axon of one cell and received by the dendrite of one or more adjoining cells. Each point of contact is called a synapse. Both electrical and chemical processes are involved when messages are transmitted among neurons.

TWO NEURONS IN SYNAPTIC CONTACT

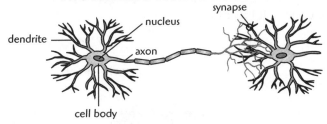

1 Which of the following best summarizes information from the passage?

(1) Messages travel from synapse to axon to dendrite.
(2) Messages travel from axon to synapse to dendrite.
(3) Messages travel from dendrite to axon to synapse.
(4) Messages travel from axon to dendrite to synapse.
(5) Messages travel from synapse to dendrite to axon.

2 In what organ in the human body are the majority of cells neurons?

(1) kidney
(2) eyes
(3) stomach
(4) brain
(5) liver

Question 3 is based on the drawing below.

The drawing below shows the lytic cycle, the attack by a virus on a living cell.

THE LYTIC CYCLE

Step 1. A virus attacks a host cell and injects the virus's genes into the cell.

Step 2. The virus's genes turn the host cell into a virus factory.

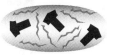

Step 3. The new viruses leave the host cell. The new viruses look for new host cells.

3 Which of the following facts *cannot* be inferred from the drawings?

(1) A virus can use a host cell to produce many more viruses.
(2) A host cell may be destroyed by the action of a virus.
(3) A virus does not reproduce in the way a cell reproduces.
(4) A virus contains genetic material.
(5) A virus can stay inactive for years.

12

Inheritable Traits in Organisms

Background Information

A trait is a physical or mental characteristic of an organism. Many characteristics, such as eye color, height, and some personality tendencies, are inherited by an offspring from its parents. Inherited characteristics are passed from parents to offspring by coded chemical messages called genes. Genes make up the chromosome strands that form DNA. DNA is the genetic material contained in the nucleus of each cell in a complex organism.

When male and female organisms mate, their offspring always receives two genes for each inheritable trait: one gene from the male parent and one gene from the female parent. Each inheritable trait depends on the presence or absence of a dominant gene. A dominant gene in a gene pair is the gene that determines the effect of the gene pair. A gene for brown eyes is dominant over a gene for blue eyes. The gene for blue eyes is called a recessive gene. A child who has inherited one brown-eye gene and one blue-eye gene will have brown eyes.

Reading Selection

Shown in the chart at right are the gene pair possibilities of a child born to

- a mother who has a brown-eye gene (Br) and a blue-eye gene (Bl)
- a father who has two blue-eye genes (Bl) and (Bl)

The child may receive any of the four possible gene pairs shown in the boxes of the chart.

Female Parent

	Br	Bl
Bl	Br Bl brown offspring	Bl Bl blue offspring
Bl	Br Bl brown offspring	Bl Bl blue offspring

Male Parent

Because the Br gene is dominant over the Bl gene, each box that contains a Br gene represents a child with brown eyes. Two boxes of the chart contain a Br gene. So each child has a 50% chance of having brown eyes and a 50% chance of having blue eyes. If this couple has two children, they might have one brown-eyed child and one blue-eyed child, or two blue-eyed children, or two brown-eyed children.

❶ Briefly describe what is meant by a dominant gene. _____

_____

❷ What is the only gene pair that a blue-eyed child may have? _____

❸ Suppose the couple represented on the chart above has four children. What are the possible eye colors of the children? _____

_____

GED Practice

1. In which pair of animals is the difference in genes most likely to be greatest?

   (1) pheasants and turkeys
   (2) robins and sparrows
   (3) bees and wasps
   (4) alligators and crocodiles
   (5) gorillas and horses

2. What statement best summarizes the role played by genes in heredity?

   (1) A gene may be either dominant or recessive.
   (2) An organism receives genes from one parent organism.
   (3) The number of an organism's genes determines which organisms can mate.
   (4) Genes carry the hereditary messages that determine inherited traits.
   (5) Different traits are represented by different numbers of genes.

3. Suppose a scientist wants to determine which personality traits are inherited and which are learned. Which of the following pairs could provide the best evidence in this study?

   (1) two adopted children who are raised in different families
   (2) an older sister and younger brother who are raised in the same family
   (3) identical twins separated at birth and raised in different families
   (4) identical twins raised in the same family
   (5) two unrelated adults who are raised in different cultures

4. Which trait is *least* likely to be an inheritable trait?

   (1) favorite sport
   (2) height
   (3) hair color
   (4) length of fingers
   (5) shape of ears

Questions 5, 6, and 7 are based on the following chart.

		Female Parent	
		Br	Bl
Male Parent	Br	Br Br brown offspring	Bl Br brown offspring
	Bl	Br Bl brown offspring	Bl Bl blue offspring

5. What color of eyes does each parent represented by the chart have?

   (1) both blue
   (2) both brown
   (3) both blue-brown
   (4) female brown, male blue
   (5) male brown, female blue

6. Suppose a child born to this couple has blue eyes. What gene pair must this child have received?

   (1) Br Bl
   (2) Bl Br
   (3) Br Br
   (4) Bl Bl
   (5) none of the pairs shown

7. Suppose the couple represented by the chart has four children. Which is the *least* likely possibility for eye color of the children?

   (1) 4 brown
   (2) 3 brown, 1 blue
   (3) 2 brown, 2 blue
   (4) 1 brown, 3 blue
   (5) 1 green, 3 brown

Classification of Species

Background Information

Biologists classify both extinct and living species of all known organisms. The most specific level of classification that identifies a single type of organism is a **species.** Human beings, sharks, pine trees, and sunflowers are each species. Species that are closely related to one another are classified together in larger groupings than species. For example, although human beings and chimpanzees are different species, they are both classified as primates.

The classification system is based on similarities in physical characteristics. This system contains many levels, and only a couple will be mentioned here. The highest level is Kingdom. Animals and plants are classified in different Kingdoms: Animalia and Plantae. The next lower level of classification is Phylum (also called Division). Humans and fruit flies, both in the Kingdom Animalia, are classified in different Divisions. Humans and chimpanzees are both in the Phylum Chordata; fruit flies are in the Division Anthropoda. As a general rule, the more similar species are in physical characteristics, the more levels of classification they have in common.

Reading Selection

Mammal is the classification of warm-blooded vertebrates (animals with backbones) that includes human beings. Mammals come in a variety of shapes and sizes. The tiniest mammals include bats, mice, and shrews. The largest mammals are blue whales and elephants. Some mammals fly, some swim, and some live entirely on land.

Although mammals may differ a great deal from one another, all mammals share the following characteristics:

- Female mammals have mammary glands with which they feed their young.
- Mammals are warm-blooded, maintaining a relatively constant body temperature.
- Mammals have specialized teeth.
- Mammals have lungs and a diaphragm to aid in breathing.
- Mammals have five senses: sight, hearing, smell, touch, and taste.
- Mammals reproduce sexually.
- Mammals protect their young.
- Mammals have complex nervous systems and large active brains.

❶ In which Kingdom would a carrot be classified? _____

❷ In which Kingdom would a mouse be classified?_____

❸ Name two ways a bat would care for its young.

_____

_____

GED Practice

Questions 1 and 2 are based on the following passage.

Until the 1960s, many scientists believed that toolmaking was a skill that separated human beings from all other species. Then researchers discovered that many animals in the wild make and use tools. For example, chimpanzees use broken branches to attack predators; they use stones to crack nuts; they wad leaves into a sort of sponge to hold drinking water; and they find or make a long stick to use in capturing ants and termites.

1 Which of the following likely changed scientists' opinions about toolmaking?

  ① pride in human accomplishments
  ② knowledge available before 1960 about animal intelligence
  ③ improvement in zoo design
  ④ observations of animals in the wild
  ⑤ observations of animals in captivity

2 Which of the following best summarizes the observations about chimpanzees?

  ① Chimpanzees may have many skills that have not yet been discovered.
  ② Chimpanzees have toolmaking skills once thought to belong only to humans.
  ③ Chimpanzees are as intelligent as human beings.
  ④ Chimpanzees are not vegetarians because they eat insects.
  ⑤ People in primitive cultures are more intelligent than chimpanzees.

3 Human beings are classified in a group called primates—mammals with a large brain and complex hands and feet. Which of the following animals is also a primate?

  ① sheep
  ② monkey
  ③ porpoise
  ④ robin
  ⑤ turtle

Questions 4 and 5 are based on the following information.

Embryos of different species can show surprising similarity during early development stages.

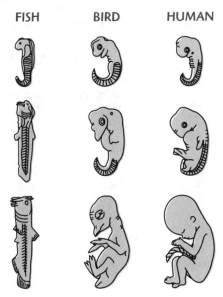

FISH   BIRD   HUMAN

4 Which structure *does not* develop in the later stage of each of the three embryos?

  ① brain
  ② eyes
  ③ backbone
  ④ lungs
  ⑤ head

5 Referring to the drawings above, which conclusion is *least* reasonable?

  ① Birds are more closely related to fish than to humans.
  ② Birds are more closely related to humans than to fish.
  ③ Different species may have similarities in their genetic codes.
  ④ Different structures can develop from similar-looking parts of different types of embryos.
  ⑤ Different species may be related biologically to one another.

Related Scientific Characteristics

Background Information

In the study of science, similar physical characteristics or similar behavior patterns are often compared and contrasted. Scientists ask, *How are things that share certain characteristics alike and how are they different?* Questions on the GED Science Test may test your ability to distinguish both similar and dissimilar characteristics of related characteristics.

Reading Selection

In the human body, a group of similar cells working together is called a tissue. Each cell in a particular tissue is very much alike in structure and function. However, the human body contains four completely different types of tissue. Each type of tissue performs its own unique function, even though each tissue has many similarities to each other type of tissue.

- *Epithelial tissue*—cells that cover and protect underlying tissues. Examples are surface skin cells and cells that line the inner surfaces of body organs such as the lungs, stomach, and blood vessels. Epithelial tissue repairs itself when cut or bruised.

- *Nerve tissue*—cells that carry nerve signals throughout the body. Examples are brain cells and cells found in sense organs. Some nerve tissue, such as that in the spinal cord, is not able to repair itself when severely damaged.

- *Muscle tissue*—cells that can contract and relax for the purpose of moving skeletal parts or in the functioning of organs such as the heart and the stomach. Muscle injury is common and most muscle tissue repairs itself. Some muscle tissue, such as that in the heart, cannot repair itself.

- *Connective tissue*—cells that join, support, cushion, and nourish organs. Types of connective tissue also form bones, cartilage, ligaments, and tendons. Damage to connective tissue in joints is common, especially among athletes. Repair to this type of damage often requires a medical operation.

1 What type of tissue is involved in the sensation of taste? _____

2 What type of tissue is the body's first defense against airborne bacteria?

_____

3 Cartilage is a type of fibrous connective tissue that is flexible and rubbery. Name a part of the human body that contains cartilage.

_____

4 What type of tissue enables you to raise your arm? _____

5 What type of tissue enables you to see? _____

6 What type of tissue is damaged in a spinal cord injury that causes paralysis?

_____

GED Practice

Questions 1 and 2 are based on the passage below.

Several plant types are described below.

- *Annuals* germinate from seeds, produce flowers, and die in one growing season.

- *Vegetable biennials* have a two-year life cycle. Seeds germinate the first year and produce roots, a short stem, and leaves. In the second year, the stem grows, and flowers, fruits, and seeds are produced. Vegetable biennials are usually harvested during their first year.

- *Flower biennials* are similar to vegetable biennials. However, flower biennials are known for their flowers and are not harvested for food.

- *Herbaceous perennials* are plants that live for more than two growing seasons. The roots grow slowly during the winter and produce new shoots each spring. Herbaceous perennials are soft and leafy and do not contain wood.

- *Woody perennials* are characterized by stiff wooden trunks and branches. They live for many growing seasons.

1 Carrots have a two-year life cycle but are usually harvested for consumption during the first year. How would you classify a carrot plant?

  ① annual
  ② vegetable biennial
  ③ flower biennial
  ④ herbaceous perennial
  ⑤ woody perennial

2 The seeds of a pea plant must be planted each year. The plant dies at the end of each growing season. How would you classify the pea plant?

  ① annual
  ② vegetable biennial
  ③ flower biennial
  ④ herbaceous perennial
  ⑤ woody perennial

Questions 3, 4, 5. and 6 refer to the information given below.

FOOT STRUCTURE VARIATIONS OF COMMON BIRDS

A   B   C   D   E

wading (Heron)   grasping (Hawk)   perching (Warbler)   swimming (Duck)   running (Rhea)

3 Which of the five birds represented is most suited to use its feet to sit on a tree branch?

  ① heron
  ② hawk
  ③ warbler
  ④ duck
  ⑤ rhea

4 Which of the five birds represented is most suited to use its feet to pick up small animals?

  ① heron
  ② hawk
  ③ warbler
  ④ duck
  ⑤ rhea

5 Which two drawings would be of most interest to someone studying birds that get their food from rivers and lakes?

  ① A and C
  ② C and E
  ③ B and E
  ④ A and D
  ⑤ D and E

6 To which of the following studies would the drawings have the *least* relevance?

  ① walking ability of birds
  ② dietary habits of birds
  ③ structural variety of bird feet
  ④ climbing ability of birds
  ⑤ flying ability of birds

Adaptive Structure of Organisms

Background Information

If organisms are to survive, they must be adapted to conditions in their environment. The most noticeable physical adaptations involve body shape, size, and color. In most organisms, there is a strong relationship between a particular physical characteristic and the function served by that characteristic.

- A shark has a shape that enables it to swim quickly through the water.
- A seagull has large wings that enable it to glide slowly above the water's surface while searching for small fish.
- A giraffe has a long neck that enables it to reach high into trees for leaves that other animals cannot reach.
- A polar bear is white in color, blending into the snow so that it cannot be seen by its prey.
- A salmon is dark-colored on the top side and light-colored on the bottom side to help hide this fish from natural predators in the ocean.

Reading Selection

Nature shows great flexibility in functions served by similar characteristics. For example, some animals have different uses for very similar body parts. While the penguin and seagull are both birds, the penguin does not fly. A penguin uses its wings only as flippers for swimming. A seagull uses its wings only for flying and gliding.

a seagull's wings used for flying

a penguin's wings used for swimming

The seagull and penguin have similar wing structures. However, each uses its wings in a way most likely to ensure its own survival in the environment in which it lives.

❶ How do a monkey and a crocodile use their tails in different ways?

_____

_____

❷ Elephants have very large ears. For what main purpose are these ears likely used?

_____

_____

❸ What survival advantage does the color of a green tree frog provide?

_____

_____

GED Practice

Questions 1 and 2 refer to the passage below.

An interesting question concerning the physical development of organisms is the discovery of vestigial organs. A vestigial organ is a small or imperfectly developed organ that seems to have no use. An example of a vestigial organ is the presence of leg bones in a snake. These small bones are absolutely useless to snakes that exist at the present time.

One explanation of vestigial organs is that animals today evolved from ancestors who needed these organs. According to this explanation, snakes inherited the genes that produce leg bones from an ancestral relative. These relatives were most likely ancient reptiles that did have legs.

1 Which phrase below best describes a vestigial organ?

   ① is small and easily identified
   ② is present in all modern reptiles
   ③ is not inherited
   ④ may have more than one use
   ⑤ does not have a known use

2 Which of the following is a hypothesis?

   ① Vestigial organs evolved from organs that were once useful.
   ② Vestigial organs are present only in reptiles.
   ③ All snakes have vestigial leg bones.
   ④ Snakes inherit organs from previous generations of snakes.
   ⑤ Vestigial organs are of no use to the animal that has them.

3 Which of the following is a vestigial organ in human beings?

   ① nose
   ② kidney
   ③ tailbone
   ④ eye
   ⑤ tongue

Questions 4, 5, and 6 refer to the following drawing.

HUMAN TEETH AND THEIR USES

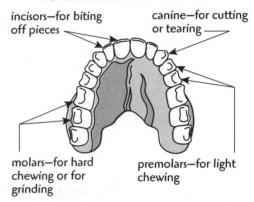

incisors—for biting off pieces
canine—for cutting or tearing
molars—for hard chewing or for grinding
premolars—for light chewing

4 Which teeth would you most likely use to take a small bite of fish which you want to taste?

   ① incisors
   ② canines
   ③ premolars
   ④ molars
   ⑤ both premolars and molars

5 Which teeth would you use to chew a very tough piece of meat?

   ① incisors
   ② canines
   ③ premolars
   ④ molars
   ⑤ both premolars and molars

6 Which are the long teeth that are more prominent in animals such as cats and dogs than they are in humans?

   ① incisors
   ② canines
   ③ premolars
   ④ molars
   ⑤ both premolars and molars

Adaptive Behavior of Organisms

Background Information

Animal traits involve not only body shape, size, and color but also patterns of behavior—actions or reactions to conditions in the environment. Complex animals have five senses: sight, smell, hearing, taste, and touch. These senses give animals a wide range of experiences unknown to plants. Also, animals can move around in ways that plants cannot. Animals can swim, fly, walk, dig, crawl, and burrow. Although no animal can do all of these well, many animals can do two or more.

The complex behavior pattern of animals is often connected with the constant struggle to survive and reproduce. The species of animals alive today are those that have been most successful in that struggle. Although many animals die young, enough usually survive and reproduce to ensure that their species does not become extinct (disappear from Earth).

Reading Selection

In order to survive against natural predators, most animals have developed one or more of the following behavioral defenses:

- *Running away*—moving quickly away from a predator. Animals such as antelopes and gazelles rely on alertness, speed, and endurance to outrun lions and other predators.
- *Fighting back*—fighting a predator. Some animals fight back by kicking, biting, or ramming. The baboon fights with sharp teeth and powerful jaws. Elk and deer fight by kicking with sharp hooves and by ramming with their antlers.
- *Playing dead*—lying motionless when attacked. When an opossum is attacked, it closes its eyes and goes limp. Most predators will not attack lifeless prey.

In addition to behavioral defenses, many animals get protection from physical adaptations.

- *Camouflage*—relying on protective skin coloring to enable an animal to blend into its surroundings. Brown toads live on the ground. Weasels have earth-colored fur in the summer and white fur in the winter.
- *Protective outer layer*—relying on a strong or menacing outer layer for protection against attack. The armadillo has a covering of tough, bony plates that predators cannot grasp. Clams and snails have shells in which they can hide.

❶ What type of defense is shown by a hyena that screams at an approaching lion?

_____

❷ What type of defense is used by a porcupine with its covering of sharp quills?

_____

❸ What type of defense is shown by a blackbird that flies away when a car horn sounds?

_____

GED Practice

Questions 1, 2, and 3 are based on the information below.

Below are five types of behavior shown by all vertebrates—animals with backbones.

Inborn behaviors

Reflex—an automatic response to a stimulus

Instinct—a complex, unlearned response that is not dependent on experience

Self-preservation—a reaction for the purpose of escaping life-threatening danger

Learned behaviors

Conditioned response—learning that connects an unusual stimulus with a desired response

Intelligent behavior—a complex response that uses past learning in new situations

1 When it saw a cat, a mouse ran for its life. What type of behavior is this?

① reflex
② instinct
③ self-preservation
④ conditioned response
⑤ intelligent behavior

2 During mating, the Adelie penguin builds a nest out of pebbles and the bones of its ancestors. What type of behavior is the penguin engaging in?

① reflex
② instinct
③ self-preservation
④ conditioned response
⑤ intelligent behavior

3 Each time Andy claps his hands, his parakeet sings. What type of behavior is the parakeet showing?

① reflex
② instinct
③ self-preservation
④ conditioned response
⑤ intelligent behavior

Questions 4 and 5 are based on the drawing below and the definitions of behavior given for questions 1, 2, and 3.

4 What type of behavior is being exhibited by the dog?

① reflex
② instinct
③ self-preservation
④ conditioned response
⑤ intelligent behavior

5 What type of behavior is being exhibited by the cat?

① reflex
② instinct
③ self-preservation
④ conditioned response
⑤ intelligent behavior

6 What type of behavior is engaged in by two people learning to play checkers?

① reflex
② instinct
③ self-preservation
④ conditioned response
⑤ intelligent behavior

7 Which sense do animals that live only underground rely on *least*?

① hearing
② sight
③ touch
④ smell
⑤ taste

Issues Concerning Population Growth

Background Information

Between the years 1800 and 2000, the world population increased from 1 billion to 6 billion people. By the year 2050, the world population is predicted to reach 9 billion. Scientists in all fields of study are worried about the consequences of the rapidly rising world population. Food and housing shortages are two major concerns. Until now, food production and housing construction in most developed countries has kept up with population needs. However, this is not true in developing countries, particularly in Africa, where droughts and famine occur often. Mass starvation in many poor countries has often resulted. Overpopulation in developed countries could reach a point where food shortages could also become a problem. Other concerns about overpopulation include excessive use of natural resources, excessive air and water pollution, excessive production of trash, and unbearable noise pollution in large population centers.

Reading Selection

In 1798, Thomas Malthus, an English clergyman and economist, wrote *An Essay on the Principle of Population*. Malthus expressed concern about overpopulation. In his essay Malthus said that food production cannot keep up with a rapidly growing population. He pointed out that food production increased in a geometric way while population increased in an exponential way. (Like comparing the geometric number series 1, 2, 3, 4, 5 . . . with the exponential number series 1, 2, 4, 8, 16 . . . Which series increases more rapidly?)

According to Malthus, the only way to prevent world famine (widespread starvation) is to limit population growth. Malthus favored late marriage and sexual abstinence as a way of limiting population growth. Malthus pointed out that, besides family planning, the only alternatives to starvation are epidemic diseases and war.

In the 1700s and 1800s, large families were considered desirable because they provided plenty of workers for farming and industry. Malthus warned that large families would actually be a drain on the economy and the available food supply and would lead to disastrous consequences if overpopulation was left unchecked.

❶ What was the main point Thomas Malthus made in his essay?

_____

_____

❷ What did Thomas Malthus believe was the best solution to the overpopulation problem?

_____

❸ What did Thomas Malthus believe would happen if overpopulation was not controlled by limiting family growth?

_____

GED Practice

Questions 1 and 2 refer to the passage below.

The world population is growing at an ever-increasing rate. Between 1810 and 1960, a period of 150 years, the world population tripled. Between 1960 and 2050, a period of only 90 years, the world population is expected to triple again. Unless population is checked, the world population could triple again in the 30 years after 2050.

❶ For a country's population to increase, which of the following must be true?

(1) The death rate must be greater than the birth rate.
(2) The birth rate must be greater than the death rate.
(3) The birth rate and death rate must be equal.
(4) The birth rate must be at least twice the death rate.
(5) The death rate must be less than half of the birth rate.

❷ What is the most sensible way of limiting the world's population?

(1) widespread starvation
(2) widespread disease
(3) widespread war
(4) widespread family planning
(5) widespread ill health

❸ Which of the following is the *least* important need of a country trying to effectively deal with overpopulation?

(1) wisely using and recycling natural resources
(2) increasing the food supply to meet all citizens' needs
(3) increasing consumer product choices
(4) educating all citizens about family planning methods
(5) improving waste-disposal systems

Questions 4 and 5 refer to the following graph.

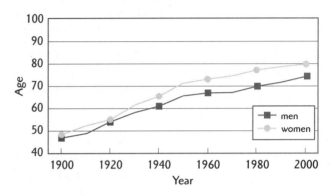

LIFE EXPECTANCY OF U.S. MEN AND WOMEN IN THE 20TH CENTURY

❹ Which of the following statements about life expectancy in the United States in the twentieth century is supported by the graph above?

(1) Life expectancies of women did not increase.
(2) Life expectancies of men did not increase.
(3) Life expectancies of women and men were equal for all years shown.
(4) Life expectancies of men were greater than life expectancies of women.
(5) Life expectancies of women were greater than life expectancies of men.

❺ Which of the following statements is true about life expectancies between the years 1900 and 2000?

(1) Life expectancies of women increased more than life expectancies of men.
(2) Life expectancies of men increased more than life expectancies of women.
(3) Life expectancies of women increased by the same number of years as life expectancies of men.
(4) Life expectancies of women increased twice as much as life expectancies of men.
(5) Life expectancies of men increased twice as much as life expectancies of women.

18

Care of Natural Resources

Background Information

Human beings depend on the resources that are available to support life. An important part of these are **natural resources**, resources provided by nature. The most important natural resources are water, air, topsoil, energy sources, and biodiversity—the wide variety of plant and animal life on Earth. Natural resources are often classified into two main types:

- *Renewable resources*—resources, such as trees, that can be used and then replaced over a relatively short time. Solar energy is the one renewable resource that is considered to be in unlimited supply.
- *Nonrenewable resources*—resources that cannot be replaced or resources that take hundreds of years or more to replace. Practically speaking, all nonrenewable resources can run out. Most minerals and fossil fuels are nonrenewable resources. Large tropical rain forests and species of animals and plants that are in danger of extinction are also considered nonrenewable resources.

Reading Selection

Recycling is the reuse of products in their original form or the reuse of the materials that make up a product. An example of reuse of an original product is a child's bicycle. The bicycle can be used by several children in one family or passed from one family to another. An example of the reuse of materials that make up a product is the recycling of aluminum soda cans. The recycled cans are returned to the can factory and melted down. The aluminum in the can is then used again in the production of new cans. Recycling of materials in this way is often called resource recovery.

Interest in recycling is growing in the United States. Yet, at the present time, the United States recycles less than 15% of its trash. Japan recycles nearly 50% of its trash, and European countries recycle about 30% of their trash.

❶ Briefly tell the difference between renewable resources and nonrenewable resources.

_____

_____

❷ Describe a situation in which you reused a product rather than throwing it away.

_____

_____

❸ Do people in your community recycle used products? If so, what products are recycled?

_____

_____

GED Practice

Question 1 refers to the following passage.

Recycling is done for several reasons.

- Recycling helps save nonrenewable natural resources such as oil, iron, and aluminum.
- Recycling helps minimize air and water pollution created during manufacturing.
- Recycling reduces the use of energy needed during manufacturing.
- Recycling decreases manufacturing waste and also the waste of discarded products.

Critics of recycling point out that using recycled products is often much more expensive for manufacturers than using raw resources. One notable exception is the recycling of aluminum. Aluminum is very expensive to obtain if you start with the raw ore that contains aluminum.

1 Which of the following is *not* mentioned as a general advantage of recycling?

  ① saving nonrenewable resources
  ② decreasing air and water pollution
  ③ reducing energy use
  ④ savings in manufacturing costs
  ⑤ reducing manufacturing waste

2 Which of the following methods of waste disposal would most likely add to air pollution?

  ① burial in a landfill
  ② incineration
  ③ sinking in an ocean
  ④ reuse in present form
  ⑤ recycling for material reuse

3 Which product would be *least* useful if it were recycled?

  ① empty aluminum soda can
  ② used plastic milk container
  ③ damaged cardboard boxes
  ④ used car oil
  ⑤ old wooden fence posts

Questions 4, 5, and 6 refer to the following graph.

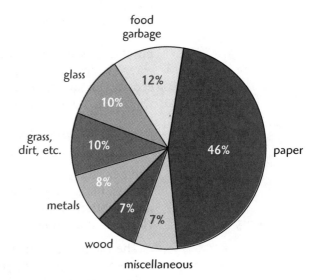

SOLID WASTE DISPOSAL IN THE UNITED STATES

food garbage 12%
glass 10%
grass, dirt, etc. 10%
metals 8%
wood 7%
miscellaneous 7%
paper 46%

4 What is the largest component of American garbage?

  ① paper
  ② glass
  ③ dirt
  ④ tin cans
  ⑤ pieces of wood

5 What percent of solid waste produced in the United States is made up of glass and metals?

  ① 10 percent
  ② 14 percent
  ③ 18 percent
  ④ 22 percent
  ⑤ 28 percent

6 What percent of solid waste produced in the United States is biodegradable (naturally decomposing): food garbage, wood, and grass?

  ① 8 percent
  ② 12 percent
  ③ 21 percent
  ④ 29 percent
  ⑤ 38 percent

19

Organisms Living Together

Background Information

The most complex relationship among a variety of plants and animals occurs in an **ecosystem**—a community of organisms where the welfare of the population of each species is dependent upon the welfare of each of the other species. All members of a particular species make up the population of that species in an ecosystem. A pond is an example of an ecosystem that has many different populations of plants and animals. Considered as a whole, an ecosystem helps each population survive, but it does not protect any individual member of each population. Said another way, an ecosystem helps ensure the survival of the many populations within the ecosystem; an ecosystem does not help ensure the survival of particular individuals within each population.

Reading Selection

A pond is a habitat, or home, for a community or organisms—an ecosystem. In and near the pond are many populations. There are populations of fish, insects, snakes, birds, and plants, both within and near the pond. Natural resources that are important in an ecosystem around a pond are adequate sunshine, clean water, clean air, and fertile soil.

The interdependence of living organisms in an ecosystem is called a food chain. In every food chain, organisms either make their own food or obtain food by eating other organisms. Algae in the pond and green plants near the pond create food through photosynthesis. They obtain nutrients through the water and the soil. Animals, on the other hand, do not make their own food. Animals eat plants and other animals that are part of their food chain.

The survival of each population in an ecosystem depends on the survival of every other population. Within a pond, small fish feed on plankton—tiny plant and animal life that float in the water. Large fish and ducks eat the smaller fish. Along the shore, insects eat plants, frogs eat insects, snakes eat frogs, and birds eat snakes. Plants depend on animals for waste products that provide nutrients.

❶ Briefly describe what an ecosystem is._____

_____

❷ A home for a community of organisms is called a _____.

❸ What is a food chain?_____

_____

❹ Suppose the snakes around a pond all mysteriously die. What will likely happen to the frog population and the insect population?

_____

_____

GED Practice

Questions 1 and 2 refer to the passage below.

Competition for limited resources is an important relationship among organisms in an ecosystem. For example, in a pond both bass and ducks eat small fish. The greater the number of fish eaten by ducks, the less food for the bass. Each animal has more than one source of food, so this competition is not likely to lead to any complete population starving. However, competition, mainly for food, does limit the size of each population. In a stable ecosystem, each population stays about the same size. The number of each species that dies is balanced by the number of newborn that survives.

1 What does the phrase "competition for limited resources" refer to in an ecosystem?

   ① the scarcity of resources
   ② the high price of available resources
   ③ the abundance of resources
   ④ the location of available resources
   ⑤ the use of available resources

2 What is a stable ecosystem?

   ① an ecosystem in which the size of each population is decreasing
   ② an ecosystem in which the size of each population is increasing
   ③ an ecosystem in which the size of each population remains constant
   ④ an ecosystem in which new populations are being introduced
   ⑤ an ecosystem in which some populations are being removed

3 Which change is *least* likely to upset the stability of a forest ecosystem in the Rocky Mountains?

   ① an earthquake
   ② a forest fire
   ③ a year of drought
   ④ increased logging
   ⑤ a hurricane

Questions 4 and 5 refer to the diagram below.

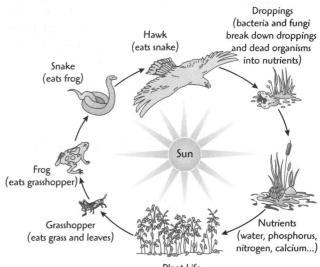

Hawk (eats snake)

Snake (eats frog)

Droppings (bacteria and fungi break down droppings and dead organisms into nutrients)

Frog (eats grasshopper)

Sun

Grasshopper (eats grass and leaves)

Nutrients (water, phosphorus, nitrogen, calcium...)

Plant Life (nourishes self through photosynthesis; needs nutrients in order to grow)

4 Which is the only organism in the food chain above that is *not* eaten by another organism in the chain?

   ① insects
   ② plants
   ③ grasshopper
   ④ hawk
   ⑤ snake

5 What would most likely happen to the animal populations if chemical spraying killed most of the mosquitoes and grasshoppers—both of which are sources of food for frogs?

   ① a decrease in both frogs and snakes
   ② a decrease in frogs and an increase in grasshoppers
   ③ an increase in both frogs and snakes
   ④ a decrease in snakes and an increase in hawks
   ⑤ an increase in both snakes and hawks

Care of the Environment

Background Information

The study of the distribution of living organisms on Earth and the relationship of organisms to their environment is called **ecology**. Ecologists are particularly interested in the interactions between organisms and their environment. Ecologists try to understand how to keep the quality of an environment at a high level to provide good health to as many species as possible. Ecologists are especially concerned about how changes in an ecosystem, many made by human intervention, can affect the long-term health of species in that ecosystem.

Reading Selection

A rain forest is an extended region of dense vegetation, characterized by a wide variety of trees that form a canopy over dense ground-covering vegetation. Rain forests are home to about two-thirds of all plant and animal species on Earth. They are characterized by high levels of rainfall—about 100 inches per year. Rain forests are thought to provide Earth with as much as 40% of the oxygen found in the atmosphere. In addition, they remove much of the carbon dioxide gas placed in the atmosphere, thus keeping Earth's temperature in a life-sustaining range.

Medical researchers have discovered that rain forests are Earth's largest supplier of natural medicines. Half of all medicines used today come from plants discovered in rain forests. The hope is that many more plant-derived medicinal drugs will be discovered in the years ahead.

Biologists have estimated that more than half of Earth's rain forests were lost to logging and agricultural clearance during the twentieth century. While rain forests used to cover about 14% of Earth's surface, they now cover only about 6%. Some scientists predict that unless they are protected, the remaining natural rain forests could disappear by the year 2050. Protection and regeneration of natural rain forests is a major goal of many environmental groups.

❶ What is the study of ecology?

_____

_____

❷ Why are rain forests important for human life on Earth?

_____

❸ What is the greatest threat to rain forests at the present time?

_____

GED Practice

Questions 1 and 2 are based on the following passage.

The giant panda is a large, cuddly-looking, black and white mammal that until recently was considered to belong to the raccoon family. During the last few years, though, scientists have come to believe that the giant panda belongs to the bear family.

The giant panda lives mainly in China and Tibet and is classified as an endangered species. Although the diet of the giant panda includes eggs and small insects, its main source of food is overwhelmingly bamboo. The giant panda is on the endangered species list because of the widespread cutting of bamboo trees for commercial use.

1 From the passage, what can you infer is the meaning of "endangered species"?

   ① a species not capable of living in a zoo
   ② a species that has natural predators
   ③ a species that is overpopulated
   ④ a species in danger of extinction
   ⑤ a species that is hunted as game

2 Which animal is most closely related to the giant panda?

   ① kangaroo
   ② black bear
   ③ raccoon
   ④ zebra
   ⑤ mule deer

3 Which factor is *least* related to providing an environment in which a wide variety of plants and animals can thrive?

   ① clean air
   ② clean water
   ③ fertile soil
   ④ biodiversity
   ⑤ land value

Questions 4, 5, and 6 refer to the following drawing.

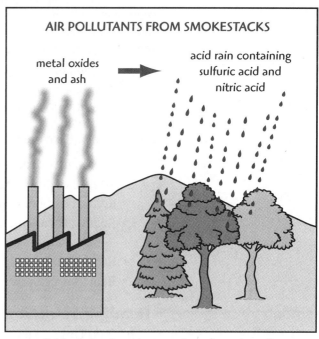

Acid rain leaches plant nutrients from the soil.
Metal oxides interfere with normal plant growth.

4 What is the most likely effect of acid rain on tree growth?

   ① tree growth temporarily stops
   ② no effect on tree growth
   ③ tree growth is increased
   ④ tree growth is decreased
   ⑤ trees die immediately

5 What is the most likely source of the sulfur contained in acid rain?

   ① impurity contained in fossil fuels
   ② naturally occurring element in air
   ③ impurity contained in soil
   ④ naturally occurring element in water
   ⑤ impurity contained in rivers

6 What is a natural occurrence that also is likely to result in acid rain?

   ① earthquake
   ② mudslide
   ③ volcanic eruption
   ④ flood
   ⑤ tsunami

Instruction Skill

21

Personal Health

Background Information

Perhaps the most important thing you can learn from your study of science is that you personally have a lot of control over how long and how well you live. Having a long and healthy life is not a matter of luck. You can plan for it. You can control many physical and mental factors that affect how you feel and how you age.

Do you know that more than half the deaths each year in the United States are caused by heart and blood vessel diseases? Do you also know that these diseases are almost unknown in many other countries? Why? The answer is related to lifestyle. Medical research says that we can do many things to prevent heart disease and obesity (excessive weight).

- Avoid fatty meat and fatty animal products.
- Reduce or stop smoking.
- Reduce alcohol consumption.
- Reduce sugar consumption.
- Reduce stress.
- Reduce body weight.
- Exercise regularly.

Reading Selection

In 1900 United States citizens could expect to live an average of 47 years. By the end of the twentieth century, the average life expectancy in the United States rose to more than 75 years. There are several reasons for this increase. First, fewer children are dying as a result of accidents at work. Laws now prohibit child labor, which was prevalent in the early 1900s. Children younger than 16 are now required to stay in school. Better nutrition and new vaccinations against disease also help ensure children's health. Also, adult Americans are healthier. Workplace safety laws have helped protect adult workers; advances in medicine have benefited adults of all ages, especially those with health insurance. Increased education has brought about a new public awareness of health and safety.

❶ At what age do you believe adults should be allowed to drink alcoholic beverages? Give a brief reason for your answer.

_____

❷ Name two things you personally can do to help ensure a healthier life for yourself.

_____

❸ What are four reasons that U.S. life expectancy increased during the twentieth century?

_____

_____

GED Practice

Questions 1, 2, 3, and 4 refer to the passage below.

A scientist placed four mice in each of two cages and fed each group the same type of food. However, he kept the food trays in cage 1 full at all times. He placed only small portions of food in cage 2. The results of his experiment are as follows:

- The mice in cage 1 lacked energy and were often ill. All died before reaching the average life expectancy.
- The mice in cage 2 were energetic and healthy. They all lived long beyond the average life expectancy.

1 What phrase best tells what this experiment tried to discover?

- (1) effect of food on sleep
- (2) effect of aging on health
- (3) effect of aging on food consumption
- (4) effect of health on aging
- (5) effect of food on health and aging

2 What conclusion can you draw from the results of the mice experiment?

- (1) The death of mice in cage 1 is related to the type of food eaten.
- (2) The mice in cage 2 would have lived a long time even if their supply of food was not limited.
- (3) Limiting feeding slows the aging process in mice.
- (4) Overfeeding slows the aging process in mice.
- (5) Neither underfeeding nor overfeeding affects the aging process.

3 Which of the following is *least* important to know before drawing conclusions?

- (1) cause of death of each mouse
- (2) size of food trays in each cage
- (3) average daily amount of food given to mice in each cage
- (4) average amount of food a typical mouse would normally eat daily
- (5) the life expectancy of a mouse that is fed an average amount of food

4 Suppose these results are applied to humans. Which statement *least* supports the opinion that overeating leads to poor health?

- (1) Overeating ensures that you have enough vitamins and minerals.
- (2) Overeating overloads your body's ability to deal with pollutants found in food.
- (3) Overeating makes you less able to get a good night's sleep.
- (4) Overeating requires a great deal of energy for digestion.
- (5) Overeating results in weight gain that is hard on the heart.

Questions 5 refers to the chart below.

RECOMMENDED DAILY VITAMIN NEEDS OF ADULTS (ages 19-30)*		
	Males	Females
Vitamin A	1,000 ug	800 ug
Vitamin E	10 mg	8 mg
Vitamin K	75 ug	62 ug
Vitamin C	60 mg	60 mg
Thiamin	1.2 mg	1.1 mg
Riboflavin	1.3 mg	1.1 mg
Niacin	1.6 mg	1.4 mg
Vitamin B$_6$	1.3 mg	1.3 mg
Folate	400 ug	400 ug
Vitamin B$_{12}$	2.4 ug	2.4 ug
Vitamin D	5 ug	5 ug
mg = milligram; ug = microgram		
*Based on figures from the National Academy of Sciences		

5 Which of the following can be inferred from the chart?

- (1) Vitamin A is more necessary than all other vitamins.
- (2) Micrograms (ug) are larger than milligrams (mg).
- (3) For good health, the human body needs a variety of vitamins.
- (4) Children don't need vitamins.
- (5) Vitamin A is important for nighttime vision.

Community Health

Background Information

Community health refers to the study and betterment of the health of a whole community or the health of a nation in general. Of particular interest are responsibilities that the government assumes to protect the health of its citizens. Some of these responsibilities are to:

- prevent widespread diseases—both physical and psychological
- provide widespread health care for all citizens
- provide widespread medical knowledge about healthful living styles
- control the distribution of non-medicinal substances such as tobacco and alcohol
- determine the safety of medical drugs given out by prescription only
- determine the safety of over-the-counter medicines such as aspirin
- provide for the safety of food, water, and air

Reading Selection

Before the year 2050, scientists may develop vaccines to eliminate most human diseases. A vaccine helps prevent a disease, not cure it. A vaccine is a dose of germ that triggers your natural immune system into action. For example, a flu vaccine consists of a small dose of flu virus. Once this vaccine is taken (a vaccination), your body responds by making antibodies, a form of protein that acts as a virus fighter. These antibodies then prevent the same flu virus from entering and attacking your body at a later time.

Vaccines that have been very successful are the DPT vaccine—which has all but eliminated the three long-feared childhood diseases of diphtheria, tetanus, and pertussis (commonly called whooping cough)—and the vaccines for pneumonia, influenza, polio, measles, mumps, German measles, and smallpox. The effectiveness of vaccines is most obvious when parents fail to have their children immunized at recommended times. When this happens, the number of children stricken with those diseases once again rises.

At the present time, scientists are working hard to develop vaccines for AIDS (Acquired Immune Deficiency Syndrome), Avian flu (bird flu), and various forms of cancer thought to be caused by viruses.

❶ What do you think the government's role should be in the control of the sale of tobacco and alcohol to youth?

_____

_____

❷ Do you personally get a flu shot each year? Why or why not?

_____

_____

GED Practice

Questions 1 and 2 are based on the passage below.

Vaccines, while considered safe overall, do have an element of risk. A small number of people who take a vaccine actually get the disease. For example, it is estimated that one child in 310,000 who takes the DPT vaccine will become ill and suffer brain damage. Yet, without the DPT vaccine, it is claimed that the incidence of death due to whooping cough would be 19 times higher than it is now. Also, the incidence of brain damage would be four times as high. Because of the potential danger of vaccines, medical research on vaccine safety is continuing. Parents are advised to check with their doctor or with a local health clinic to see which vaccines are appropriate for themselves and their children.

1 What risk does the passage describe in getting vaccinated for a disease?

(1) being overcharged
(2) getting the wrong vaccine
(3) not needing the vaccine
(4) getting the disease
(5) the vaccine not working

2 Which statement below is only an opinion that can be neither proved nor disproved with evidence?

(1) Vaccines have been successful in preventing the spread of many diseases.
(2) Because of risk, all vaccinations should be halted until vaccines can be made perfectly safe.
(3) Research is being done to develop vaccines to prevent cancer.
(4) The success of vaccines has been partly due to the work of chemists involved in medical research.
(5) In most cases, the health of children is put at risk if they do not receive recommended vaccines.

Questions 3 and 4 refer to the graph below.

The line graph below shows how the amount of antibodies (pathogen-fighting cells) in a person's blood varies between the first exposure to a pathogen (such as that provided by a vaccine) and a later, second exposure.

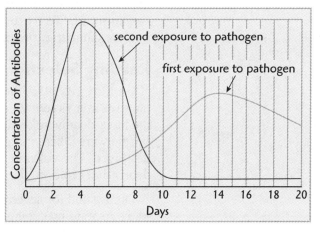

IMMUNE RESPONSE

3 What can you infer to be the meaning of the word *pathogen*?

(1) a type of blood disease
(2) a type of vaccine
(3) a disease caused by a vaccine
(4) a virus or bacteria that can prevent a disease
(5) a virus or bacteria that can cause disease

4 What can you conclude about the human immune system?

(1) The immune system may not destroy all of a pathogen during the first infection.
(2) The immune system reacts differently to different pathogens.
(3) The immune system remembers an invading pathogen.
(4) The immune system itself can come under attack.
(5) Second exposures to a pathogen are more dangerous than first exposures to the same pathogen.

Natural Disasters

Background Information

Perhaps nothing can have a more devastating effect on a local population than a **natural disaster**. Examples of natural disasters are volcanic eruptions, earthquakes, forest fires, mudslides, tornados, and hurricanes. During and after a natural disaster, the natural forces at work within Earth result in a serious threat to the life and health of all local residents as well as all other organisms in the area. What's more, a disaster brings all of our science into use. We react with immediate medical care, with rescue and recovery, and with reconstruction of our homes and communities. We try to better understand how the forces of nature work and learn how we can better predict and deal with these forces in the future.

Reading Selection

On May 18, 1980, the top one-third of Mount St. Helens in southern Washington blew off in a violent volcanic eruption. The eruption of Mount St. Helens was the most deadly volcanic eruption in the history of the United States. Fifty-seven people were killed and 200 homes, 47 bridges, and 185 miles of highway were destroyed. The volcano resulted in an avalanche of ash, mud, trees, and other debris that replaced the summit of the mountain with a mile-wide crater.

During and for several weeks after the eruption, ash fell like rain from the sky into surrounding communities. Portland, Oregon, the largest nearby community, was quickly covered with more than a foot of ash. For weeks after the eruption, Portland residents shoveled ash from the tops of homes, from yards, and from streets. During this time, many Portland residents wore breathing masks to protect their lungs from the ash. Hospitals had to deal with great numbers of patients with respiratory problems.

Mount St. Helens became active again in autumn 2004. Thousands of small, localized tremors were followed by several visible emissions of steam and ash. Throughout the summer of 2005, activity was recorded on the mountain and steam was often seen rising from the lava dome in the crater. Scientists remain alert for any more significant signs of future eruptions.

❶ What natural disaster is most likely to happen where you live?

_____

❷ How can citizens best prepare themselves for survival during a time following a natural disaster—a time when grocery stores may be closed, water pipes may be destroyed, and electric power lines may be down?

_____

_____

_____

GED Practice

Questions 1 and 2 are based on the following passage.

Hurricane Katrina was a category 5 hurricane (the strongest category) that lasted from August 23, 2005, to August 31, 2005. Katrina came ashore on August 29 near New Orleans, Louisiana. The accompanying storm surge breached the levee system that protected New Orleans from nearby Lake Pontchartrain and the Mississippi River. Most of New Orleans was then flooded with both sea water and lake water. Heavy damage also occurred along the Mississippi and Alabama coasts. Katrina was the most destructive and costliest natural disaster in the history of the United States.

Hurricane Katrina left an estimated 5 million people without power. The official death toll was 1,325. Damage was estimated to be over 100 billion dollars. It may be decades before the city of New Orleans is completely rebuilt.

1 What is the first need of people who are in a hurricane?

  ① replacement of lost valuables
  ② rescue and movement to a safe location
  ③ permanent new housing
  ④ getting children back in school
  ⑤ letting relatives know they are safe

2 What is the safest preventive measure people can take in the days before a powerful hurricane strikes?

  ① buy extra food and water
  ② lock the doors of their home
  ③ place boards over windows
  ④ move to a safe location, out of town if necessary
  ⑤ keep updated on weather reports

3 Which organization below works to help people who are victims of natural disasters?

  ① Special Olympics
  ② Chamber of Commerce
  ③ Red Cross
  ④ National Football League
  ⑤ Humane Society

Questions 4 and 5 are based on the picture below.

4 What is the first responsibility of elected officials when a natural disaster is predicted?

  ① to warn citizens and provide them with safety
  ② to reassure everyone that the city is safe
  ③ to let people know who's in charge
  ④ to leave the danger area
  ⑤ to close local stores

5 What type of natural disaster most likely caused the damage shown above?

  ① flood
  ② volcanic eruption
  ③ forest fire
  ④ mud slide
  ⑤ tornado

6 In a poor country hit by a natural disaster, which of the following would *not* be an immediate health or safety issue?

  ① lack of property insurance
  ② lack of food
  ③ shortage of medical supplies
  ④ shortage of safe water
  ⑤ housing shortage

Human-Created Hazards

Background Information

The survival of all organisms, including human beings, depends on the quality of their environment. Healthy life depends on the presence of safe water, safe air, safe food, and a safe working environment. Unfortunately, the realities of our world make attaining these goals difficult. Industry, which is so necessary for jobs, very often produces either products or byproducts that pose health risks. Industry is responsible for much of the air and water pollution that affects our lives. Government regulations appear to be the surest way to protect all citizens from the pollutants which we ourselves create.

Reading Selection

Love Canal is a 36-square-block neighborhood in Niagara Falls, New York. In 1978 the president of the Love Canal Homeowner's Association led an effort to investigate community concerns about health problems of local residents. These residents had extremely high rates of cancer and birth defects. School children were constantly ill, and residents complained of strange outdoor odors and unknown substances seeping into their yards.

In a three-year fight, Love Canal residents were able to prove that toxic chemicals buried as long as 40 years before by the Hooker Chemical Company were responsible for the residents' health problems. On August 7, 1978, United States president Jimmy Carter declared a federal emergency at Love Canal. On May 17, 1980, the EPA (Environmental Protection Agency) announced results of their investigation. The EPA concluded that the residents of Love Canal had chromosome damage related to toxic chemicals. This chromosome damage meant that Love Canal residents were at an increased risk of having cancer, reproductive problems, genetic damage, and birth defects—the same types of problems being reported.

Eventually the federal government relocated more than 800 families from Love Canal. Congress passed the Superfund Law, which held polluters liable for any health problems resulting from their pollution. Occidental Petroleum, owner of Hooker Chemical Company, paid more than $200 million to clean up the site. Even now, though, a chain-link fence separates toxic areas of Love Canal from the safer area that people have moved back to.

❶ Name two health problems that can result from exposure to toxic chemicals.

_____

❷ What is the Superfund Law? _____

_____

❸ There are still many toxic waste dumps in the United States. Are you willing to pay more money in taxes so that the government can clean these up?

_____

_____

GED Practice

Questions 1, 2, and 3 refer to the passage below.

On April 26, 1986, an accident occurred at the Chernobyl nuclear power plant in the Soviet Union. A reactor had a catastrophic steam explosion. Then a series of fires and additional explosions occurred. Soon, a nuclear reactor overheated and melted. Lethal radioactive gas and debris spread throughout the plant and escaped into the atmosphere. The contaminated gas drifted over western parts of the Soviet Union, Europe, Scandinavia, the United Kingdom, and the eastern United States.

The accident claimed 31 workers at the plant during the first few days. In the days following, 200,000 local residents were moved to other cities. Since the accident, an unknown number have died from their exposure to the escaped radioactive materials. It is estimated that thousands, perhaps tens of thousands, more will die in the years ahead. This is because the effects of nuclear radiation poisoning lead to cancers that can take years to develop.

1 What is the main danger to humans from a nuclear power plant accident?

  ① burns suffered from hot steam
  ② smoke inhalation from fire
  ③ being hit by falling debris
  ④ drowning from resulting floods
  ⑤ nuclear radiation poisoning

2 Why is it difficult to accurately estimate the number of deaths caused by the Chernobyl accident?

  ① The investigation of the accident takes years to complete.
  ② Resulting cancers can take many years to develop.
  ③ A nuclear power plant takes years to construct.
  ④ It is difficult to locate all the people present at the time of the accident.
  ⑤ The health effects of radiation poisoning are not really known.

3 Which of the following people are at highest risk for health problems due to radioactive waste poisoning?

  ① residents of nearby towns who were resettled in other communities
  ② residents of England, where radioactive waste was detected
  ③ Soviet officials responsible for the safety of nuclear power plants
  ④ workers involved in cleaning up the Chernobyl plant after the accident
  ⑤ people who designed the Chernobyl nuclear power plant

Questions 4 and 5 refer to the drawing below.

4 What health warning is at the bottom of the paint thinner can?

  ① Paint thinner can be used safely.
  ② Paint thinner should not be mixed.
  ③ Paint thinner is poisonous.
  ④ Paint thinner is not expensive.
  ⑤ Paint thinner is not toxic.

5 Which of the following is true?

  ① Household products can create both safety and health risks.
  ② Household products are always safe for young children.
  ③ All household products contain warnings.
  ④ A product that is sold in a store carries no risk to a consumer.
  ⑤ Inexpensive household products carry no safety or health risks.

Human Aspects of Science

Background Information

Science is a human endeavor that seeks to understand our world. Tens of thousands of years ago, primitive people feared or worshipped the Moon. In our time, astronauts have flown to the Moon, walked on the lunar surface, and brought moon rocks back to Earth. It is hard to believe how far our understanding and technology have progressed.

Science today is done by people just like you. Scientists are excited by new discoveries and are disappointed when science does not live up to its promises. Listen to the words of two famous scientists:

> Why does this magnificent applied science, which saves work and makes life easier, bring us so little happiness? The simple answer runs: Because we have not yet learned to make sensible use of it.
>
> —Albert Einstein (1879–1955) American physicist and Nobel prize winner

> There will come a time when the world will be filled with one science, one truth, one industry, one brotherhood, one friendship with nature . . . This is my belief.
>
> —Dimitry Mendeleyev (1834–1907) Russian chemist, father of modern genetics

Reading Selection

From the time of primitive people to the present, personal beliefs, particularly religious beliefs, have played a role in science. When science was in its infancy, scientific discoveries often were in disagreement with religious teachings. When that happened, religious beliefs were often considered correct and further scientific inquiry was stopped.

Today, science and religion have come a long way from those earlier times. Now the questions of science do not need to overlap questions of faith.

- Science deals with questions of the natural world, questions for which experiments can be performed. For example, "Is there life on Mars?"
- Faith deals primarily with questions of values, questions for which science cannot give answers. For example, "Should we do medical experimentation on animals if the animals are harmed by the research?"

In the twenty-first century we realize that the most difficult questions are questions of values, not science. Science will give us many new choices, but it will not provide an answer to questions about how science is used.

❶ Describe an issue that concerns you that involves both science and personal values.

_____

_____

GED Practice

Questions 1 and 2 are based on the following quotation.

Science investigates; religion interprets. Science gives man knowledge, which is power; religion gives man wisdom, which is control.

—Martin Luther King, Jr. (1929–1968)

1 What did Martin Luther King, Jr., believe was the source of knowledge?

(1) power
(2) control
(3) science
(4) wisdom
(5) religion

2 What did Martin Luther King, Jr., believe was the source of wisdom?

(1) power
(2) religion
(3) knowledge
(4) science
(5) control

3 Which word or phrase would *not* be a good characteristic of a scientist?

(1) curious
(2) proud of his or her work
(3) willing to share ideas
(4) secretive
(5) honest

4 Which of the following types of research is a scientist *least* likely to be involved in today?

(1) medical drug research
(2) research on health effects of exercise
(3) research on animal intelligence
(4) research on nutritional value of food
(5) research on a polio vaccine

Questions 5 and 6 are based on the following label.

> **SURGEON GENERAL'S WARNING**
> Quitting Smoking Greatly
> Reduces Serious Health Risks

5 A scientist supports keeping this warning on all tobacco products. What concern is this scientist responding to?

(1) community health
(2) restrictions on free speech
(3) government taxation
(4) tobacco company profits
(5) house-fire danger

6 A tobacco company scientist claims that there is no firm medical evidence that links smoking with serious health risks. Which concern is this scientist most likely responding to?

(1) personal health
(2) personal job security
(3) community health
(4) religious values
(5) air pollution

7 Which of the following do scientists have the *least* control over?

(1) the number of hours they work
(2) the type of work they choose to do
(3) how often they share their findings with other scientists
(4) how they report their findings to the general public
(5) how scientific discoveries are used by society

Traces of Ancient Life

Background Information

A **fossil** is the preserved remains or traces of an ancient living thing. Fossils provide evidence of organisms that once lived on Earth but that are now extinct. By studying fossils, scientists find clues as to how today's organisms are related to extinct organisms. Scientists have used fossils to confirm that slow evolution does seem to take place as proposed by Darwin's theory of evolution. Fossils also indicate that punctuated equilibrium—sudden evolutionary changes brought about by catastrophic events such as an asteroid striking Earth—is an important part of the evolutionary process.

Fossils tell us many things about an organism:

- when the organism first appeared on Earth
- how the organism differed from the ancestors from which it evolved
- characteristics of the organism's life
- how long the organism was on Earth until it became extinct
- what caused the organism to become extinct

Reading Selection

During its life, every organism absorbs two types of carbon: stable carbon-12 and radioactive carbon-14. While it is alive, an organism keeps its body level of each type of carbon at a constant level. From the time of death on, however, the level of carbon-14 in an organism slowly decreases without being replaced. This fact enables scientists to determine when an organism died by examining its fossil remains. The time of death is related to the amount of carbon-14 remaining in the fossil compared to the amount of carbon-12 in the fossil.

Carbon-14 decreases at a constant rate. Half of any carbon-14 remaining in a fossil disappears each 5,730 years. This is called the half-life of carbon-14. By measuring the amount of carbon-14 remaining, a scientist knows how many half-lives have passed.

- If the amount of carbon-14 is $\frac{1}{2}$ of the amount seen in a living organism, the fossil is of an organism that died 5,730 years ago.
- If the amount of carbon-14 is $\frac{1}{4}$ of the amount seen in a living organism, the fossil is of an organism that died 11,460 years ago (2 half-lives, or $2 \times 5,730$).
- If the amount of carbon-14 is $\frac{1}{8}$ of the amount seen in a living organism, the fossil is of an organism that died 17,190 years ago (3 half-lives, or $3 \times 5,730$).

❶ What is a fossil? _____

❷ Give two reasons why fossils are important to study.

_____

❸ What is meant by the phrase "half-life of carbon-14"?

_____

GED Practice

Questions 1, 2, and 3 refer to the passage below.

Fossils tell us that about 400 million years ago organisms began appearing on land, having first started in the ocean. First came plants, then simple amphibians, perhaps ancestors of today's frogs and salamanders. Reptiles such as lizards, snakes, and dinosaurs appeared about 300 million years ago. The first mammals appeared about 100 million years ago. Mammals, though, would not come to be a dominant species until the extinction of dinosaurs about 70 million years ago.

1 What can you infer from information given in the passage?

    ① Life on Earth most likely started in a water environment.
    ② Life on Earth most likely started in a land environment.
    ③ Life on Earth most likely started in both a water and land environment.
    ④ Life on Earth did not start in water.
    ⑤ Life cannot start on land.

2 Which of the following statements can you conclude to be true?

    ① Mammals were on Earth before the emergence of dinosaurs.
    ② Mammals and dinosaurs were never on Earth at the same time.
    ③ Early mammals were on Earth at the same time as dinosaurs.
    ④ The emergence of mammals led to the extinction of dinosaurs.
    ⑤ The emergence of dinosaurs led to the extinction of early mammals.

3 How would you classify this statement: "Modern birds may actually be living dinosaurs"?

    ① nonsense
    ② scientific fact
    ③ hypothesis
    ④ opinion
    ⑤ evidence

Questions 4 and 5 refer to the drawing below and the information given for questions 1, 2, and 3.

Spinal column vertebrae from a Tyrannosaurus Rex

4 Which of the following is the most likely age of the pictured fossil?

    ① 100 years old
    ② 10,000 years old
    ③ 100,000 years old
    ④ 1,000,000 years old
    ⑤ 100,000,000 years old

5 What part of the animal is represented by these fossils?

    ① skull
    ② backbone
    ③ front leg
    ④ rear leg
    ⑤ foot

6 Dinosaur egg fossils have been found. What living animals do you think are most likely to be related to ancient dinosaurs?

    ① goats and gorillas
    ② horses and pigeons
    ③ ducks and alligators
    ④ antelopes and sharks
    ⑤ frogs and kangaroos

Advances in Medicine

Background Information

There is probably no other area in science that affects you more directly than advances in medicine. Not only has life expectancy in the United States almost doubled during the last century, but also the quality of your life has been enhanced by advances in medicine.

Medical advances have occurred in many areas: health care, medical technology, diagnosis, medicinal drug therapy, surgical procedures, and follow-up therapy. For example, only a few years ago, most forms of cancer were not treatable. Today, many forms of cancer can be cured if detected early enough. And, for some cancers, cancer-fighting drugs have been developed that target specific cancer cells. Invasive surgeries and chemical assaults on the entire body are no longer necessary.

Reading Selection

One medical procedure for a heart that is irreversibly damaged by heart disease or infection is a heart transplant—the replacement of a disabled heart with a healthy human heart. The healthy heart comes as a donated organ from a recently deceased organ donor.

The world's first heart transplant was performed by Dr. Christian Bernard in 1969. In an operation performed in South Africa that lasted nine hours, Dr. Bernard worked with a team of 30 assistants to replace the ailing heart of 55-year-old Louis Washkansky. Mr. Washkansky received the heart of a young woman who was killed in an auto accident. Washkansky lived for just 18 days following the operation. He died of pneumonia induced by the medicinal drugs he was taking to aid his recovery.

Dr. Bernard also pioneered heart/lung transplants, artificial heart valves, and the use of animal hearts for temporary emergency situations.

Today, more than 2,000 heart transplants are performed in the United States each year. Thousands more patients would benefit from a heart transplant if more donated hearts were available. About 3 out of 4 heart transplant recipients are male.

❶ What is Dr. Christian Bernard remembered for? _____

❷ What limits the number of heart transplants performed in the United States each year?

_____

❸ What is your personal opinion about becoming an organ donor—a person who gives a doctor permission to remove viable organs from his or her body at the time of his or her death? These organs would then be used to help other patients in need.

_____

_____

GED Practice

Questions 1, 2, and 3 are based on the following passage.

Radiation (high-energy rays similar to X-rays) has long been used to fight cancer. The problem with this method has been that beams of radiation strike not only cancer cells, but also surrounding healthy tissue and organs.

One of the newest weapons in the fight against cancer is targeted beams of radiation, called IMRT (intensity modulated radiation therapy). Instead of bombarding cancerous regions of the body with large doses of radiation, IMRT is directed by a computer to target very specific cancerous cells. Like drug therapy that targets specific cells, IMRT may be a breakthrough in cancer treatment that could help eliminate the traditional side effects of radiation therapy ranging from nausea to organ damage and even paralysis.

1 What is IMRT used to do?

  ① prevent nausea
  ② repair organ damage
  ③ kill cancer cells
  ④ block X-rays
  ⑤ repair damaged tissue

2 How does IMRT differ from traditional radiation therapy?

  ① IMRT attacks body cells.
  ② IMRT targets specific cells.
  ③ IMRT is a weapon against cancer.
  ④ IMRT is always successful.
  ⑤ IMRT costs less.

3 What is one disadvantage of traditional radiation treatment of cancer?

  ① cancer cells are not always killed
  ② excessive cost of treatment
  ③ a lack of trained specialists
  ④ less effective than drug treatment
  ⑤ damage to non-cancerous organs

Questions 4 and 5 are based on the following information.

One of the keys to good health is maintaining good blood pressure—the pressure that blood exerts against the walls of a person's arteries during the heartbeat cycle. Blood pressure is given as two numbers such as 135/85 (read as 135 over 85):

- The first number is systolic pressure, the point of highest blood pressure during the heartbeat cycle.
- The second number is diastolic pressure, measured just before the heart beats.

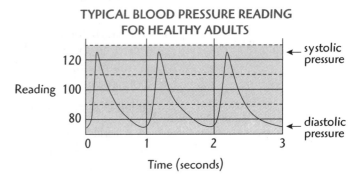

TYPICAL BLOOD PRESSURE READING FOR HEALTHY ADULTS

4 What does blood pressure measure?

  ① the difference in pressure between blood flowing in arteries and blood flowing in veins
  ② the pressure that blood exerts on the walls of arteries
  ③ the pressure with which blood flows from a wound
  ④ the amount of a person's blood
  ⑤ the weight of a person's blood

5 What is the blood pressure reading shown on the graph above?

  ① 135/85
  ② 130/90
  ③ 130/75
  ④ 125/75
  ⑤ 120/75

Historical Perspectives in Life Science

Background Information

Science slowly progresses over a long period of time. Sometimes new discoveries occur one after another. Other times, hundreds of years pass before a theory is replaced by a more correct and complete understanding. Often we find that the theories of early thinkers in science are somewhat humorous. We easily forget how difficult it is to move beyond one's beliefs, even in the face of new evidence. Did you know, for example, that two hundred years ago many people believed that insects and worms came from rotting soil? And did you know that people believed that frogs formed in clouds and fell to Earth during rainstorms? Only in the last 150 years have people come to understand that life comes only from life, each organism coming from the reproduction of parent organisms.

Reading Selection

Galen (131–201 A.D.), a Greek physician, is one of the most famous medical doctors in history. Galen's conclusions on how the human body worked were accepted as correct for 1,400 years. It wasn't until the work of Englishman Dr. William Harvey (1578–1657) that some of Galen's theories were changed to more correctly agree with new discoveries.

Galen did make several important discoveries that were correct:

- Arteries carry blood, not air as had been believed up until Galen's time.
- The brain controls the human voice.
- Different muscles are controlled at different levels along the spinal cord.

Galen was completely wrong about one function. Although he studied the heart, Galen believed that the liver was the main organ of the vascular (blood carrying) system. He also concluded that blood moves from the liver to the outer skin, where it forms skin. Galen did not realize that blood continually circulates through the body.

❶ For what reason might people believe that insects and worms came from rotting soil?

_____

❷ What is a surprising thing about Galen's medical theories?

_____

❸ Suppose Galen noticed that skin burns were very slow to heal. Which organ would Galen likely suspect to be diseased?

heart   eye   brain   stomach   liver

❹ What does the reading selection imply that Dr. William Harvey is remembered for?

_____

GED Practice

Questions 1 and 2 refer to the following passage.

Before the publication of Darwin's theory of evolution, Jean Lamarck, a French biologist, proposed a different theory on how species evolved. According to Lamarck, an individual organism could acquire certain traits by its own efforts. Lamarck believed that these traits would then be inherited by all of the organism's future offspring.

Lamarck's often cited example is a giraffe. He claimed that giraffes once had short legs and short necks. But then as they stretched to reach high in the trees, giraffes stretched their necks and legs a little at a time. In this way, the bodies of giraffes changed shape. When these "stretched" giraffes reproduced, their offspring were born with long necks and long legs.

Scientists today do not accept Lamarck's ideas. Although organisms can condition their bodies to their environment in some ways, they cannot pass these changes on to their offspring.

1 According to Lamarck, which factor most influenced a change in the shape of giraffes?

   ① the extinction of natural predators
   ② lots of vegetation near the ground
   ③ rivers caused by frequent floods
   ④ a lack of vegetation near the ground
   ⑤ the size of natural predators

2 According to scientists today, which of the following is *not* a trait that is passed on to offspring?

   ① wing speed of a hummingbird
   ② green color of a tree frog
   ③ muscle tone of a weight lifter
   ④ swimming ability of a whale
   ⑤ thick white fur of a polar bear

Questions 3 and 4 refer to the passage below.

In the seventeenth century, Francesco Redi performed an experiment to see if rotting meat would change into maggots. His experimental setup is shown below.

EXPERIMENT BEGINS

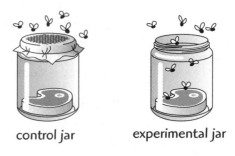

control jar   experimental jar

SEVERAL WEEKS LATER

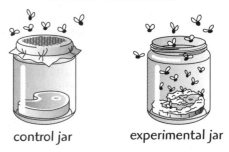

control jar   experimental jar

3 Why is cloth placed over the control jar?

   ① to keep dirt off the meat
   ② to contain the smell of rotting meat
   ③ to keep fresh air in the control jar
   ④ to keep flies away from the meat
   ⑤ to keep maggots from escaping

4 What conclusion can be drawn from the results of Redi's experiment?

   ① Maggots appear on rotting meat only after hatching from fly eggs.
   ② Maggots turn into flies only when they hatch on rotting meat.
   ③ The cloth slows down the rotting process.
   ④ Rotting meat turns into maggots only in the presence of fresh air.
   ⑤ Flies lay eggs only on rotting meat.

Phases of Matter

Background Information

A chemical formula, such as H_2O, tells what atoms make up a molecule. A molecule of water, H_2O, contains 2 hydrogen atoms and 1 oxygen atom. Unfortunately, the formula does not tell us much about the water. For example, steam, running water, and ice are all forms of water. Each is represented by the chemical formula H_2O.

Steam, running water, and ice are three forms, called **phases**, of water—gas, liquid, and solid. Each phase is determined by energy shared among its atoms or molecules. When the energy is very low, a substance is typically a solid. When the energy is moderate, the substance is typically a liquid. When the energy is high, the substance becomes a gas.

Reading Selection

To understand the properties of different phases of matter, think about everyday objects.

- *Solids:* Pick up a metal coin. The coin has two properties of all solids: definite shape and definite volume. Using a coin does not change its shape or size. This is because the atomic structure of the coin is very rigid. Atoms stay where they are.

- *Liquids:* Pour some water into a drinking glass. The water takes the shape of the glass. Water has two properties of all liquids: definite volume but not definite shape. The volume of water will not change if it is moved to a second glass of different shape. The liquid always takes the shape of the container that holds it, but the volume of liquid does not change. This is because the atoms and molecules in a liquid are able to move around each other easily but they do not change their average distance apart.

- *Gases:* Add air to a soccer ball. The ball does not change shape. The entering air takes the shape of the ball and crowds in as necessary. Air has two properties of all gases: neither definite shape nor definite volume. A gas spreads out or contracts to fill any container that encloses it. This is because the molecular structure of a gas is relatively loose, allowing atoms to move farther apart or closer together independently of each other.

❶ Identify the phase of matter of each common object below.

helium in a balloon _____   milk _____

hot tea _____   spoon _____

shell on the seashore _____   gasoline _____

dinner plate _____   air _____

chicken broth _____   newspaper _____

GED Practice

Questions 1, 2, and 3 refer to the passage below.

Viscosity is a measure of how much a fluid resists flowing. Think of viscosity as being a measure of the "thickness" of a liquid. For example, at room temperature the viscosity of syrup is much greater than the viscosity of water; the syrup pours more slowly than water. However, if syrup is heated, it pours more easily than water. At an increased temperature, the viscosity of syrup is less than that of water.

Viscosity is determined by the strength of chemical bonds that hold molecules of a liquid together. These bonds form a resistance that retards the movement of molecules past one another. Heating causes molecules to move more quickly and weakens the bonds that join them.

1 Which of the following fluids has the greatest viscosity at room temperature?

  ① milk
  ② toothpaste
  ③ oxygen gas
  ④ grape juice
  ⑤ car oil

2 What is the main property of a liquid that determines how its viscosity changes?

  ① shape of container in which liquid is placed
  ② color of liquid
  ③ weight of liquid
  ④ amount of liquid
  ⑤ temperature of liquid

3 What property determines which of two liquids has the greatest viscosity at room temperature?

  ① type of container liquid is in
  ② strength of chemical bonds
  ③ weight of liquid
  ④ what liquid is used for
  ⑤ boiling point of liquid

Questions 4 and 5 refer to the diagrams below.

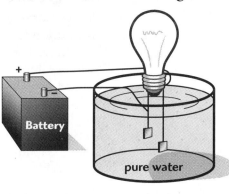

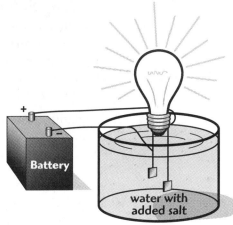

4 What is the key point made in the illustration?

  ① Salt dissolves in pure water only when an electric current is flowing.
  ② Electric appliances will be harmed by being placed in salt water.
  ③ Dissolved salt changes pure water into a nonconductor of electricity.
  ④ Dissolved salt changes pure water into a conductor of electricity.
  ⑤ All pure water contains salt.

5 When is the surface of your skin most likely to be a good conductor of electricity?

  ① when you are sweating
  ② right after you have bathed
  ③ when you are shivering
  ④ while you are sleeping
  ⑤ when you are talking

Chemistry of Life

Background Information

On the morning of July 20, 1976, the *Viking I* lander slowly drifted, with parachutes open, down to the dusty, red surface of the plains of Chryse on the planet Mars. On September 3, *Viking I* was joined by *Viking II*, which touched down on the Martian plain of Utopia. A major goal of both landers was to search the Martian soil for signs of life. Disappointingly, neither spacecraft found any evidence of molecules that contain the element carbon—the element found in all organisms on Earth. A visit by the more complex *Pathfinder* spacecraft on July 4, 1997, also failed to find signs of life. With several proposed new voyages during the next decade, NASA's Mars Exploration Program continues. The hope of finding either traces of extinct life or evidence of living organisms remains strong.

Reading Selection

All living things on Earth contain the element carbon. Because of this, the study of molecules that contain carbon is very important. This study is given the name **organic chemistry**. The word *organic*, from the word *organism*, refers to any molecule that contains one or more atoms of carbon. Organic chemistry is often called the chemistry of life.

Scientists know that organic molecules form easily in a wide range of environments that are rich in carbon and water. And surprisingly, on Earth at least, some type of life usually forms wherever carbon and water are found. Organisms have formed deep on the bottom of the ocean, deep in polar ice, and deep in volcanic hot springs. Now excitement is growing about the possibility of life on Mars. Scientists have discovered that Mars contains both water and carbon dioxide (gas made up of oxygen and carbon). The polar ice caps of Mars contain both frozen water and frozen carbon dioxide; the atmosphere of Mars is rich in carbon dioxide gas. The presence of water and carbon dioxide on Mars certainly gives rise to the possibility of organic molecules on Mars. Whether life in any form has ever existed on Mars is a question that is likely to intrigue humans for decades to come.

❶ What element is found in all organisms on Earth? _____

❷ What is organic chemistry? _____

❸ What two substances found on Mars are known to be important for the existence of life as we know it on Earth?

_____

❹ Do you believe that life existed on Mars in ancient times? Explain why or why not.

_____

_____

GED Practice

Questions 1 and 2 refer to the passage and illustration below.

Because of the ease with which carbon atoms can bond to one another, carbon molecules can take a variety of shapes. Some carbon molecules, called isomers, have the same number of carbon atoms but different molecular structure—different arrangements of atoms. Isomers differ in their physical, chemical, and biological properties. An example of isomers is shown below: normal butane (written as *n*-butane) and isobutane, with short line segments showing atom-to-atom bonds.

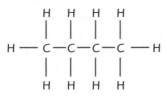

n–Butane

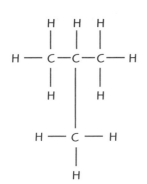

Isobutane

1 Which of the following properties is the same in isomers?

(1) number of all atoms
(2) number of carbon atoms
(3) chemical properties
(4) biological properties
(5) arrangement of atoms

2 How does an *n*-butane molecule differ from an isobutane molecule?

(1) number of carbon atoms
(2) number of hydrogen atoms
(3) total number of atoms
(4) arrangement of carbon atoms
(5) number of atom-to-atom bonds

Questions 3 and 4 refer to the passage and graph below.

Ancient forests and foliage of all kinds after tens of thousands of years of being buried, compressed, and heated were turned into the fossil fuels that we use today: coal, natural gas, and petroleum (oil). Each type of fossil fuel is made up mainly of molecules containing only carbon and hydrogen.

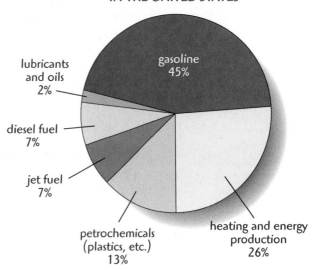

PERCENT BREAKDOWN OF PETROLEUM USE IN THE UNITED STATES

3 What is the main petroleum product used in the United States?

(1) petrochemicals
(2) diesel fuel
(3) heating and energy production
(4) jet fuel
(5) gasoline

4 What total percent of petroleum is used for the production of transportation fuels?

(1) 7 percent
(2) 14 percent
(3) 59 percent
(4) 72 percent
(5) 98 percent

Physical and Chemical Changes

Background Information

In nature, change continually takes place. Some changes, such as ice cream melting, do not change the properties of a substance. Some changes, such as trees burning in a forest fire, do change the properties of a substance. In general, changes are classified as either physical or chemical.

- *Physical change*—does not produce a new substance. During a physical change, a substance may change shape, size, color, and state. The substance may look different, but it is the same substance. For example, when ice cream melts, it changes from a solid to a liquid. The ice cream changes appearance and temperature, but it is still ice cream. Its color, taste, and chemical properties do not change.
- *Chemical change*—does produce a new substance. During a chemical change, a substance changes on a molecular level, may combine with other substances, and becomes a new substance. The new substance has different properties than the original substance. For example, when wood burns, the ash, carbon dioxide gas, and water that remain are no longer wood. No simple act can change the ashes back to wood.

Reading Selection

Fire is a form of chemical change called combustion. During combustion, a fuel substance, such as wood, undergoes rapid oxidation—a chemical change in which wood combines with oxygen. During combustion, both heat and light energy are given off. When wood burns, hydrocarbon molecules (molecules made up of hydrogen and carbon atoms) that make up the wood combine with oxygen, forming different types of molecules than those found in wood. The substances that result are ashes, carbon dioxide gas, and water.

Fire starts when a fuel is subjected to heat in the presence of oxygen. Fire continues only if there is both an oxygen supply and a continual supply of fuel. The heat required is given off by the burning fuel itself. The flaming part of a fire can actually conduct electricity. This presents an added danger when large fires are burning in the vicinity of electrical power lines. Fire can be extinguished by removing either the heat, oxygen, or fuel.

❶ What type of change is combustion? _____

❷ What three things are necessary for combustion to occur?

_____

❸ What two types of energy are given off during a fire?

_____

❹ Why does throwing water on a small campfire cause the fire to go out?

_____

GED Practice

Questions 1 and 2 refer to the passage below.

Lighting a match and making toast are both examples of chemical changes. Breaking the burned match into two pieces and cutting the toast in half are both examples of physical changes.

1 Which of the following statements is true?

  ① Both chemical changes can be reversed.
  ② Neither chemical change can be reversed.
  ③ Only the outward appearance of the toast is changed by heat.
  ④ Only the outward appearance of the match is changed by heat.
  ⑤ Both chemical changes are destructive and serve no purpose.

2 Which action will produce additional chemical changes?

  ① blowing out the lit match
  ② throwing the match away
  ③ eating the toast
  ④ placing jam on the toast
  ⑤ cutting the toast into small squares

3 When iron (Fe) combines with water and oxygen, it rusts. Which action will lead to this chemical change in a nail?

  ① Place the nail in a warm, dry place.
  ② Heat the nail until it glows red.
  ③ Run electricity through the nail.
  ④ Place the nail in a cool, dry place.
  ⑤ Place the nail in a cool, wet place.

4 Which action will produce a chemical change in sugar that is placed on a piece of bread about to become cinnamon toast?

  ① toasting the bread
  ② cutting the toasted bread
  ③ mixing the sugar and cinnamon
  ④ spreading the sugar on the bread
  ⑤ spreading cinnamon on the sugar

Questions 5, 6, and 7 refer to the diagram below.

ELECTROLYSIS

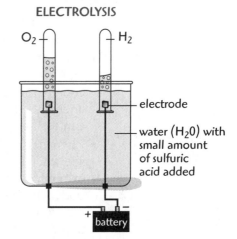

5 What two gases are involved in an electrolysis reaction?

  ① sulfur and water
  ② sulfur and oxygen
  ③ hydrogen and water
  ④ hydrogen and oxygen
  ⑤ carbon and oxygen

6 What type of reaction is electrolysis?

  ① a physical reaction in which water is broken down into oxygen and hydrogen
  ② a physical reaction in which oxygen and hydrogen are combined to form water
  ③ a chemical reaction in which water is broken down into oxygen and hydrogen
  ④ a chemical reaction in which oxygen and hydrogen are combined to form water
  ⑤ a chemical reaction in which water is used to create an electric current

7 What would likely increase the rate at which electrolysis occurs?

  ① using a lower voltage battery
  ② using a higher voltage battery
  ③ disconnecting the battery
  ④ increasing the size of the inverted tubes
  ⑤ decreasing the amount of water

32

Energy Flow in Chemical Reactions

Background Information

Energy is a very important part of our world.

- Energy plays a key role in the universe as a whole, keeping galaxies from collapsing due to gravitational force.
- On Earth, energy plays a key role in our lives. Types of energy that we see daily are sun energy, wind energy, the kinetic energy of moving cars, light energy from electric lights, and sound energy from a stereo. These forms of energy are involved in activities that take place on a human scale, things we can feel, see, and hear.
- Energy also plays a big role in the part of our lives that we don't normally see: chemical reactions, activity that occurs on a molecular level. A common example is the digestion of food. Molecules of food provide the human body with both the nutrients and the energy required for survival. Chemical reactions involving food molecules provide the energy that humans need to move around and think, as well as the energy needed to keep the human body healthy.

Reading Selection

In a chemical reaction, atoms or molecules of one or more substances combine in new ways to form new substances. In every chemical reaction, one or more chemical bonds are broken and new bonds are formed. Each time a bond is broken or a new bond is formed, energy is either absorbed or released. As a chemical reaction proceeds, energy is being given off in some parts of the reaction, and energy is being absorbed in other parts of the reaction. At the completion of the reaction, a net amount of energy is either given off or absorbed.

- *Exothermic reaction*—more energy is produced than is used, and energy is released as a result of the reaction. For example, when wood burns, both heat and light energy are given off. Burning wood is an exothermic reaction.
- *Endothermic reaction*—more energy is used than is given off. An endothermic reaction requires heat or light energy from an outside source in order to take place. For example, when bread bakes, a source of heat must be provided for the reaction to take place. Baking bread is an endothermic reaction.

❶ The chemical equation for the fermentation of alcohol is as follows:

$$C_6H_{12}O_6 \longrightarrow 2C_2H_3OH + 2CO_2 + heat$$

What type of reaction is the fermentation of alcohol? _____

❷ The chemical equation for photosynthesis is as follows:

$$6O_2 + 12H_2O + light \longrightarrow C_6H_{12}O_6 + 6O_2 + 6H_2O$$

What type of reaction is photosynthesis? _____

GED Practice

Questions 1, 2, 3, and 4 refer to the passage below.

Many chemical reactions that are self-sustaining (keep themselves going) begin only when a certain activation energy is reached. One example is a match. A match does not burst into flame until it is scratched on a hard surface. The scratching adds the heat energy needed by the chemicals in the match before they will ignite. Another example is the burning of paper. A piece of paper, placed near a heat source, continues to warm until it reaches a temperature of about 450°F, at which point it bursts into flame.

1 What is the best definition of activation energy?

① energy needed to stop a chemical reaction
② energy given off by a chemical reaction
③ energy needed to start a chemical reaction
④ energy absorbed during a chemical reaction
⑤ the type of energy produced during a chemical reaction

2 Which of the following requires an activation energy before it is self-sustaining?

① a warm hair dryer
② a cold freezer
③ an electric light that is on
④ a lit fire in a fireplace
⑤ a turned-on flashlight

3 What form of activation energy is responsible for lighting a candle?

① light
② heat
③ sound
④ microwave energy
⑤ electricity

4 What occurs if a needed activation energy is not supplied?

① A reaction stops halfway.
② A reaction slows down.
③ A reaction speeds up.
④ A reaction does not begin.
⑤ A reaction is delayed by several minutes.

Question 5 is based on the illustration below and the definitions given on page 86.

5 Which of the following best describes the type of reaction taking place above?

① neither an endothermic nor an exothermic reaction
② an exothermic reaction in which heat energy is supplied by the egg
③ an endothermic reaction in which heat energy is supplied by the egg
④ an exothermic reaction in which heat energy is supplied by the hot water
⑤ an endothermic reaction in which heat energy is supplied by the hot water

Question 6 is based on the illustration and the passage for questions 1 through 4.

6 Which of the following best describes the reaction pictured above?

① activation energy being used to start an exothermic reaction
② activation energy being used to start an endothermic reaction
③ activation energy being used to stop an exothermic reaction
④ activation energy being used to stop an endothermic reaction
⑤ activation energy being used to start a reaction that is neither exothermic nor endothermic

Mixture of Elements

Background Information

If you had to choose a single word to describe the mixture of elements that appear on and within Earth, that word would be *solution*. A **solution** is a mixture of one or more substances dissolved in another substance. In a solution, the mixture is the same throughout the solution. A solution is a uniform mixing of substances. Solutions are everywhere in nature.

- Air is a solution of gases.
- Ocean water is a solution of water, salt, and other minerals.
- Earth's interior is a molten solution of elements, primarily iron and other heavy metals.

Although solutions are very common, not every mixture forms a solution. For example, when you mix sand with water, the sand appears to go into a solution. However, if you wait a few minutes, the sand will settle to the bottom. Sand does not dissolve in water.

Reading Selection

When you drop a cube of sugar into water, the sugar disappears. However, the sugar is not gone. When you taste the water, you discover a sweet taste. The sugar is in the water even though you can no longer see it. The molecules of sugar have separated from one another and have become equally distributed throughout the molecules of water. Because of this, sugar water is equally sweet in every part of the solution.

The two components of a solution are the solute and the solvent.

- The solute is the substance that is dissolved.
- The solvent is the substance that dissolves the solute.

In a sugar solution, sugar is the solute and water is the solvent. The water dissolves the sugar. When no more of a solute can be dissolved in a solvent, the solution is saturated. When no more sugar will dissolve in a glass of water, the water is saturated with sugar.

❶ What is a solution? _____

❷ What is meant by the words *solute* and *solvent*? _____

_____

❸ Why doesn't sand mixed with water form a solution? _____

_____

❹ What does it mean when we say that a solution is saturated? _____

_____

GED Practice

Questions 1 and 2 are based on the passage below.

There are several types of solutions:

Gases dissolved in gases—Air is a solution of gases dissolved in gases. Gases in air include nitrogen, oxygen, hydrogen, and helium.

Liquids dissolved in liquids—Water is used to thin latex paint.

Gases dissolved in liquids—In carbonated soft drinks, carbon dioxide gas is dissolved in water along with sugar and flavor additives.

Solids dissolved in liquids—Sugar water is made by dissolving solid sugar in water.

Solids dissolved in solids—Metal alloys are made by dissolving one metal in another. To form an alloy, two or more metals are melted and then mixed as liquids. The solution of liquid metal is cooled and solidified. Brass is an alloy that is made by dissolving zinc in copper. Brass has qualities that are a mixture of the qualities of zinc and copper. Brass is stronger than copper but is less flexible.

1 Powdered punch mix is added to water to make punch. How do you classify the punch solution?

(1) gas dissolved in gas
(2) liquid dissolved in liquid
(3) gas dissolved in liquid
(4) solid dissolved in liquid
(5) solid dissolved in solid

2 What type of solution is a carbonated soft drink?

(1) gas dissolved in gas
(2) liquid dissolved in liquid
(3) gas dissolved in liquid
(4) solid dissolved in liquid
(5) solid dissolved in solid

Questions 3, 4, and 5 are based on the drawing below.

water sweetened with sugar

sugar

3 Which statement best explains why sugar is on the bottom of the glass?

(1) The water is saturated with sugar.
(2) Sugar was placed in the glass before the water was added.
(3) Water was placed in the glass before the sugar was added.
(4) Sugar does not dissolve in water.
(5) Sugar will dissolve in water only when the water is heated.

4 Suppose the water is saturated with sugar. What feature of the solution will not change if more sugar is added to the glass?

(1) the amount of sugar on the bottom of the glass
(2) the weight of the glass and its contents
(3) the height of the water in the glass
(4) the total amount of sugar in the glass
(5) the sweetness of the water

5 What is one way to permanently decrease the amount of sugar on the bottom of the glass?

(1) Stir the water.
(2) Take water out of the glass.
(3) Add water to the glass.
(4) Cover the glass.
(5) Add sugar to the glass.

Chemistry and the Origin of Life

Background Information

A question of great interest to biologists, chemists, other scientists, and religious leaders is the question of how life on Earth began. How is it possible that elements that make up land, air, and water can combine to become the building blocks of life? Can life really come from nonliving chemicals, or must life come from other forms of life? Over the centuries, two main scientific theories have been proposed.

The earliest theory of life's origin is known as the theory of spontaneous generation. According to this theory, living organisms sometimes arise from nonliving matter. The Greek philosopher Aristotle (384–322 B.C.) first proposed this theory and it went unchallenged for 2,000 years. Aristotle noted that many animals seem to come from decaying matter, that plant lice arise from the dew on plants, that mice come from dirty hay, that beetles come from cow dung, and so on. Aristotle based his belief on his own observations.

In the seventeenth century, experiments showed that spontaneous generation did not occur, at least not with visible organisms. Life seemed to come only from other living organisms. However, in the twentieth century, a second explanation was offered. The Russian biologist Alexksandr Oparin (1894–1980) proposed that water and simple gases in Earth's early atmosphere may have combined to form basic organic molecules such as amino acids—molecules that form the basis of life. The energy that caused these chemical reactions came from sunlight or lightning. Oparin's ideas are still the basis of experiments performed today.

Reading Selection

In 1953, the American chemists Stanley Miller and Harold Urey built upon Oparin's ideas. They performed an experiment with water and with gases believed to be present in early Earth's atmosphere. The chemists tried to simulate early Earth conditions in a laboratory. They wanted to find out if organic molecules such as amino acids would result.

The Miller-Urey experiment used water (H_2O), methane gas (CH_4), ammonia (NH_3), and hydrogen gas (H_2). Water vapor and the three other gases were mixed and then exposed to electric sparks that simulated lightning. The results were amazing! After sparking, about 15% of the carbon in the mixture was now in organic compounds, some of which had formed amino acids—the building blocks of proteins found in living cells. The experiment proved for the first time that early Earth could have produced the building blocks of life from a mixture of nonliving chemicals activated by an energy source.

❶ What is the theory of spontaneous generation? _____

_____

❷ What did the Miller-Urey experiment demonstrate? _____

_____

GED Practice

Questions 1 and 2 refer to the passage below.

The discovery of the microscope in the seventeenth century helped lead scientists away from the theory of spontaneous generation. With careful experimentation, scientists discovered that even microbes such as bacteria could be killed by boiling, and once killed they did not lead to new life forms.

The death of the theory of spontaneous generation led to the work of the French biologist Louis Pasteur. Pasteur showed that if matter was sterilized and prevented from being contaminated, then bacteria and other microscopic life forms did not arise on their own. Pasteur's discoveries have great importance today in the sterilization of hospital instruments prior to surgery. Pasteur's discoveries also led to widespread pasteurization of milk (and other liquid foods)—the killing of possible harmful bacteria in milk before human consumption.

1 How is milk most likely pasteurized?

(1) by freezing
(2) by sterilizing the container before milk is added
(3) by boiling
(4) by adding flavor additives
(5) by rapid shaking

2 What is the reason for sterilizing medical instruments?

(1) to kill microbes floating in the air
(2) to kill microbes possibly present on the instruments before surgery
(3) to prepare a clean place for the growing of microbes
(4) to kill microbes present in a dirty wound
(5) to protect doctors from microbes possibly present on unsterilized instruments

Questions 3, 4, 5, and 6 refer to the diagram below.

OPARIN'S THEORY OF THE ORIGIN OF LIFE

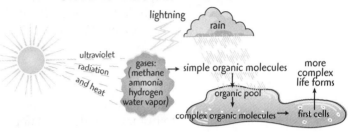

3 Which of the following atmospheric gases did Oparin *not* consider important for his theory?

(1) ammonia
(2) hydrogen
(3) water vapor
(4) methane
(5) nitrogen

4 According to Oparin's theory, which of the following would have had to come first?

(1) rocks containing fossils
(2) a multicellular organism
(3) the first living cell
(4) an atmosphere containing methane
(5) a pool containing organic material

5 According to Oparin's theory, where did the first cells form?

(1) in streaks of lightning
(2) in sunshine passing through clouds
(3) in rain passing through gases
(4) in pools of water
(5) in clouds during a rainstorm

6 What event does Oparin's theory most directly try to explain?

(1) the creation of the first living cells
(2) the creation of Earth's early atmosphere
(3) the creation of liquid water on Earth's surface
(4) the creation of carbon compounds on Earth
(5) the creation of cell specialization

35

Chemistry and Human Health

Background Information

The properties of substances we use in our daily lives are determined by their chemistry. Iron is hard because of the strength of bonds that hold iron atoms in a crystal lattice. Wood burns because, in the presence of heat, its atoms can combine with oxygen. Water is a liquid because the strength of bonds between its molecules is so weak that these molecules can move freely past one another.

Many substances react with each other because of their chemical properties. Also, many substances react with tissues and organs of the human body. This fact makes medicines possible, but it also means that many substances can be harmful to human health and safety. For this reason, it is very important to read and follow the advice of warning labels placed on all household chemicals, especially household cleansers and chemical additives such as paint thinner, antifreeze, brake fluid, and so on.

Reading Selection

Two important types of chemical substances that are often related to human health and safety are acids and bases.

- *Acid*—a substance that releases hydrogen ions (H^+) when mixed with water. Food acids, also called organic acids, are sour to the taste. The citric acid found in oranges, grapefruits, and lemons is an example. Acetic acid found in vinegar is another. Inorganic acids, on the other hand, can be dangerous. If ingested, inorganic acids can be poisonous. If spilled on the skin, inorganic acids can cause severe burns. Sulfuric acid is an inorganic acid used in car batteries. Hydrochloric acid is used as a metal cleaner.
- *Base*—a substance that produces hydroxide ions (OH^-) in water. A base will combine with an acid and neutralize its effect, usually producing water and a neutral salt. Baking soda, a weak base, can be used as a cleanser and as a mild stomach antacid. Stronger bases, such as ammonia and bleach, are used as high-strength cleansers and can be harmful if touched or ingested.

A neutral salt is neither an acid nor a base. Also, pure water is neither an acid nor a base. Because of this, pure water can be used to dilute the strength of either an acid or a base.

❶ What is a good safety rule regarding the use of a strong household cleanser?

_____

❷ If a small amount of baking soda is added to freshly-squeezed orange juice, how do you think the taste will change?

_____

❸ If you are working with a strong inorganic acid, why is it a good idea to have both water and baking soda nearby?

_____

GED Practice

Questions 1, 2, 3, and 4 refer to the following passage.

Carbon monoxide is a gas produced as a byproduct of the combustion of fossil fuels. Carbon monoxide is present in the exhaust fumes of automobiles and in the gases given off by burning coal.

Carbon monoxide can be fatal if inhaled. It prevents oxygen from being absorbed in the lungs. Both odorless and tasteless, carbon monoxide is difficult to detect when breathing. A victim first becomes drowsy and then unconscious, with death occurring within a few minutes.

1 Which word or phrase does *not* describe carbon monoxide gas?

① smelly
② tasteless
③ odorless
④ dangerous
⑤ hard to detect

2 What is the main source of carbon monoxide?

① uncontrolled nuclear reactions
② burning of fossil fuels
③ respiration in animals
④ exposure of oxygen gas to sunlight
⑤ photosynthesis in plants

3 In which situation is the risk of carbon monoxide poisoning the greatest?

① visiting a fossil fuel electric power plant
② living near a traffic intersection
③ starting a car in a closed garage
④ starting a car in an open parking lot
⑤ burning wood in a fireplace

4 What is the cause of death from carbon monoxide poisoning?

① drowning
② heart failure
③ cancer
④ lack of oxygen
⑤ too much oxygen

Questions 5, 6, and 7 are based on the information below.

The strength of an acid or a base is measured on a pH scale. Number 7 is the middle point, representing a substance that is neither acidic nor basic. Substances with a pH less than 7 are acids; those with a pH greater than 7 are bases. When an acid mixes with an equal amount of base, the pH takes the average value.

pH Scale

5 What might be the pH level of freshly-squeezed orange juice?

① 6
② 7
③ 8
④ 9
⑤ 10

6 An antacid is used to reduce indigestion caused by excessive stomach acid. What property does the active ingredient in an antacid have?

① neither acidic nor basic
② not dissolvable in water
③ a pH of 7
④ a pH less than 7
⑤ a pH greater than 7

7 Baking powder is mainly sodium bicarbonate ($NaHCO_3$) which reacts with an acid to produce carbon dioxide gas and water. What type of substance is sodium bicarbonate?

① an acid
② a base
③ a neutral substance
④ neither an acid nor a base
⑤ both an acid and a base

91

36 Historical Perspectives in Chemistry

Background Information

The chemists of the Middle Ages (500–1600 A.D.) were known as alchemists. These early chemists were mainly interested in turning different metals into gold. They also tried to create a medicine that would keep people from aging. Although alchemists failed in their attempts, their work did help speed the development of modern chemistry.

With the discovery of the atom, chemists began to understand the properties of natural substances, many of which were in common use. One example was the bark of the willow tree. During the seventeenth and eighteenth centuries, Native Americans used the bark of willow trees as a treatment for fever. No one knew why it worked. By studying the properties of the bark, chemists discovered that salicylic acid in the bark was the chemical responsible for the pain-relieving effect. Chemists then began to produce this acid in their laboratories. The drug proved to be helpful in easing pain, but it had unpleasant side effects, including stomach irritation. Chemists were able to reduce this irritation by adding another element to salicylic acid. The resulting drug, acetylsalicylic acid, is what we know today as aspirin.

Chemists have also been able to create materials not found in nature. One example is plastic. Plastic has proven to be one of the most durable, inexpensive, and versatile materials known. Milk containers, computer parts, children's toys, and clothes are just some of the products that are now made of plastic.

Reading Selection

Long before chemists understood the atom, ancient Greek philosophers believed that every substance could be broken down into a smallest piece. Democritus (460–370 B.C.) called these smallest particles *atomos,* from the Greek word *atoma,* meaning "indivisible." Democritus believed that *atomos* (atoms) moved about in empty space and were indestructible. He thought that atoms were made of the same matter but differed in shape, size, weight, and arrangement. Differences in substances were accounted for by the arrangement of atoms in space, not in differences among atoms. Democritus believed that properties such as taste were related to the size and arrangement of atoms. He thought that a sharp or bitter taste meant that atoms of a substance were small and pointed; that a sweet taste meant that atoms were large and round. Today, we understand that differences in substances occur because of differences in atoms. An atom of copper is not the same as an atom of iron, even though each atom is made up of only three particles: electrons, protons, and neutrons.

1 What did alchemists attempt to do? _____

_____

2 What did Democritus think accounted for the observed differences in substances?

_____

GED Practice

Questions 1, 2, and 3 refer to the passage below.

Friedrich Wohler (1800–1882) was a pioneer in the field of organic chemistry. Wohler showed that urea, a waste product created by many living organisms, could be created in a laboratory from ammonium cyanate, a chemical substance that did not come from living organisms. Before Wohler's discovery, scientists believed that organic substances—substances made by living organisms—could be made only from other organic substances.

1 From information given in the passage, what can you infer about urea?

  ① Urea is another name for ammonium cyanate.
  ② Urea cannot be made in a laboratory.
  ③ Urea is an organic substance.
  ④ Urea is not an organic substance.
  ⑤ Urea is a useful substance.

2 What is another way of stating Wohler's discovery?

  ① Organic substances cannot be made from nonorganic substances.
  ② Organic substances cannot be created in a laboratory.
  ③ Organic substances always break down into nonorganic substances.
  ④ There is no difference between organic and nonorganic substances.
  ⑤ Organic substances can be made from nonorganic substances.

3 Which word likely represents how other scientists felt upon hearing of Wohler's results?

  ① surprised
  ② happy
  ③ disappointed
  ④ jealous
  ⑤ angry

Questions 4 and 5 refer to the illustration below.

CHANGING VIEW OF AN ATOM

Ancient Greeks (2,400 years ago)

solid sphere

Rutherford Model (early 20th century)

planetary system

Schrodinger Model (present-day model)

cloud of orbiting electrons

cloud of nuclear particles

mathematical description telling most-probable location of atomic particles

4 What is Rutherford's idea of electrons orbiting a nucleus modeled after?

  ① a system of swinging weights
  ② musical notes in a scale
  ③ the solar system
  ④ patterns of water waves
  ⑤ patterns seen in wind-blown sand

5 Which phrase best describes how the model of the atom has changed from the time of the ancient Greeks to the present?

  ① from a solid sphere to a planetary-type system
  ② from an unusual mathematical model to a solid sphere
  ③ from an unusual mathematical model to a planetary-type system
  ④ from a solid sphere to an unusual mathematical system
  ⑤ from a planetary-type system to a solid sphere

Motion and Forces

Background Information

In the study of matter, **force** is defined as an influence that changes the motion or position of an object. The study of force was one of the earliest studies in physics. The most important advance in this study was made by Isaac Newton (1642–1727), an English mathematician and physicist. Newton made several discoveries that are today known as Newton's laws of motion. These laws can be stated in three parts:

- *Law of inertia:* If no force is applied, an object at rest will remain at rest. An object in motion will move in a straight line at a constant speed.
- *Law of acceleration:* Part 1. An object's speed increases in proportion to the amount of force that is applied. Part 2. For the same amount of applied force, a lighter object accelerates—increases its speed—at a greater rate than a heavier object.
- *Law of interaction:* For every action there is an equal and opposite reaction.

Reading Selection

There are many forces in nature. One, the electrical force, is very important in our daily lives. Electrical force occurs because all matter is made up of charged particles: negatively-charged electrons and positively-charged protons. Like charges repel each other while unlike charges attract each other. Most matter is electrically neutral, having the same number of electrons and protons. The gravitational force between two charged particles is much weaker than the electrical force. Here are two examples of uses of electric force:

- *Static electricity*—When you rub a comb through your dry hair, the comb picks up weakly-held electrons. These electrons electrically stick to the comb and can then make your now slightly positively-charged hair stand on end. The electric force (attraction between negative and positive charges) causes your hair to lift up. When you walk across a carpet, your body can pick up weakly-held electrons from the carpet. You can get a shock by touching a metal door handle as electrons jump from your fingers to the metal.
- *Electric current*—Electrons in metal such as copper can be made to flow. Although a copper wire is electrically neutral, a battery can be used to make electrons flow through the wire. The battery supplies an electric force to which the freely moving electrons in the wire will respond. These flowing electrons can be used to create light and heat, or to do work such as to power an electric vacuum cleaner.

❶ Which of Newton's laws of motion explains why it's easier to throw an apple than a brick?

_____

❷ Which type of electricity is used when you plug a radio into a wall socket?

_____

❸ Which type of electricity is responsible for lightning?

_____

GED Practice

Questions 1 and 2 refer to the passage below.

Newton used his laws of motion to help discover and explain the properties of gravity. His discovery is called the law of universal gravitation. This law can also be written in three parts:

Part 1. Gravitational force is an attractive force, a force that pulls two objects toward one another.

Part 2. Gravitational force is greater for heavy objects (objects with more mass) than for light objects.

Part 3. The force of gravity decreases as the distance between objects increases.

1 Which of the following is *not* explained by the law of universal gravitation?

   ① the path through the air of a thrown baseball
   ② the orbit of the Moon around Earth
   ③ the colors in the rainbow
   ④ the weight of an astronaut on the Moon
   ⑤ the orbit of Earth around the Sun

2 If two electrons are brought close together, they strongly repel each other. What can you infer from this fact?

   ① The gravitational force between electrons is a repulsive force.
   ② There is no gravitational force between electrons.
   ③ The gravitational force between electrons is equal in strength to the electrical force.
   ④ The gravitational force between electrons is much weaker than the electrical force.
   ⑤ The gravitational force between electrons is much stronger than the electrical force.

Questions 3, 4, and 5 refer to the illustration below.

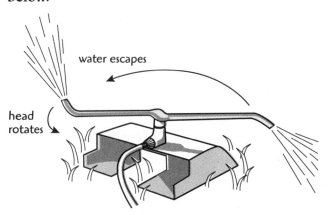

The head of the sprinkler rotates as a reaction to the force of escaping water.

3 What exerts force on the sprinkler head, causing it to twist?

   ① the garden hose
   ② gravity
   ③ air pressure
   ④ electricity
   ⑤ the flowing water

4 Which of the following would cause the sprinkler head to twist more rapidly?

   ① placing the sprinkler on a hill
   ② increasing the rate at which the water is flowing
   ③ decreasing the rate at which the water is flowing
   ④ placing the sprinkler in the sunshine
   ⑤ placing small weights on the rotating arms of the sprinkler

5 What law is demonstrated by the action of the sprinkler?

   ① the law of inertia
   ② the law of acceleration
   ③ the law of interaction
   ④ the law of gravity
   ⑤ the law of the lever

38

Interaction of Energy with Matter

Background Information

Energy is key to everything that happens on Earth and in the universe as a whole. All living organisms require a source of energy for survival. Plants need energy to produce sugar and nutrients both for their own survival and for the survival of animals that eat plants. Humans rely on both plants and animals as food—sources of energy and nutrients that make human life possible. Humans also need energy for daily living, for use with everything from heating homes to powering vehicles. We also need energy for powering the devices we use in our work and home lives. If life is ever discovered on another planet, you can be sure of one thing: a source of energy has led to the growth and survival of that life.

Earth itself has two main energy sources. One is the Sun, Earth's main source of heat and light. The second is Earth's hot interior, the fiery liquid region just below the surface mantle. This hot region gives rise to the movement of the hard plates that form Earth's crust. The grinding of these plates against one another causes earthquakes, volcanoes, and ocean tsunamis. This molten liquid region beneath the mantle is also the source of heat energy that causes natural hot springs. Weather conditions on Earth, including extreme conditions such as hurricanes and tornadoes, result from energy both from the Sun and from the rotation of Earth on its axis.

Every star in every galaxy in the universe is a source of energy. Within each star, including the Sun, nuclear energy heats the star and keeps it from collapsing due to the force of gravity. Meanwhile, each star's own energy and the gravitational force between the star and other stars work together to keep the star within a path inside its own galaxy.

Reading Selection

As a science term, the word *energy* means "the capacity to do work"—the capacity to make things move. Examples of energy include the movement of vehicles such as cars and buses, and the movement of molecules (the creation of heat) in gas, liquids, or solids.

Energy is a property of matter; it is not an object or a substance you can hold. For example, a moving car has energy, but it ceases when the car stops. An ocean wave has energy, but it ceases when the ocean surface becomes calm. A stream of moving electrons (electric current) has energy, but it ceases when the current is switched off. A beam of light is pure energy, the light and its energy being absorbed together. In each case, energy does not disappear; it simply changes form and may no longer be noticeable.

❶ What are the two main sources of energy for Earth?_____

_____

❷ How does energy differ from a substance? _____

_____

GED Practice

Questions 1 and 2 refer to the passage below.

Heat is the most common form of energy in our daily lives. Heat is the energy of movement of atoms and molecules. When atoms or molecules move rapidly, an object is hot. When atoms or molecules move slowly, the object is cold.

Temperature is a measure of heat energy. When an object absorbs heat, its temperature rises. When an object gives off heat, its temperature falls.

When two objects of different temperature are brought into contact, heat energy flows from the warmer object to the colder object. This heat flow continues until both objects reach the same temperature.

All other forms of energy can be changed to heat energy. Light energy changes to heat on your skin when you sit in the sun. Electricity is changed to heat by a stove. Chemical energy is changed to heat by a firecracker. Nuclear energy is changed to heat in a nuclear power plant, the heat being used to create steam, which then drives turbines that create electricity.

1 What is the best definition of heat?

  ① the total energy of an object
  ② a measure of temperature
  ③ the movement of nuclear particles
  ④ the energy of movement of atoms and molecules
  ⑤ a flow of energy between objects

2 When a piece of hot iron (350°F) is thrown into a barrel of cold water (50°F), what will happen?

  ① Heat will flow from the water to the iron until both are the same temperature.
  ② Heat will flow from the iron to the water until both are the same temperature.
  ③ The water will be heated to 350°F.
  ④ The iron will be cooled to 50°F.
  ⑤ Nothing will happen because heat can't flow from iron to water.

Questions 3 and 4 refer to the illustration below.

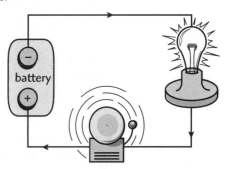

A copper wire connects a light and a ringer with a battery.

3 What carries the energy produced by the battery to the light and ringer?

  ① a moving stream of electrons in the copper wire
  ② a moving stream of copper atoms in the copper wire
  ③ a moving stream of air surrounding the copper wire
  ④ a sound wave in the copper wire
  ⑤ light created by the glowing bulb

4 Which forms of energy take part in the electric circuit shown above?

  A. chemical
  B. heat
  C. light
  D. electrical
  E. sound

  ① only one of the listed forms
  ② only two of the listed forms
  ③ only three of the listed forms
  ④ only four of the listed forms
  ⑤ all five of the listed forms

Conservation of Energy

Background Information

By studying interactions of energy in various forms, physicists discovered one of the most important laws in science: the law of **conservation of energy**.

> During any interaction, energy may change from one form to another, but no energy is lost. The total amount of energy present remains constant.

Here are two examples:

- When you turn on a lamp, electricity flows to the bulb. At the bulb, the electrical energy is changed to both light and heat, two other forms of energy. The total amount of electrical energy used is equal to the total amount of energy that is produced as light and heat.
- When a car increases speed from a standstill to 25 miles per hour, gasoline chemical energy is used. The gasoline chemical energy is changed to kinetic (moving) energy of the car and to heat energy caused by friction of the car moving through the air. Friction changes some kinetic energy of the car to heat energy in the surrounding air.

Reading Selection

There are two types of energy involved in the movement of physical objects:

- *Kinetic energy* is energy of motion. A kicked soccer ball has kinetic energy.
- *Potential energy* is stored energy. A book sitting on the edge of a table has potential energy—stored gravitational energy. If the book is pushed off the table, its potential energy changes to kinetic energy as the book falls.

Throughout the book's fall, energy changes form but is not lost. At any point, the sum of the different forms of energy present has not changed.

- While sitting on the table, the book has only gravitational potential energy.
- Just before the book hits the floor, the book has only kinetic energy; its potential energy is almost 0. When the book hits the floor, all of its kinetic energy suddenly changes to sound energy and to heat energy. The sound energy is the noise you hear; the heat energy is molecular-vibration energy that occurs in the book and in the floor. This heat energy results from the collision of the book with the floor.

❶ In your own words, state the law of conservation of energy._____

_____

❷ What type of energy does a falling book have when it's halfway to the floor?

_____

GED Practice

Questions 1 and 2 refer to the passage below.

Five forms of energy are listed below.

Electrical—energy carried by a moving stream of electrons

Light—energy-carrying waves that can travel through a vacuum

Sound—energy vibrations that travel through air or other substances

Heat—energy of molecular motion

Chemical—potential energy that can be released during a chemical reaction

1 How does energy change form during photosynthesis—the process in which plants convert sunlight to sugar?

① light energy is changed to heat
② light energy is changed to chemical energy
③ heat energy is changed to light energy
④ chemical energy is changed to light energy
⑤ chemical energy is changed to electrical energy

2 Which of the following is an example of light energy changing to heat energy?

① turning on a flashlight
② sitting in sunshine
③ heating an electric oven
④ taking a photograph
⑤ playing music

3 After striking a building, a wrecking ball hangs motionless on its cable. What type of energy was created by the ball when it struck the building?

① both gravitational potential energy and kinetic energy of the ball
② frictional energy only
③ kinetic energy of the moving ball
④ gravitational potential energy of the ball and crane
⑤ kinetic energy used to break apart the building, sound, and heat

Questions 4 and 5 refer to the illustration below.

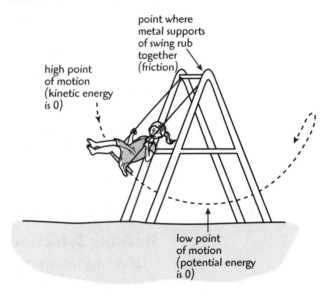

4 Suppose the girl just rides the swing without moving her legs. What will cause the swinging to stop?

① the change of potential energy to kinetic energy
② the change of kinetic energy to potential energy
③ air friction only
④ air friction and friction caused by metal parts rubbing
⑤ only friction caused by metal parts rubbing

5 At the point where the girl is halfway between the low point and high point of the swinging, what type of energy does she have?

① kinetic and potential energy
② potential energy only
③ kinetic energy only
④ heat energy only
⑤ frictional energy only

Change and Constancy in Nature

Background Information

Change, perhaps more than any other property, characterizes our world. Many things around us are in a constant state of change: children grow, leaves change color and fall from trees, rivers carve canyons, house paint fades, and so on. In the pursuit of knowledge, scientists study every type of change.

Constancy, the tendency for certain things to remain unchanged, is also of interest to scientists. For example, mathematical laws don't change. The fact that $2 + 2 = 4$ is as true today as it was 10,000 years ago. Also, laws of nature don't change. The law of gravity hasn't changed since the beginning of the universe. After all, gravity is what holds the universe together! Biological processes don't change. The passing on of traits from one generation of organism to the next has been occurring since the beginning of life. Finally, laws of chance don't change. Today you have a 50% chance of a flipped coin landing heads-up. This same chance will be true of a coin flipped 10,000 years in the future.

Reading Selection

There are two special types of change. Cyclical change occurs over and over again without human intervention. Cyclical changes are of great interest to scientists. Here are a few examples:

- Daily changes, such as ocean tides coming in and going out on a predictable time schedule
- Seasonal changes, such as the falling of leaves in autumn and new growth in spring
- Yearly changes, such as the annual migration of whales and birds

Evolutionary change is change that occurs slowly over time, change that does not repeat over a given period of time. Evolutionary change takes place in living organisms over a long period of time as they become better adapted to their environment. Evolutionary change takes place on Earth itself as continents slowly drift on the mantle, forming both earthquakes and volcanoes and forever changing Earth's surface. Evolutionary change takes place in the universe as a whole, with the universe in a state of expansion. Galaxies slowly move away from one another with stars being born and dying in the process.

❶ Define and give an example of constancy.

_____

❷ What is the difference between cyclical change and evolutionary change?

_____

_____

_____

GED Practice

Questions 1 and 2 refer to the passage below.

Equilibrium is a condition in which change takes place, but not in an obvious way. In a state of equilibrium, change takes place in equal but opposite ways. Suppose you place enough salt in a glass of water to create a saturated solution. Suppose now that you add even more salt. An equal amount of "extra salt" will condense on the bottom of the glass. As the glass sits there, the amount of salt on the bottom will not change. However, if you could look at the salt on a molecular level, you would find that salt is continually condensing on the bottom and dissolving into the water at the same time.

1 Which of the following is true about a state of equilibrium?

① Change takes place only during the beginning phase.
② Change takes place at a slower-than-predicted rate.
③ Change takes place in equal but opposite ways.
④ Change does not take place at all.
⑤ Change takes place in a cyclical cycle.

2 Which of the following is the best example of equilibrium?

① daily temperature variations
② yearly seasons on Earth
③ the 24-hour rotation period of Earth
④ the cooling of milk in a refrigerator
⑤ constant human body temperature

3 What would be one result if the force of gravity were very slowly increasing?

① Your weight would slowly increase.
② Your height would slowly increase.
③ The laws of mathematics would change.
④ Evolutionary changes would no longer take place.
⑤ The universe would cease to exist.

Questions 4 and 5 refer to the drawings below.

A container of low-temperature gas is brought into contact with a container of high-temperature gas.

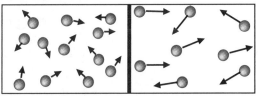

Low Temperature   High Temperature

Later that day

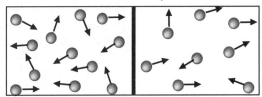

Each container is at the same temperature.

4 The two containers are brought into contact and temperature equilibrium slowly occurs. What can you infer led to the equilibrium condition?

① The number of gas molecules in each container became equal.
② The average energy of each gas molecule became equal.
③ The average weight of each gas molecule became equal.
④ The average distance between gas molecules in each container became equal.
⑤ The average diameter of each gas molecule became equal.

5 What process made it possible for temperature equilibrium to occur?

① gravity acting on gas molecules
② the cooling of each gas
③ the intermixing of gas molecules
④ the flow of heat
⑤ the absorption of light

Differences Between Technology and Science

Background Information

Technology is the use of knowledge, materials, and tools to make products that help solve human problems and that provide for human needs and wishes. Technology gives us many types of products:

- Consumer products, from groceries and clothes to automobiles, compact discs, and cellular telephones
- Scientific research products, from microscopes and telescopes to the space shuttle and the orbiting space station
- Multipurpose products, such as computers, that are popular with consumers but also have many other uses at work, in science, and in industry

Science, on the other hand, is a search for understanding. The goal of science is to understand the natural world, not necessarily to use that knowledge in any practical way. The study of life on Earth is just one part of science. Much scientific research is done in fields of science that have no practical benefits for human beings.

The goal of technology is to improve human life; the goal of science is to increase human understanding of the world of nature. Because of this, most people feel the immediate impact of technology more than they feel the impact of science.

Reading Selection

Like many inventions before it, the typewriter has almost disappeared from offices and from homes. Invented in 1868, the typewriter offered people an alternative to handwriting. By printing or impressing type characters on paper, the typewriter produced text more quickly and far more legibly than written words.

With the invention of personal computers in the 1970s, everything changed. The typewriter began to give way to electronic word processors whereby documents can be electronically created, corrected, stored, printed, and sent as e-mail (electronic mail). Word processing is a standard feature on today's personal computers and is the main business and home use of most computers.

❶ Give a brief definition of technology. _____

_____

❷ Give a brief definition of science. _____

_____

❸ What has led to the reduced use of typewriters in the workplace?

_____

GED Practice

Questions 1 and 2 refer to the passage below.

During the last few decades, technology has advanced more rapidly than ever before. As a result, things have become possible that were once imagined only in science fiction. Along with scientific understanding has come technology that may conflict with your values. Some of these areas are the following:

- *Genetically altered food*—Scientists have learned how to alter the properties of foods by injecting them with genes from a different organism. When you eat a genetically altered food, you are eating a food that is in a form that nature did not create.

- *Nuclear weapons*—To end World War II, the United States dropped atomic bombs on Japan, killing more than 100,000 people immediately. These bombs were the first of a terrible new kind of weapon. Since that time, even more powerful nuclear weapons have been developed.

1 What is a major concern about rapid technological advance?

  ① the cost of new consumer products
  ② the quality of new consumer products
  ③ the rate at which technology is improving our lives
  ④ the conflict between new knowledge and personal values
  ⑤ the difficulty in keeping technological secrets

2 What is the major concern involving the development of nuclear weapons?

  ① their possible use in war
  ② the cost of research
  ③ the difficulty of storage
  ④ the use of nuclear materials for medical purposes
  ⑤ the shortage of nuclear materials

Questions 3, 4, and 5 refer to the drawings below.

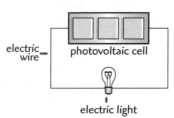

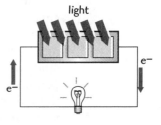

3 What is the purpose of a photovoltaic cell?

  ① to change chemical energy into electrical energy
  ② to change electrical energy into light energy
  ③ to change light energy into electrical energy
  ④ to change light energy into chemical energy
  ⑤ to change chemical energy into light energy

4 Which device uses a photovoltaic cell?

  ① clinical thermometer
  ② electric train
  ③ microwave oven
  ④ sunglasses
  ⑤ solar-powered calculator

5 If the number of solar panels on the photovoltaic cell is increased, what would be the most likely result?

  ① an increase in electric current
  ② a decrease in electric current
  ③ an increase in sunlight
  ④ a decrease in sunlight
  ⑤ no noticeable change

Historical Perspectives in Physics

Background Information

From the time of ancient Greek philosophers 2,500 years ago, people have wanted to understand the natural world. Why, for example, do objects drop to the ground? Why does the Moon have different shapes at different times each month? Why are there seasons: summer, fall, winter, and spring? Why is the sky blue? Why do some rocks (natural magnets) attract each other, and then repel if one rock is turned the other direction? With little knowledge of the natural world and very little mathematics to use as a language, early physicists could make little progress.

A major breakthrough in the study of both mathematics and physics, now called the Scientific Revolution, occurred during the sixteenth and seventeenth centuries. The invention of the telescope and microscope enabled both physicists and biologists to see things never before seen. The telescope made possible the study of celestial objects such as the Moon and the planets; the microscope made possible the study of cells, the fundamental unit of living organisms. Encouraged by these discoveries and with the development of mathematics, other scientists began to examine the nature of light and the nature of magnetism. It wasn't long before electricity was discovered and the Scientific Revolution was well under way.

Reading Selection

Considered by many to be the greatest scientist who has ever lived, Isaac Newton (1642–1727) was an English physicist, astronomer, alchemist, and mathematician.

- Among his major scientific accomplishments was the advancement of the idea that the Sun is at the center of all celestial objects. Newton likely believed that the Sun was at the center of the universe because the nature of the solar system was not yet understood.
- Perhaps Newton is most remembered for his theory of universal gravitation and the laws of motion. Newton was the first scientist to really understand that laws governing objects on Earth would also govern celestial objects. For example, the force that holds a person on Earth's surface would be the same type of force that holds the Moon in orbit around Earth.
- Newton also made scientific advancements in the study of light. Newton proved that the spectrum of colors seen when sunlight is passed through a prism comes from the sunlight itself. The colors are not added by the prism, as other scientists had claimed.

❶ What two inventions helped start the Scientific Revolution?

_____

❷ What did Newton believe about the Sun's location in the universe?

_____

❸ What did Newton prove to be true about sunlight?

_____

GED Practice

Questions 1, 2, and 3 refer to the passage below.

About 2,600 years ago, the Greek philosopher Thales was the first scholar to try to understand nature in a scientific way. Before Thales, the Greeks explained the origin and nature of the world through myths of gods and heroes. Thales rejected these ideas and tried to explain common events in terms of natural causes.

Thales taught that Earth was a flat disk floating on water, the universal element. Earthquakes, he believed, were caused by rough waves, not angry gods who shook Earth. Thales believed that water was the main substance in the universe and that everything came from water.

1 What did Thales most likely see that led him to his theory of the Earth being a flat disk in water?

  ① the full moon
  ② the jagged coastline of Greece
  ③ the height of mountains in Greece
  ④ the surface of the sea near Greece
  ⑤ the numerous rivers in Greece

2 Which scientific steps could Thales *not* do in his study of the Moon?

  ① observe the shape of the Moon each night for a month
  ② describe the shape he saw during each observation
  ③ determine the distance of the Moon from Earth
  ④ estimate the time the Moon appears over the horizon each night
  ⑤ see the Moon from different parts of Greece

3 What did Thales believe was the universal element?

  ① life force
  ② heat
  ③ air
  ④ soil
  ⑤ water

Questions 4 and 5 refer to the following passage.

Archimedes (287–212 B.C.) was a Greek mathematician and inventor. He is best known today for his discovery of the law of hydrostatics. This law states that a body immersed in a liquid loses weight equal to the weight of the water it displaces (takes the place of). Archimedes very likely discovered this law while taking a bath.

4 In which of the following is Archimedes' discovery an important factor?

  A. the design of a submarine
  B. the anatomy of a fish
  C. the design of a space rocket

  ① A only
  ② B only
  ③ C only
  ④ both A and B
  ⑤ both A and C

5 According to Archimedes, which of the following is true for an object that is floating in water?

  ① The weight of the displaced water is equal to the weight of the object.
  ② The weight of the displaced water is less than the weight of the object.
  ③ The weight of the displaced water is more than the weight of the object.
  ④ The weight of the displaced water is twice the weight of the object.
  ⑤ The weight of the displaced water is half the weight of the object.

6 In 1752, Benjamin Franklin flew a kite during a lightning storm. What was Franklin trying to learn more about?

  ① the strength of kite string
  ② the nature of electricity
  ③ the strength of wind
  ④ the flying properties of kites
  ⑤ the strength of gravity

Origin of Earth

Background Information

Scientists estimate that Earth has existed for about 4.6 billion years. If present theories are correct, Earth and all other planets and moons in the solar system were created by the gravitational collapse of a cloud of interstellar gas and dust, called the solar nebula. The Sun, comets, and asteroids most likely formed from this same nebula.

Horsehead Nebula

Earth's atmosphere most likely was formed as volcanic eruptions on the hardening surface brought carbon monoxide, carbon dioxide, water vapor, and methane out of the developing crust and mantle. Impacts from meteorites and comets added carbon, hydrogen, and oxygen. The atmosphere made possible the slow emergence of life about 3.5 billion years ago. Early forms of life slowly changed Earth's atmosphere to become more like it is today.

Earth's oceans began forming about 4 billion years ago. As Earth's surface cooled, water vapor from volcanic eruptions and ice from comets added water to the surface and to the atmosphere. As the cooling began, rain began to form and stay on the surface. For the first several million years after that, Earth did not have continents, only a water-covered surface.

Reading Selection

The Moon is Earth's single orbiting natural satellite. The origin of the Moon is uncertain, but three theories have been proposed. The first theory is that the Moon broke off from Earth's developing crust—that the Moon was originally part of Earth. The second theory is that the Moon and Earth formed together, both forming from the same material that was condensing to form Earth. The third theory is that the Moon formed from molten material that was ejected from the surface of Earth during Earth's collision with a huge asteroid the size of Mars. This third theory is the one that most scientists believe is probably correct.

❶ What is the approximate age of Earth?_____

❷ How do scientists think Earth developed?_____

_____

❸ How do most scientists think Earth's moon developed? _____

_____

GED Practice

Questions 1, 2, and 3 refer to the passage below.

Scientists have a theory about why the solar nebula began its collapse. They believe that a disturbance, possibly from a nearby supernova, sent shock waves through the nebula. These shock waves caused much of the gas and dust in the nebula to be pushed toward the center of the nebula. As the nebula compressed, a point was reached at which gravitational forces overcame the internal pressure of the nebula's hot gases. The resulting gravitational collapse resulted in a spinning pancake shape of hot gas with a bulge in the middle. The dense hot center portion would become the Sun. The heavy, rocky material pulled in strongly by gravity stayed near the central bulge. This heavy material would become the inner planets. The lighter elements, mainly hydrogen, stayed near the outer edge and would become the outer planets.

1 What does the proposed model for the formation of the solar system try to explain?

① why Pluto is farthest from the Sun
② why all of the planets are mainly gaseous
③ why inner planets are gaseous and outer planets are made up of heavy elements
④ why inner planets are made up of heavy elements and outer planets are gaseous
⑤ why planets have moons

2 What made it possible for the solar nebula to collapse?

① gas pressure overcoming gravity
② gravity overcoming gas pressure
③ electrical force overcoming gravity
④ gas pressure overcoming electrical force
⑤ nuclear force overcoming gas pressure

3 What is most likely the main element found in gaseous outer planets?

① carbon
② oxygen
③ hydrogen
④ helium
⑤ nitrogen

Question 4 refers to the illustration below.

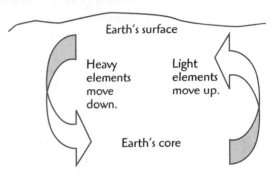

4 Which of the following does the diagram help explain?

① the temperature of Earth's core
② the formation of continents on Earth's surface
③ the distribution of elements within Earth's core
④ the presence of oceans on Earth's surface
⑤ the presence of an atmosphere on Earth's surface

5 Which of the following is most likely true?

① The Moon was never a molten sphere of liquid elements.
② The Moon is less than ten million years old.
③ The Moon is mainly light elements such as hydrogen.
④ The Moon formed before Earth formed.
⑤ The Moon was once a molten sphere of liquid elements.

6 Which statement supports the theory that the Moon formed from material ejected from Earth's surface?

① The Moon is made of the same elements found on Earth's surface.
② The Moon is made of different elements than those found on Earth's surface.
③ The Moon formed before Earth.
④ The interior of the Moon is solid, not liquid.
⑤ Craters on the Moon were formed by asteroids.

The Evolving Earth

Background Information

Earth can be compared to a gigantic sculpture being shaped by the forces of nature. This comparison is especially meaningful to anyone who has seen the awe-inspiring canyons in the southwestern United States, the breathtaking waterfalls at Niagara Falls in New York, or photographs of the powerful volcanic eruptions at Mount St. Helens in Washington in 1980—eruptions that blew off the top one-third of the mountain.

At first glance, the land part of Earth's surface looks unchanging. However, although we don't usually notice it, change does take place on a daily basis. The Grand Canyon itself was once a highland plateau that was crossed by the Colorado River. Then, during millions of years—but one day at a time—the river, wind, and rain combined to carve and shape the mile-deep canyon that is now one of the natural wonders of the world.

Earth's surface is changed by two types of processes. One type takes place rapidly and violently, processes such as earthquakes, volcanoes, tornadoes, and tsunamis. The other type takes place slowly and gently, processes such as the slow carving effects of rain, water, and wind.

Reading Selection

Wind, water, and gravity together bring about changes in Earth by the processes of weathering and erosion.

- *Weathering* is the breaking down of rock into smaller pieces by natural processes. Weathering helps produce soil, a mixture of tiny rock fragments and organic materials produced by living things. Most organic materials in soil are the decaying remains of plants and animals. Weathering may bring about both physical and chemical changes in rock. Physical weathering (also called mechanical weathering) causes changes such as breaking, in which a rock does not change into other types of rocks or substances. Chemical weathering is the softening and crumbling of rocks caused by chemical changes. Chemical changes create new substances not originally part of the rocks.

- *Erosion* is the natural movement of rock fragments over the surface of Earth. The three main causes of erosion are gravity, wind, and water.

❶ What types of processes bring about rapid, violent changes in Earth's surface features?

_____

❷ What is soil made of? _____

❸ What two types of changes can weathering cause?_____

_____

❹ Name two places that erosion is constantly occurring. _____

_____

GED Practice

Questions 1, 2, and 3 refer to the following definitions below.

Physical weathering—weathering (the breaking up of rocks) that does not involve chemical changes

Chemical weathering—weathering that results in chemical changes

Gravity erosion—rock movement that is caused by gravity

Wind erosion—rock movement that is caused by wind

Water erosion—rock movement that is caused by the flow of water

1 What is the main process that creates patterns of sand high on a beach?

① physical weathering
② chemical weathering
③ gravity erosion
④ wind erosion
⑤ water erosion

2 Trapped carbon dioxide gas in a mineral reacts with water, forming an acid that causes the mineral to crumble. What process is occurring here?

① physical weathering
② chemical weathering
③ gravity erosion
④ wind erosion
⑤ water erosion

3 What process is mainly responsible for the slow carving of the Snake River Canyon in Idaho?

① physical weathering
② chemical weathering
③ gravity erosion
④ wind erosion
⑤ water erosion

Questions 4, 5, and 6 refer to the illustration below and the definitions at left.

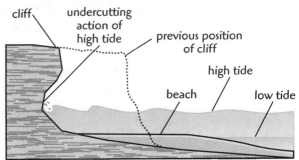

The Action of Ocean Tides on a Beach

4 What two types of processes are the main subjects of the drawing above?

① water erosion and chemical weathering
② wind erosion and gravity erosion
③ wind erosion and physical weathering
④ physical weathering and chemical weathering
⑤ water erosion and physical weathering

5 What is one result of the action of the high tide waves on the cliff?

① an increase in the height of the cliff
② a decrease in the amount of beach
③ an increase in the amount of beach
④ a decrease in the height of the cliff
⑤ an increase in the height of the tide

6 Which of the following would be the *best* alternate title for the illustration?

① Weather Along Ocean Coasts
② The Movement of Ocean Tides
③ Changing Ocean Shorelines
④ Changing Ocean Shoreline Sand
⑤ Solar Heating of Ocean Water

Geochemical Cycles and Earth's Energy

Background Information

Earth consists of a relatively fixed number of atoms of each element such as carbon. The amount of carbon on and in Earth today is about the same amount as when Earth formed. And carbon, like every other element, is found in several chemical storehouses.

- Carbon occurs in the atmosphere as carbon dioxide gas.
- Carbon occurs in carbon-bearing rocks such as limestone.
- Carbon is found in water as dissolved carbon dioxide.
- Carbon is found in all organic molecules.

The movement of elements from one chemical storehouse to another is referred to as a **geochemical cycle**. Movement of carbon among its storehouses is driven by Earth's internal and external energy sources.

- Earth's internal energy comes from two primary sources—the gravitational energy from Earth's formation which led to a high-temperature core and radioactivity. The heat produced in the core is carried to the mantle both by radiation (light energy) and by convection (moving) currents of molten rock, mainly liquid iron and other heavy metals. The internal energy is responsible for earthquakes and for volcanoes that release gases containing carbon into the atmosphere.
- Earth's external energy comes from the Sun. Solar energy is responsible for the heating of the atmosphere. The heating of the atmosphere, together with Earth's energy of rotation, causes wind, rain, ocean currents, and other forms of weather.

Reading Selection

The movement of carbon between some carbon storehouses may involve processes that take millions of years. Limestone, marble, and chalk are examples. Each of these is a common type of rock that is composed mainly of calcium carbonate. The carbon contained in these rocks comes from the bodies of marine organisms that were alive millions of years ago. These organisms took carbon from the atmosphere, water, and soil. When they died, their remains eventually became part of sedimentary rocks, such as limestone, marble, and chalk, formed during millions of years.

Today, when deposits of limestone, marble, or chalk weather, the calcium carbonate chemically reacts with water. The byproducts of this reaction are carbon dioxide gas and carbonic acid. Carbon returns both to the atmosphere and to oceans and lakes.

❶ What is a geochemical cycle? _____

_____

❷ What carbon-based chemical is contained in limestone, in marble, and in chalk?

_____

GED Practice

Questions 1, 2, and 3 refer to the passage below.

Phosphorous is an element that also takes part in a geochemical cycle. Phosphorous occurs in nature mainly in chemicals called phosphates. Most phosphates occur as salts in ocean sediments or in rocks.

Land plants absorb phosphates from soil; ocean plants absorb phosphates from sea water. Plants are eaten by herbivores (plant-eating animals). Herbivores are eaten by carnivores (meat-eating animals). After death, both plants and animals decay, and the phosphates in each organism return to the soil or to the ocean.

Geological processes also play a role in this cycle. These processes bring ocean sediments to land, while weathering and runoff often carry phosphates back to the ocean. In the ocean, phosphates once again become part of bottom sediments; on land, phosphates may, over time, again become part of rocks.

1 What element is found in phosphates?

  ① sulfate
  ② protons
  ③ photons
  ④ phosphorous
  ⑤ carbon

2 In what commercial product would you most likely find phosphates?

  ① jet fuel
  ② dish soap
  ③ garden fertilizer
  ④ house paint
  ⑤ wood glue

3 What processes move phosphorous from living organisms back to its storehouses in the ocean and in rock?

  ① death and decay
  ② birth and growth
  ③ heat and pressure
  ④ cooling and freezing
  ⑤ light and heat

Questions 4, 5, and 6 refer to the illustration below.

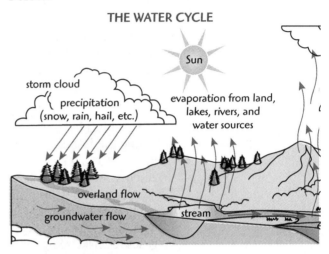

THE WATER CYCLE

4 What is the source of energy that drives the water cycle?

  ① Earth's internal energy
  ② water vapor
  ③ rain
  ④ sunshine
  ⑤ weather conditions

5 How do clouds form?

  ① Water falls from clouds as rain.
  ② Water flows from streams, bringing fresh water to the oceans.
  ③ Water evaporates from lakes and oceans.
  ④ Water vapor on land condenses into water droplets.
  ⑤ Atmospheric water vapor condenses into water droplets, forming clouds.

6 What is Earth's greatest storehouse of water?

  ① freshwater lakes
  ② the oceans
  ③ polar icecaps
  ④ freshwater streams
  ⑤ clouds

The Greenhouse Effect and Global Warming

Background Information

Life on Earth is made possible by a delicate balance of many factors. If this balance is upset, extinction of all living organisms could result. One factor is temperature. Earth's surface temperature must stay in a range in which organisms can live, not too hot and not too cold. The mild temperature range presently found on Earth's surface results from two effects: the heating of the surface from sunlight and the insulating and warming properties of the atmosphere. The two effects working together are often called the **greenhouse effect**.

Scientists have discovered that Earth's atmosphere has been warming slowly during the last century. One possible cause is an increase in air pollution that has been occurring since the beginning of the Industrial Revolution during the nineteenth century. Scientists believe that industrial air pollution can actually cause the greenhouse effect to overheat Earth's surface. Today, the slow rise in atmospheric temperature is referred to as **global warming**. The air pollution leading to global warming is mainly excess carbon dioxide gas and, to a lesser extent, several other gases. Considered together, these gases are referred to as greenhouse gases.

Reading Selection

The planet Venus, a close neighbor of Earth, has experienced a high temperature increase over the centuries that makes the possibility of life on Venus very unlikely. Like Earth, Venus has both a solid surface of minerals and an atmosphere. You might think Venus is a planet where organisms could develop and grow. However, the surface temperature of Venus is about 900°F—much too hot for any form of life that we know.

Venus is very hot because of a high level of carbon dioxide gas in its atmosphere. Venus cannot cool as Earth cools: by sending excess heat back into space. On Venus, heat energy radiating from the surface is absorbed by the excess carbon dioxide gas in the atmosphere.

❶ What is the greenhouse effect?_____

_____

❷ What is global warming?_____

_____

❸ What do scientists believe is one possible cause of global warming?_____

_____

❹ In what two ways is the planet Venus similar to Earth?_____

_____

GED Practice

Questions 1 and 2 are based on the passage below.

Scientists have discovered that the amount of carbon dioxide gas in Earth's atmosphere has increased almost 30% in the last one hundred years. At this rate, the level could increase another 40% by the end of the twenty-first century. If this happens, several things may occur:

- The average surface temperature of Earth will increase, perhaps by as much as 3.6°F.
- Glacial ice will melt and ocean levels will rise by several feet.
- World rainfall patterns will change. The United States could become an arid, parched desert.

1 Which of the following may result from global warming on Earth?

(1) the slow melting of polar ice caps
(2) an increase in carbon dioxide gas in the atmosphere
(3) a decrease in carbon dioxide gas in the atmosphere
(4) a decrease in the average ocean depth
(5) the freezing of Earth's oceans

2 Which of the following would be of *least* importance to a scientist studying global warming?

(1) any change in the average thickness of ice at locations in Antarctica
(2) any change in the average air temperature near the coast of Alaska
(3) any change in efforts designed to protect polar bears from extinction
(4) any change in average summer and winter temperatures at the North Pole
(5) any change in the average level of high and low tides in San Francisco Bay

Questions 3 and 4 refer to the following passage.

Forest vegetation plays a role in the greenhouse effect. Plants absorb carbon dioxide gas from the atmosphere for use in photosynthesis. As a byproduct, plants release oxygen gas to the atmosphere. When large areas of tropical rain forests are cleared for logging or other purposes, an increase in the usual level of carbon dioxide gas in the atmosphere may result. Because of this, tropical rain forests have long played a role in maintaining Earth's present temperature range.

3 How do tropical rain forests play a role in helping to maintain Earth's normal temperature range?

(1) by decreasing the amount of all gases in the atmosphere
(2) by producing plant sugar through the process of photosynthesis
(3) by increasing the level of carbon dioxide gas in the atmosphere
(4) by providing cleared areas of land
(5) by helping to reduce excess carbon dioxide gas in the atmosphere

4 Which of the following is implied by this passage?

(1) The cutting of tropical rain forests could lead to the greenhouse effect.
(2) The cutting of tropical rain forests could lead to an increase in global warming.
(3) The cutting of tropical rain forests could lead to a decrease in global warming.
(4) The cutting of tropical rain forests could lead to changes in ocean current flow.
(5) The cutting of tropical rain forests could lead to an increase in the average oxygen content of the atmosphere.

113

Historical Perspectives in Earth Science

Background Information

For much of human history, people thought that Earth was a fearful place, a place ruled by an assortment of gods, giants, and demons. Storms, volcanoes, earthquakes, and even the Sun itself were not features to study and understand. They were warnings and punishments to be feared. Human and animal sacrifices often were used as a form of communication and peacemaking between human beings and their gods.

- In the valley of Mexico before the arrival of Spanish conquerors in the sixteenth century, the Aztecs offered human sacrifices to the Sun.
- In ancient Iceland, Norsemen believed that earthquakes resulted from quarrels among their gods.
- Ancient Polynesian islanders believed that the goddess Pele and her sister Namakaokahai battled across the Pacific Ocean and that a scar of each battle created each of the Hawaiian Islands.
- Ancient Europeans believed that the lava that erupted from Iceland's most active volcano, Hekla, or Hell's Gate, contained the souls of the damned.

Ancient peoples around the world mixed religious beliefs with attempts at understanding in ways that may seem strange to us. Remember, though, ancient peoples tried to explain their world in ways that made sense to them. This is also what we do today. Luckily, we have the advantage of basing our present understanding on a wealth of scientific discoveries and on a well-understood scientific method for obtaining new knowledge.

Reading Selection

Accurate timepieces were first invented in the seventeenth century. Before this, the motion of the Sun across the sky was used as a basis for measuring time. At any locality, noon occurs when the Sun is at the highest point in the sky. The time between noon on one day and the next was, by custom, divided into 24 hours. With the invention of accurate timepieces, time could be kept mechanically. Measuring the position of the Sun in the sky became unnecessary. Perhaps the most important use of accurate timepieces was in the lives of sailors. Accurate timepieces enabled sailors to determine their exact location while sailing across an ocean.

❶ How did fear play a role in the beliefs of ancient peoples? _____

_____

❷ Before the use of accurate timepieces, what limited the measurement of time?

_____

❸ How did accurate timepieces help sailors? _____

GED Practice

Questions 1 and 2 refer to the passage below.

About 1900, Western thinkers, unlike Greek thinkers before them, came to believe that Earth had a beginning. They believed there must be a way to describe how Earth began and to estimate Earth's age.

One such early influential thinker was Georges Leclerc (1707–1788), a French mathematician, biologist, and cosmologist. Leclerc proposed that all planets, including Earth, had been formed by comets colliding with the Sun. He also suggested that the age of Earth was much more than 6,000 years, as proclaimed at the time by the church. By measuring the cooling rate of an iron ball, Leclerc calculated that Earth must be about 75,000 years old. For this, he was condemned by the church and his books were burned.

Modern dating methods, based on radioactivity, show the age of Earth to be about 4.6 billion years.

1 What does the first paragraph imply about what early Greek thinkers believed?

    ① Earth's surface is flat.
    ② Earth is too large to measure.
    ③ Earth will exist forever.
    ④ Earth has a beginning but its age is impossible to know.
    ⑤ Earth has existed forever and has no beginning.

2 What model can you infer that Leclerc used to represent Earth in his experiments to determine Earth's age?

    ① a comet
    ② a collision of objects
    ③ a thermometer
    ④ a hot iron ball
    ⑤ a radioactive element

Questions 3 and 4 refer to the graph below.

Scientists have found evidence that indicates that the average sea level has varied over the past 35,000 years as shown on the graph below. This graph is consistent with evidence of ice ages in Earth's past during which the ocean level falls and glaciers increase in size.

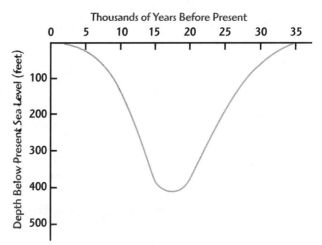

ONE ICE AGE CYCLE

3 According to the graph, about how long ago was the peak of this ice age?

    ① within the last 1,000 years
    ② about 10,000 years ago
    ③ about 18,000 years ago
    ④ about 26,000 years ago
    ⑤ about 35,000 years ago

4 If the graph represents one ice age, about how many years did this ice age last?

    ① 35,000 years
    ② 25,000 years
    ③ 15,000 years
    ④ 5,000 years
    ⑤ 1,000 years

Celestial Objects in the Universe

Background Information

Astronomy, one of the oldest sciences, is the general study of all celestial objects in the universe—the planets and their moons, stars, comets, meteoroids, asteroids, interstellar clouds of material, and a host of strange objects that are just beginning to be understood.

The part of the universe that is nearest to us is the solar system—the Sun and the objects that revolve around it: the planets with their moons, asteroids, and comets.

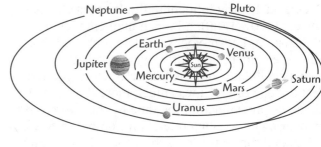

OUR SOLAR SYSTEM

- The largest planets are Jupiter, Saturn, Uranus, and Neptune.
- Four smaller planets—Mercury, Venus, Earth, and Mars—are those closest to the Sun.
- Not much is known about Pluto, the smallest, outermost planet. Pluto's eccentric orbit sometimes crosses the orbit of Neptune.

Reading Selection

Stars—the fiery hot gaseous objects that fill the night sky—are born, have a lifetime, and eventually die. Although a long lifetime for a human being may be 100 years, the life of a star may be many millions or even billions of years. A star forms from a cloud of interstellar dust and gas, goes through a life cycle, and then ceases to exist, often with much of the star's material returning to interstellar space. The exact life cycle of a star depends on the amount of material from which the star is made.

Stars are made up mainly of hot hydrogen gas that slowly converts to helium gas. The conversion process is a nuclear reaction in which tremendous energy in the form of heat and light is given off. When all of the hydrogen is consumed, the normal life of a star is over.

1 Name the planets in order, starting with the planet closest to the Sun.

_____

2 Not counting Pluto, what is one difference between the inner planets (planets closest to the Sun) and the outer planets?

_____

3 What is the main element from which stars are made? _____

4 What is the source of energy in a star? _____

GED Practice

Questions 1 and 2 refer to the following passage.

As stars age, they may explode or may turn into unusual but often beautiful structures.

- *Supernova*—a flash of light caused by the explosion of a massive star that has become too hot. Heavy elements are formed in supernova explosions.

- *Neutron star*—a very dense, small star made up entirely of neutrons from the leftover materials near the center of a supernova. A teaspoonful of neutron star would weigh one billion tons if brought to Earth.

- *Pulsar*—a neutron star that spins. A pulsar sends out beams of pulsing radiation that are detected on Earth.

- *Black hole*—the collapsed leftovers of a supernova. The gravity of a black hole is so strong that it may pull in material from nearby stars. Not even light can escape from a black hole.

- *Quasar*—celestial objects that emit great amounts of light energy. No one knows what a quasar is, but it is possibly a small galaxy surrounding a massive black hole.

❶ What is the name of the celestial object that cannot be seen directly because it traps light that might otherwise emanate from it?

(1) supernova
(2) neutron star
(3) pulsar
(4) black hole
(5) quasar

❷ What is the name of the flash of light created when a massive star explodes?

(1) supernova
(2) neutron star
(3) pulsar
(4) black hole
(5) quasar

Questions 3, 4, and 5 refer to the following illustration.

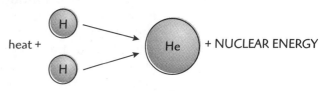

In a star, hydrogen is converted to helium, releasing nuclear energy.

❸ When hydrogen is converted to helium in a nuclear reaction, how many atoms of hydrogen are needed to make one atom of helium?

(1) one
(2) two
(3) three
(4) four
(5) five

❹ Which of the following statements can you infer to be true about the nuclear reaction that takes place in stars?

(1) All the nuclear energy that is created stays in the star as heat.
(2) The nuclear energy that is released is less than the heat energy needed to start the reaction.
(3) The nuclear energy that is released is equal to the heat energy needed to start the reaction.
(4) All the nuclear energy that is created leaves the star as light.
(5) The nuclear energy that is released is greater than the heat energy needed to start the reaction.

❺ At the end of a star's life, what element will the star mainly contain?

(1) water
(2) hydrogen
(3) carbon
(4) helium
(5) oxygen

The Evolving Universe

Background Information

The concept of **evolution**—gradual change due to natural processes—is believed to apply to the universe as a whole. Most space scientists believe that the universe had a beginning and that it has been slowly evolving ever since. Stars are born, stars die, and strange new celestial objects form. And, while all this change is taking place, galaxies slowly move away from one another. What drives this evolutionary process and whether it will ever end are questions of interest to both scientists and religious leaders.

Reading Selection

Today, scientists do know that the universe is still expanding and cooling. However, no one knows if this expansion will continue. There are three models of what may eventually happen as the universe evolves. No one knows which model is correct.

- *Open universe*—a universe that continues to slowly expand forever
- *Flat universe*—a universe that at some future time reaches a constant size
- *Closed universe*—a universe that at some future time begins to contract and eventually collapses to its original state

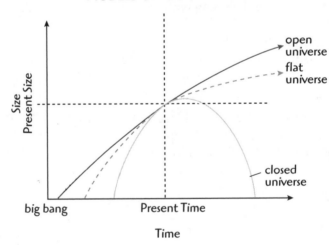

MODELS OF THE UNIVERSE

❶ The model that the universe will expand forever is called _____.

❷ The model that the universe will eventually collapse is called _____.

❸ The gradual change that takes place in the universe is called _____.

GED Practice

Questions 1, 2, and 3 refer to the following passage.

By extrapolating the expansion of the universe back in time, scientists have come up with an interesting idea: the universe appears to have started at a single point and at a single instant! The theory that the universe began in this way is called the big bang theory.

According to the big bang theory, the universe started about 14 billion years ago as a very dense, hot, compact mass under extreme pressure. In an instant, this mass exploded and the universe and all that is in it was born. Within the first fraction of a second, all the elements that make up today's universe were created.

Although it is difficult to understand, the big bang theory is accepted by most space scientists as being the best scientific theory we have about how the universe began.

1 According to the big bang theory, what is the approximate age of the universe?

　① 75 billion years
　② 14 billion years
　③ 40 million years
　④ 140,000 years
　⑤ 6,000 years

2 According to the big bang theory, how soon after the initial explosion did the elements form?

　① elements are still forming
　② 14 billion years later
　③ about 90 days later
　④ a few days later
　⑤ within the first fraction of a second

3 Scientists jokingly use the phrase "the big crunch" to refer to a model of the universe. To what model are they most likely referring?

　① the big bang theory
　② a universe that expands forever
　③ a universe that has a constant size
　④ the closed universe theory
　⑤ the accelerated universe theory

Questions 4, 5, and 6 refer to the passage and drawing below.

The expansion of the universe is often compared to dots on a balloon. Suppose you draw many dots on the surface of a balloon before you fill it with air. Then you fill the balloon with air and watch what happens to the dots as the balloon expands.

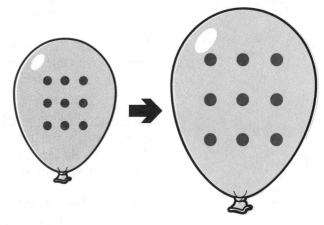

4 What happens to the dots on the balloon as you fill it with air?

　① They disappear.
　② They move closer together.
　③ They move farther apart.
　④ They form one large dot.
　⑤ They stay the same distance apart.

5 According to the passage, what do the dots on the balloons most likely represent?

　① elements
　② galaxies
　③ energy
　④ planets
　⑤ protons

6 In the balloon diagram, what does the balloon itself represent?

　① the universe
　② Earth
　③ a star
　④ the solar system
　⑤ an atom

50

Historical Perspectives in Space Science

Background Information

The earliest thinkers based their ideas about celestial objects on the motions of planets and stars seen by the naked eye. The Greek philosopher Aristotle (384–322 B.C.) believed that Earth was the center of the universe and that everything else rotated around it in orbits that were perfect circles. This is what naked-eye observation suggests is the case. Aristotle's model of the universe was considered correct until after the invention of the telescope.

The telescope was invented by an unknown Dutch eyeglass lens maker in about 1608. However, it was Galileo Galilei (1564–1642), an Italian astronomer, who made his own telescope in 1609 and first used a telescope to view celestial objects. From Galileo's observations came the discoveries that forever changed how scientists view the universe.

Since the time of Galileo, scientists have discovered that the universe is filled with clusters of billions of stars that we now call galaxies. These galaxies are filled not only with familiar stars but also with strange and interesting objects. Early scientists would never have dreamed of the existence of quasars, pulsars, blazers, radio galaxies, neutron stars, and black holes.

Reading Selection

Galileo Galilei did not invent the telescope, but he is believed to be the first scientist to use it to observe the night sky. Galileo made many important discoveries:

- The planet Jupiter has moons in orbit around it.
- The planet Venus orbits the Sun and exhibits a full set of phases like Earth's moon.
- The Moon's surface is characterized by mountains and craters, the lunar surface being uneven in the same way that Earth's surface is uneven.
- Galileo reported seeing sunspots, although he had no idea what caused them.
- Galileo was the first scientist to realize that the Milky Way is a band of countless stars.

Galileo's observations agreed strongly with the work of Nicolaus Copernicus (1473–1543), a Polish astronomer who proposed that the Sun, not Earth, was at the center of the solar system. In agreeing that the Sun was at the center of the solar system, Galileo was bringing science directly into conflict with religious teachings that held that Earth was the center of the universe and of creation in general. The full acceptance of Galileo's beliefs would take decades.

❶ What invention led to changing views of the universe? _____

❷ Who is credited as being the first scientist to use the telescope to study celestial objects?

_____

❸ What conflict of values did Galileo's discoveries lead to? _____

_____

Questions 1 and 2 refer to the passage below.

Seen through a telescope, Mars appears as a red and orange disk. White ice caps can be seen at the north and south poles. Dust, blowing in the Martian atmosphere, gives the impression of color changes and changing surface features. Before spacecraft in the late twentieth century, this was the limit of our understanding of Mars.

Early in the twentieth century, astronomers believed they saw canals on the Martian surface. An American astronomer, Percival Lowell, believed that these canals were built by an advanced civilization on Mars. He wrote books expounding his belief. Lowell proposed that canals were built on Mars to carry water from wet polar regions to dry equatorial deserts.

Spacecraft visits to the Martian surface during the last decade have shown that no canals exist on Mars. And, as far as we now know, it is not likely that any life form has ever existed on Mars.

1 Which of the following can you infer from the passage?

① Mars does not have a solid surface.
② Mars does not have a gaseous atmosphere.
③ Mars has a gaseous atmosphere.
④ Mars used to have liquid oceans.
⑤ Mars has running water in its polar regions.

2 What invention led to the greatest jump in understanding about Mars?

① electron microscope
② high-mountain telescopes
③ space-based telescopes
④ spacecraft circling Mars
⑤ spacecraft landing on Mars

3 Why does Mars appear to observers on Earth as a red-orange planet?

① Mars contains active volcanoes that spew red-orange magma.
② Red-orange light is reflected by the gaseous atmosphere of Mars.
③ Mars has a high surface temperature.
④ Mars is a glowing star.
⑤ Mars has a solid surface.

Question 4 refers to the passage below.

The ancient Greeks made the following observations:

A. The Sun rises in the morning and sets at night.
B. The Sun and the Moon look about the same size.
C. The bright part of the Moon changes shape during the days of each month.
D. Earth does not seem to move.

4 Which of the above observations could the ancient Greeks use to support their belief that the Sun moved around Earth?

① A and B only
② A and C only
③ B and C only
④ B and D only
⑤ A and D only

Question 5 refers to the following passage.

Seen by the naked eye, planets appear as faint lights that cross the night sky. Yet, unlike stars, planets do not give off their own light.

5 Knowing this, which of the following facts would Galileo have needed in order to explain how people on Earth could see the other planets?

A. Planets close to the Sun have higher surface temperatures than planets farther away.
B. Five planets are farther from the Sun than Earth while three are closer.
C. Planets reflect part of the sunlight that strikes them.
① A only
② B only
③ C only
④ A and C only
⑤ B and C only

Taking the GED Test

Congratulations on completing the instruction section of *Top 50 Science Skills for GED Success*. You are now familiar with the types and difficulty levels of questions you will see on the GED Science Test. As you ready yourself for the GED Science Test, you may want to think about these good test-taking strategies:

- Get a good night's sleep before the test.

- Eat breakfast before the test, especially if you are taking the test in the morning.

- Arrive at the testing center a few minutes early. If you have never been to the testing center, visit it before the day of the test so that you can find it easily.

- Read the test directions carefully. Read each question carefully and be sure you understand what is being asked. Then select the answer that matches that question.

- Grid your answers carefully, ensuring that you mark each answer in the place provided for it. If you erase an answer, be sure you erase it completely.

- If you are not sure of an answer, make an educated guess. When you leave a question unanswered, you will always lose a point, but you may gain the point if you make a correct guess.

- During the test, work quickly and accurately. If you do not know the answer to a question, try to eliminate any choices that do not make sense and select the best answer from the remaining choices.

- All questions on the test have the same point value. Because of this, make sure you answer all of the easier questions. In other words, don't spend a lot of time on a more difficult question. If you find yourself spending a lot of time on a single question, stop working on that item. Put a question mark beside the question number or write the number on your scratch paper. Then mark the answer you think is most likely correct, and go on to the next question. If you have time at the end of the test, go back to the difficult questions and check your answers.

- If you find yourself feeling nervous or unable to focus, close your eyes for a moment or two and take a few deep breaths. Then return to the test.

About the GED Posttest

This GED Posttest is a review of the 50 skills presented in this book. It is parallel in form to the Pretest you took at the beginning of this book. It will demonstrate what you have learned from the specific skills you practiced throughout this book and will identify any areas you need to review before taking the GED Science Test.

Take this test just as you would the GED Test. On the GED Test, you will have 80 minutes to read the passages, charts, and graphs and complete the 50 questions. For best practice, allow yourself 80 minutes to complete the Posttest in this book.

Answer every question on this Posttest. When time is up, mark the questions you did not finish. Then take extra time to answer those questions, too. That will give you an idea of how much faster you need to work on the actual test.

After you finish, turn to the Answer Key on page 178 to check your answers. Then use the GED Posttest Evaluation Chart (pages 138–139) to figure out which skills to review in the instruction section of this book. You may also use the pages from Contemporary's *GED Science* for further practice and review.

GED Posttest

Questions 1, 2, and 3 are based on the following diagrams.

FRATERNAL TWINS
Two genetically different individuals develop within separate fetal sacs.

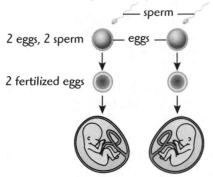

2 eggs, 2 sperm — sperm — eggs

2 fertilized eggs

IDENTICAL TWINS
Cell division results in two genetically identical individuals who develop in the same fetal sac.

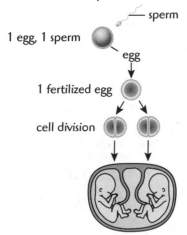

1 egg, 1 sperm — sperm — egg

1 fertilized egg

cell division

1 Which of the following characteristics is *least* likely to be shared by identical twins?

  (1) height
  (2) shoe size
  (3) eye color
  (4) favorite color
  (5) gender (male or female)

2 From which fact can you deduce that twin girls are fraternal twins, not identical twins?

  (1) Both girls are in the first grade.
  (2) One girl prefers cake for dessert while her sister prefers ice cream.
  (3) One girl is slightly heavier than the other.
  (4) The twin girls have brothers who are identical twins.
  (5) One girl's earlobes are shaped differently than her sister's.

3 Which of the following is a correct summary of how identical twins form?

  (1) Identical twins form from the fertilization of two egg cells.
  (2) Identical twins form from the division of a single fertilized egg cell.
  (3) Identical twins form from the fertilization of two egg cells by two sperm.
  (4) Identical twins form from the fertilization of one egg cell by two sperm.
  (5) Identical twins form from the fertilization of two egg cells by a single sperm.

Questions 4 and 5 are based on the following passage and diagram.

A tide is a periodic movement of ocean water that changes the level of the ocean's surface. High tides occur on the part of Earth nearest to the Moon and the part of Earth farthest from the Moon. Low ocean tides occur on each side of Earth between the positions of the high tides.

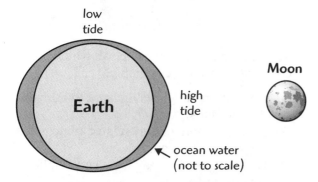

Before Isaac Newton formulated his laws of motion and his law of universal gravitation, the causes of tides were not understood. Newton's ideas helped scientists understand how the Moon and Earth interact at a distance, as well as how Earth and the Sun interact.

4 What did Isaac Newton most likely conclude was the cause of ocean tides on Earth?

① the shape of the Moon
② the phases of the Moon
③ the gravitational attraction of the Moon
④ the shape of the Moon's orbit
⑤ the rotation of the Moon on its axis

5 A spring tide, the highest and the lowest of tides, occurs each time Earth, the Moon, and the Sun are approximately in a straight line. How many times each month does a spring tide occur?

① one time
② two times
③ three times
④ four times
⑤ more than four times

Question 6 is based on the following passage.

There is a special class of single-cell organisms called prokaryotes. Prokaryotes are organisms whose cells do not contain a nucleus or any other specialized cell structures. Bacteria and mildew are examples. However, although bacteria cells do not contain a nucleus, they do contain genetic material scattered throughout the cell. Bacteria reproduce by a process called binary fission. During binary fission, a bacteria cell simply divides into two identical cells, each cell receiving a share of the genetic material.

6 What property of bacteria makes it very unlike most other plant cells?

① the smaller than normal size
② the absence of a cell wall
③ the absence of a nucleus
④ the presence of genetic material
⑤ the fact that the cell divides

7 Ancient astronomers may have noticed that constellations (patterns of stars) seen in countries north of the equator are different from constellations seen in countries south of the equator.

Which statement below best explains this observation?

① Countries in the Northern Hemisphere have summer while countries in the Southern Hemisphere have winter.
② Constellations have been observed both in the Northern Hemisphere and in the Southern Hemisphere.
③ The noonday Sun is higher in the sky in summer months than in winter months.
④ Earth's northern regions point to a different part of the universe than do Earth's southern regions.
⑤ The distance between Earth and the Sun changes as Earth revolves around the Sun.

Question 8 is based on the following passage.

The Kashmir earthquake (also known as the northern Pakistan earthquake) occurred on October 8, 2005, in the disputed territory of Kashmir—the area being claimed by both Pakistan and India. A month later, the official death toll was set at about 90,000. Most of the affected region had limited access due to its remoteness and mountainous terrain, and impeded access due to landslides caused by the quake. The situation was made even worse by the upcoming winter snows. It will be years before this region returns to normal.

8 What is the major problem that relief workers faced when trying to help survivors of the Kashmir earthquake?

① knowing when a disaster occurs
② knowing where a disaster occurs
③ knowing what kinds of needs survivors will have
④ burying those who have died
⑤ getting aid to those who were injured

Question 9 is based on the following passage.

Boyle's law states that the volume taken up by a gas decreases as the pressure applied to the gas increases. As an example, if you double the pressure on a fixed amount of gas, you will decrease its volume by half.

9 Applying Boyle's law, what advantage does a high-pressure container offer for the storage of oxygen gas?

① A lot of oxygen gas can be stored in a relatively small container.
② Oxygen can be kept separate from other gases in the room.
③ The temperature of the oxygen can be carefully controlled.
④ The container prevents the gas from catching fire.
⑤ The container prevents the gas from escaping into the atmosphere.

Question 10 is based on the drawing below.

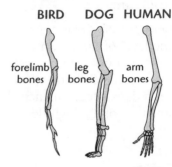

10 Referring to the drawings above, which conclusion is *least* reasonable?

① Dogs are more closely related to humans than to birds.
② Birds are more closely related to dogs than dogs are to humans.
③ Different species may have very similar genetic codes.
④ Different physical functions among different species can be performed by similar physical structures.
⑤ Different species may be related biologically to one another.

11 For life to have formed on another planet, scientists believe that several things must be present. Which of the following is *not* one of these things?

① a source of carbon
② a source of water
③ a source of energy
④ a source of hydrogen gas
⑤ a favorable temperature range

Questions 12, 13, and 14 are based on the following illustration and passage.

VOLCANO

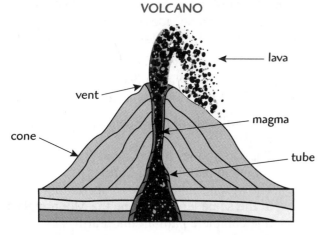

A volcanic eruption is an explosion through Earth's surface of molten rock called magma—a fiery liquid-rock solution of mainly silicon-based compounds. Magma forms in the mantle from heat that radiates from Earth's core. Magma flows as convection currents of molten rock in a relatively solid mantle below Earth's crust.

Near Earth's surface, magma flows through tubular cracks in Earth's crust. Magma, together with hot gas and steam, is under high pressure and can blow a vent (hole) in the surface. Gases released into the atmosphere include water vapor, sulfur dioxide, carbon dioxide, carbon monoxide, hydrogen, hydrogen sulfide, hydrogen chloride, and hydrogen fluoride.

Magma often breaks through the surface with enough force to blast a large part of a mountain out of its way. This is what happened in the 1980 eruption of Mount St. Helens in the state of Washington.

Magma that emerges through the surface is called lava. A volcanic eruption usually forms a cinder cone made of fragments of ejected rocks and lava around the vent.

⑫ What important role did volcanoes likely play in the early development of Earth?

① Volcanoes removed water vapor from the developing atmosphere.
② Volcanoes helped send extra heat from Earth's surface to space.
③ Volcanoes contributed heat to the cooling, hardening surface.
④ Volcanoes contributed heat to Earth's liquid interior.
⑤ Volcanoes contributed gases to the developing atmosphere.

⑬ Which statement best explains what happens during a volcanic eruption?

① Material on Earth's surface moves through the crust and into the mantle.
② Material below Earth's crust moves through the crust onto Earth's surface.
③ Material breaks off of Earth's crust and gets deposited on Earth's surface.
④ Material breaks off of Earth's surface and becomes part of the crust.
⑤ Material from the top of a mountain is shaken loose and slides down the sides of the mountain.

⑭ What is the source of energy that causes a volcanic eruption?

① heat energy from the Sun
② gravitational energy from the Moon
③ heat energy from Earth's core
④ chemical energy from Earth's solid crust
⑤ Earth's rotational energy

Questions 15 and 16 are based on the following chart.

MOHS SCALE OF MINERAL HARDNESS		
Mineral	*Hardness*	*Property*
Talc	1	can be scratched
Gypsum	2	by a fingernail
Calcite	3	can be scratched
		by a copper penny
Fluorite	4	can be scratched
Apatite	5	by a piece of glass
Feldspar	6	can scratch a piece
Quartz	7	of glass or a knife
Topaz	8	blade
Corundum	9	
Diamond	10	can scratch all other
		common materials

15 According to the Mohs scale, which mineral could be part of a rubbing compound used to smooth a roughly cut piece of glass?

1 feldspar
2 calcite
3 fluorite
4 talc
5 apatite

16 Which of the following is best classified as an opinion rather than a fact or a hypothesis?

1 One test of hardness of a mineral is to determine what it will scratch.
2 Diamonds are the hardest of all listed minerals in the chart.
3 Diamonds are the prettiest of all minerals.
4 The hardness of a mineral is related to the strength of the mineral's molecular bonds.
5 The hardness rating of many minerals depends on temperature.

17 As the Moon formed, most likely from ejected matter from Earth's surface, an interesting thing slowly occurred: the Moon's motion became such that the same side of the Moon always faces Earth. A person standing on Earth never sees the backside of the Moon.

Which of the following must be true for the same side of the Moon to always face Earth?

1 The dark side of the Moon never faces Earth.
2 The Moon does not rotate as it makes one complete path around Earth.
3 The Moon rotates twice on its rotation axis in the same length of time the Moon makes one complete path around Earth.
4 The Moon rotates once on its axis in the same length of time it takes the Moon to make one trip around Earth.
5 Only one side of the Moon is ever lit by sunlight.

Question 18 is based on the following passage.

In vitro fertilization (IVF) is a procedure for fertilizing an egg outside of a woman's body. IVF is a major treatment for infertility when other methods of achieving pregnancy have failed.

In IVF, the egg and sperm are taken from the couple and are put together in a container of special fluid. The resulting fertilized egg is transferred to the woman's uterus where the fetus then develops.

18 Why might a couple choose in vitro fertilization instead of adoption?

1 the desire to reduce total costs
2 the desire to spend less time and less effort in the entire procedure
3 the desire to have a healthy child
4 the desire to choose the gender of the child
5 the desire to have a child that is genetically their own

Questions 19 and 20 are based on the following passage.

A pandemic is a global epidemic—a global outbreak of an infectious disease that affects people over extensive geographical regions. According to the World Health Organization, a pandemic is possible when three conditions are met:

- A disease emerges that is new to the world's human populations.
- The disease can affect humans and cause serious illness.
- The disease spreads easily and substantially among humans.

Well-known pandemics of the past include the Black Death that started in Europe in the mid-1300s and killed about one-third of Europe's population. The Black Death is believed to have been an outbreak of bubonic plague, a plague possibly caused by bacteria spread by fleas. A recent pandemic was the Hong Kong flu in 1968–69, which caused about 34,000 deaths in the United States. The Hong Kong flu was an outbreak of influenza, a virus-caused disease of the lungs and upper airways.

Avian influenza, also known as bird flu, is a type of influenza virus that is mainly hosted by birds. However, it is known that avian influenza can also infect several species of mammals that come into contact with infected birds. Avian influenza is the first possible pandemic that scientists believe may spread through the world in the early part of the twenty-first century.

19 What distinguishes a pandemic from other forms of community health problems?

① the type of symptoms that infected humans show
② the extent, seriousness, and speed of transmission of illness
③ the country of origin
④ the type of bacteria or virus that causes the illness
⑤ the difficulty in preparing enough vaccine for all affected countries

20 Which of the following is an unstated assumption made by the writer of this passage?

① The avian influenza virus can jump from an animal host to humans.
② The avian influenza virus cannot jump from an animal host to humans.
③ All viruses can jump from animal hosts to humans.
④ No virus can jump from an animal host to humans.
⑤ All viruses are easily spread from human to human.

21 Which of the following would be the best way for humans to address the problem known as global warming?

① Manage forests in order to prevent lightning fires.
② Place restrictions on the use of fireplaces.
③ Develop cars that get high gas mileage.
④ Reduce human dependence on all types of fossil fuels.
⑤ Place high taxes on all types of fossil fuels.

22 What values come into conflict with the problems posed by global warming and the desire to drive a car rather than take public transportation?

① personal values versus conflicting legal values
② religious values versus conflicting freedom of speech
③ the need for affordable health care for all versus personal economic needs
④ the needs of the poor versus the need for feeling economically secure
⑤ societal needs versus a sense of personal freedom

Questions 23, 24, and 25 are based on the following passage.

Following publication of Darwin's theory of evolution, a search took place for a fossil that could prove the existence of an evolutionary ancestor of both humans and apes. No one knew if this ancestor, often referred to as the missing link, even existed.

Then in 1912, near Piltdown, England, an ape-like fossil was found that seemed to be the missing link. The scientific community was astounded. Charles Dawson, an amateur naturalist, gained instant fame from this discovery.

It wasn't until 1953 that Piltdown Man, as the fossil came to be known, was proved to be a fake. Dating techniques, which first became available in 1953, showed the skull bones of Piltdown Man to be only several hundred years old rather than the million or more years that a genuine missing-link fossil would be.

Scientists discovered that the fake fossil was really made up of the cranium of a human and the jaw of an ape. The pieces of skull had been stained and sanded to give them a very aged appearance.

23 What characteristics would a scientist expect to find in a real missing-link fossil?

① characteristics of a human-like vertebrate that has no similarity to either a human skull or an ape skull
② characteristics that are those solely of an ape skull
③ characteristics that are those solely of a human skull
④ characteristics that show similarities between a human skull and an ape skull
⑤ characteristics that show no similarities between a human skull and an ape skull

24 What pressure on Charles Dawson likely led him to carry out the Piltdown Man hoax?

① the need for professional recognition
② the need to prove Darwin correct
③ the need to contribute to his society
④ the need to care for his family
⑤ the need to prove Darwin wrong

25 For what reason did the Piltdown Man hoax go undetected for so many years?

① lack of confirming evidence
② lack of interest by scientists
③ inadequate dating techniques
④ secrecy regarding the discovery
⑤ existence of confirming evidence

Question 26 is based on the following information.

Polymers are long-change hydrocarbons—molecules made up of only carbon and hydrogen atoms in which the carbon atoms are in a single line. Two common polymers are shown below.

PROPANE   BUTANE

26 Suppose you know the number of carbon atoms in a polymer molecule. What rule tells you how many hydrogen atoms are in that same molecule?

① twice the number of carbon atoms
② twice the number of carbon atoms plus two
③ twice the number of carbon atoms minus two
④ three times the number of carbon atoms minus two
⑤ five times half the number of carbon atoms

Questions 27 and 28 refer to the following information.

Physical changes do not result in the creation of new chemical compounds.

Chemical changes do result in the creation of new chemical compounds.

Endothermic reactions are reactions that use more energy than they release.

Exothermic reactions are reactions that give off more energy than they use.

Below are examples of these definitions.

(A) Car engine combustion

$$2C_8H_{16} + 25O_2 \longrightarrow 16CO_2 + 18H_2O + \textit{energy}$$
gasoline oxygen   carbon water
                          dioxide

(B) Acid rain creation

$$SO_3 + H_2O \longrightarrow H_2SO_4$$
sulphur water   sulfuric
trioxide   acid vapor

(C) Ice melting

$$\textit{heat} + H_2O \longrightarrow H_2O$$
          ice   water

(D) Ozone creation

$$\textit{ultraviolet} + 3O_2 \longrightarrow 2O_3$$
\textit{light}   oxygen   ozone

27 Which reaction is a physical change, but not a chemical change?

① A only
② B only
③ C only
④ D only
⑤ None of the above

28 Which reactions are endothermic reactions?

① A and B only
② A and C only
③ B and C only
④ B and D only
⑤ C and D only

Question 29 is based on the following passage and drawing.

Ancient sailors used Polaris (often called the North Star) as a guide when sailing at night. As shown on the drawing below, Polaris is almost directly in line with Earth's rotation axis.

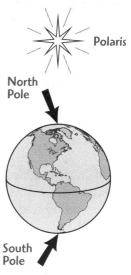

29 To use Polaris as a direction finder at night, what must a sailor assume to be true?

① Polaris is the brightest evening star.
② Polaris can be located by first finding the group of stars called the Big Dipper.
③ Polaris is as easily seen during daytime as it is during nighttime.
④ Polaris stays in the same position in the sky at all hours of the night.
⑤ Polaris stays in the Milky Way galaxy at a constant distance from the Sun.

Question 30 is based on the following illustration.

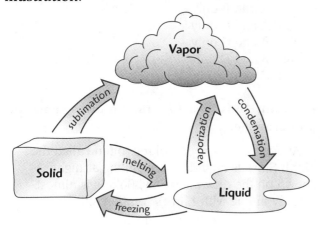

30 What change of phase takes place during the process called sublimation?

① from solid to gas
② from solid to liquid
③ from gas to liquid
④ from gas to solid
⑤ from liquid to solid

31 A tablespoon of sugar is added to each of two glasses. One glass contains warm water, and the other glass contains cold water. The sugar dissolves more quickly in the warm water. Which phrase best describes how the rate of dissolving is affected by temperature?

① Dissolving decreases with increasing temperature.
② Dissolving increases with increasing temperature.
③ Dissolving is not dependent on temperature.
④ Dissolving increases with stirring.
⑤ Dissolving decreases with stirring.

Question 32 is based on the following passage.

The *Exxon Valdez* was an oil tanker owned by the former Exxon Corporation. On March 23, 1989, the tanker left Valdez, Alaska, with a full load of oil. In the early morning of March 24, the vessel was damaged when it hit the Bligh Reef in Prince William Sound. The result was the most devastating domestic oil spill in United States history.

About 30 million gallons of crude oil spilled into the ocean and onto the Alaskan coastline. As a result, an estimated 250,000 sea birds, 2,800 sea otters, 300 harbor seals, 250 bald eagles, and 22 whales perished in the days and weeks after the spill. Researchers have concluded that some habitats will take more than 30 years to recover from this unnecessary disaster.

32 In the *Exxon Valdez* oil spill, what most likely was the cause of the deaths of so many birds?

① poisoning due to eating oil
② burning in fires occurring on the ocean surface
③ inability to escape the pollution after landing due to oil-soaked wings
④ being accidentally killed during cleanup efforts
⑤ being unable to get to food sources hidden by floating oil

33 Which of the following is a goal of science but may not be a goal of technology?

① to develop faster computers
② to improve the sound of the speaker's voice on cellular phones
③ to improve the quality of medicines
④ to improve gas mileage of automobiles
⑤ to determine if life ever existed on Mars

Questions 34 and 35 are based on the following passage.

Ascorbic acid is an organic acid with antioxidant properties, now known to be important in the fight against many types of cancer. Also known as vitamin C, ascorbic acid is important to the human body in the production of connective tissue and is necessary for healthy functioning of the nervous system and the adrenal glands.

Vitamin C is also needed for the prevention of symptoms collectively known as scurvy, a widespread problem that sailors in previous centuries suffered while spending long periods of time at sea. Symptoms of scurvy include loose teeth, easy bleeding, poor healing, anemia, and general sickness. Luckily, scurvy is easily prevented with a diet rich in vitamin C.

Vitamin C is found in citrus fruits, tomatoes, many dark green vegetables, and vegetables from the mustard family including cabbage, broccoli, and cauliflower. Cooking or drying food destroys much of its natural vitamin C.

34 To obtain a rich source of vitamin C, which of the following foods would be recommended?

   ① a smoked salmon snack
   ② a dish of canned corn
   ③ a fresh orange
   ④ a hamburger steak
   ⑤ a fresh banana

35 What fact of sailing in ancient times was related to widespread occurrence of scurvy?

   ① the cost of obtaining fresh fruit
   ② the difficulty in storing fresh fruit on board during a long sail
   ③ the difficulty in reaching a destination in the estimated time
   ④ the uncertainty of which types of food would be available at each port
   ⑤ the difficulty in preparing food in the cramped quarters of a sailing ship

Question 36 is based on the following information and diagram.

The law of reflection governs the behavior of light rays reflecting off of a surface:

- *Specular reflection* occurs when light reflects off a smooth surface such as a mirror. All reflected light rays are parallel to one another. Specular reflection makes it possible to see a reflected image.
- *Diffuse reflection* occurs when light reflects off a rough surface such as a carpet. In this type of reflection, reflected light rays leave the surface in all directions. No visible image occurs in diffuse reflection.

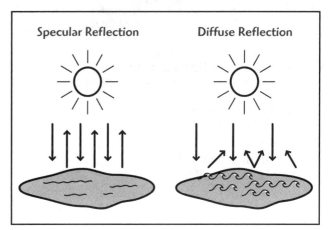

36 Which of the following statements can you infer to be true?

   ① Light does not reflect off a rough surface.
   ② A rough surface reflects only some of the light rays that strike it.
   ③ Specular reflection can occur on the surface of a lake.
   ④ Specular reflection is the most common type of reflection.
   ⑤ Diffuse reflection does not occur when sunshine is the light source.

Question 37 is based on the graph below.

ANIMAL SPECIES ON EARTH

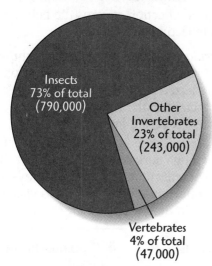

Insects
73% of total
(790,000)

Other
Invertebrates
23% of total
(243,000)

Vertebrates
4% of total
(47,000)

37 Approximately how many total species of animals are known to exist on Earth?

   ① about 1.7 million
   ② about 1.5 million
   ③ about 1.3 million
   ④ about 1.1 million
   ⑤ about 0.9 million

Question 38 is based on the following passage.

One of the strangest objects in the universe is known as a black hole. A black hole is believed to be the very dense remains of a large star that has collapsed to a fraction of its original size. The gravitational field of a black hole is so strong that even light cannot escape from it.

A black hole is surrounded by a spherical boundary called a horizon. Light can enter the horizon but can never escape. Therefore, a black hole appears totally black, its outer radius extending to its horizon.

38 How would a black hole appear to an astronomer who tries to see it?

   ① as a large, bright object in the sky
   ② as a small, bright object in the sky
   ③ as an object blinking on and off
   ④ as a dark void in the sky
   ⑤ as an object slowly becoming darker

Questions 39 and 40 refer to the following passage.

One type of cause-and-effect relationship that occurs with organisms is known as the principle of stimulus-response. According to this principle, an organism will respond when acted on by a stimulus—anything that can be felt, seen, heard, or smelled. An organism will respond to each stimulus in a way that best ensures its own well-being.

39 A young girl throws a cracker into a pond. Which of the following is the best example of an organism's response to this stimulus?

   ① A circular water wave slowly spreads from the point where the cracker hit the water.
   ② The girl yells to her parents.
   ③ Fish at the other end of the pond pay no attention.
   ④ The cracker starts to dissolve in the water.
   ⑤ Ducks swim toward the cracker.

40 Which of the following is true about every stimulus-response reaction?

   ① The response occurs at exactly the same time as the stimulus.
   ② The response always occurs before the stimulus.
   ③ The stimulus always occurs before the response.
   ④ The purpose of a stimulus is to help an organism survive.
   ⑤ The purpose of a response is to attract attention.

Questions 41 and 42 are based on the following passage and illustration.

Newton's first law of motion states, in part, that a body in motion will stay in motion until acted upon by an external force.

The illustration below shows what happens to a driver and a car when acted on by an external force—a collision with another car or object.

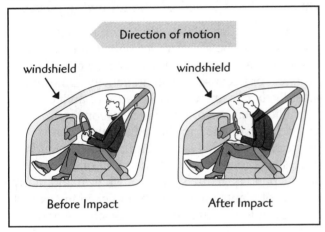

Direction of motion

windshield   windshield

Before Impact   After Impact

41 Which of the following best describes what would most likely happen during a hard collision if the car did not have an air bag and the driver was not wearing a seat belt?

① The car stops; the driver stops because he or she is sitting in the seat.
② The car stops; the driver keeps going, stopped only by impact with the steering wheel, dashboard, and windshield.
③ The car stops; the driver is thrown into the back seat.
④ The car stops; the steering wheel impacts the driver, holding him or her firmly in the seat.
⑤ The car stops; the driver holds himself or herself in the seat by holding onto the steering wheel.

42 The law of conservation of energy states that energy is not lost during an interaction. How does this law apply to the driver of the car represented by the illustration?

① The law applies to the car, not the driver.
② The driver does not have energy, either before or after the crash.
③ The driver's energy stays with the driver.
④ The driver's energy is transferred to the car, through the seat belt and the airbag.
⑤ The driver's energy disappears when the car stops.

Question 43 is based on the following chart.

Blood alcohol level is given as a percent of alcohol in blood.

0.05%	Impaired judgment
0.1%	Difficulty walking and driving
0.2%	Abnormal emotional behavior
0.3%	Impaired vision and hearing
0.45%	Unconsciousness
0.65%	Death

43 Which of the following statements is supported by information given on the table?

① The legal blood alcohol level defining drunk driving is usually set too low.
② Drinking alcohol can affect both normal body functions and behavior.
③ Over time, alcohol use can damage cells in the liver.
④ Drunken drivers are a menace on public highways.
⑤ Alcohol consumption has less effect on a heavy person than it does on a thin person.

Questions 44 and 45 refer to the following passage and illustration.

Shown below are two types of elephants: the African savannah elephant and the Asian elephant (also known as the Indian elephant). The easiest way to distinguish between the two types is the size of the ears. Ears on elephants are full of blood vessels that help in cooling when the ears are flapped.

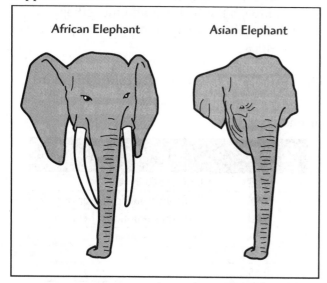

African Elephant   Asian Elephant

44 What can you infer to be true about the habitats of the elephants shown?

① The Asian elephant lives in a much wetter habitat than the African savannah elephant.
② The African savannah elephant lives in a much wetter habitat than the Asian elephant.
③ The Asian elephant lives in a much warmer habitat than the African savannah elephant.
④ The habitats of both African savannah and Asian elephants are about the same average temperature.
⑤ The African savannah elephant lives in a much warmer habitat than the Asian elephant.

45 What is one type of adaptive behavior shown by both species of elephants?

① growth of a long trunk
② growing to great weight
③ periodic flapping of ears
④ ability to run quickly
⑤ presence of a good memory

Question 46 is based on the following passage.

Many scientists believe that each species of organism may be on Earth for only a limited time. A species can become extinct because of natural disasters or because of human activity. Dinosaurs most likely became extinct because of an ice age 70 million years ago. Passenger pigeons were hunted to extinction in the 1800s by human hunters. During this same century, buffalo herds were slaughtered almost to the point of extinction. Today, pandas, many species of whales, and many species of plants are in danger of becoming extinct as tropical forests are cut down. Scientists now wonder if human beings may also soon become in danger of extinction, considering the poor quality of care humans give to the environment.

46 What does the writer imply in this passage?

① Human activity can help cause or can help prevent extinction of human beings.
② Human beings do not have the ability to control natural disasters.
③ Dinosaurs were the first animals to ever become extinct.
④ Extinction means that an animal or plant species disappears for a few years.
⑤ Scientific discoveries such as cloning may help prevent the extinction of human beings in the future.

Questions 47, 48, 49, and 50 are based on the following passage and drawing.

A wildlife biologist placed a number of young trout in Fern Lake, a lake that previously had no trout. The graph below shows the growth of the trout population over many years. Also shown is the estimated trout population that might have grown in the absence of population-limiting factors—things that kill trout before they reach the end of their natural life span.

TROUT POPULATION IN A LAKE

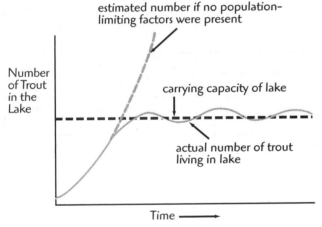

47 Which of the following would *least* likely be classified as a population-limiting factor?

① water pollution in the lake
② bacteria in the lake that cause diseases in fish
③ a lack of adequate food resources for trout in the lake
④ the presence of many insect species along the shore of the lake
⑤ the presence of other species in the lake that feed on trout eggs

48 Which of the following natural resources most directly affects the long-term health of fish in Fern Lake?

① the forest on the south side of Fern Lake that was recently opened up to logging
② Fern Mountain, a granite mountain nearby from whose peak visitors often take photographs of Fern Lake
③ the Long Tom River, a river that flows into the north end of Fern Lake
④ Green Lake, a popular boating lake about two miles from Fern Lake
⑤ Emerald Falls, a 120-foot high waterfall that is on the Emerald River, a river flowing out of Fern Lake

49 After the trout capacity is reached, what will be true about Fern Lake?

① Fern Lake will be an ecosystem where an average number of trout can coexist with other organisms for only a short time.
② Fern Lake will be an ecosystem where the average number of trout will slowly increase over time.
③ Fern Lake will be an ecosystem where the average number of trout will slowly decrease over time.
④ Fern Lake will not be an ecosystem because the actual number of trout varies over time.
⑤ Fern Lake will be an ecosystem where a stable average number of trout can coexist with stable average numbers of other organisms.

50 Which of the following human activities is most likely to decrease the trout capacity of Fern Lake?

① picnicking activities on the shore
② waterskiing on the lake
③ canoeing on the lake
④ building cabins along the shore
⑤ fishing from the shore

137

Posttest Evaluation Chart

After you complete the GED Posttest, check your answers with the Answer Key on page 178. Then use this chart to figure out which skills you need to review. In column 1, circle the numbers of the questions you missed. The second and third columns tell you the name of the skill and its number in the instruction section of the book. The fourth column tells you the pages to review. From the fifth column, use the pages from Contemporary's *GED Science* for further study if necessary.

Question Number	Skill Name	Skill	Pages	GED Science
3	Summarize the Main Idea	1	22–23	49–56
46	Identify Implications or Inferences	2	24–25	57–58
39	Apply Scientific Concepts	3	26–27	59–64
16	Distinguish Facts from Hypotheses or Opinions	4	28–29	67–72
40	Identify Cause and Effect	5	30–31	73–76
20	Recognize Unstated Assumptions	6	32–33	71–72
15	Draw a Conclusion from Supporting Evidence	7	34–35	77–80
2	Evaluate Scientific Evidence	8	36–37	81–85
22	Understand the Influence of Personal Values	9	38–39	86–87, 105–108
9	Understand Inductive and Deductive Reasoning	10	40–41	88–92
6	Cellular Basis of Life	11	42–43	162–169
1	Inheritable Traits in Organisms	12	44–45	171–174
37	Classification of Species	13	46–47	175–181
10	Related Scientific Characteristics	14	48–49	182–199
44	Adaptive Structure of Organisms	15	50–51	209–216
45	Adaptive Behavior of Organisms	16	52–53	200–205
47	Issues Concerning Population Growth	17	54–55	124–127
48	Care of Natural Resources	18	56–57	120–123
49	Organisms Living Together	19	58–59	206–208
50	Care of the Environment	20	60–61	129–134
43	Personal Health	21	62–63	115–119
19	Community Health	22	64–65	115–119
8	Natural Disasters	23	66–67	129–134
32	Human-Created Disasters	24	68–69	129–134
24	Human Aspects of Science	25	70–71	139–143
23	Traces of Ancient Life	26	72–73	213–216

Question Number	Skill Name	Skill	Pages	GED Science
18	Advances in Medicine	27	74–75	229–235
25	Historical Perspectives in Life Science	28	76–77	144–155
30	Phases of Matter	29	78–79	276–278
26	Chemistry of Life	30	80–81	272–275
27	Physical and Chemical Changes	31	82–83	279–282
28	Energy Flow in Chemical Reactions	32	84–85	283–286
31	Mixture of Elements	33	86–87	281–282
11	Chemistry and the Origin of Life	34	88–89	272–275
34	Chemistry and Human Health	35	90–91	229–235
35	Historical Perspectives in Chemistry	36	92–93	144–155
41	Motion and Forces	37	94–95	292–301
36	Interaction of Energy with Matter	38	96–97	289–291, 305–332
42	Conservation of Energy	39	98–99	302–306
5	Change and Constancy in Nature	40	100–101	37–38
33	Differences Between Technology and Science	41	102–103	95–114
4	Historical Perspectives in Physics	42	104–105	144–155
12	Origin of Earth	43	106–107	342–344
13	The Evolving Earth	44	108–109	345–366
14	Geochemical Cycles and Earth's Energy	45	110–111	347–352
21	The Greenhouse Effect and Global Warming	46	112–113	134–136
29	Historical Perspectives in Earth Science	47	114–115	144–145
38	Celestial Objects in the Universe	48	116–117	370–378
17	The Evolving Universe	49	118–119	379–382
7	Historical Perspectives in Space Science	50	120–121	144–155

Structure of Matter

For most of recorded history, people have wondered about the structure of matter. Even you may have asked the following question or one like it:

> Suppose a piece of gold is divided into smaller and smaller pieces. What does the smallest possible piece of gold look like?

Experiments performed in the nineteenth and twentieth centuries answered this question. Scientists discovered that all matter, including the matter that makes up all living organisms, is made from one or more of about one hundred different **elements**. Each element is a single type of substance.

Some substances, such as gold, are single elements. Other substances, such as water, are made of more than one element. Water is made of two elements: hydrogen and oxygen. As you may know, hydrogen and oxygen occur in nature as gases. When combined, though, hydrogen and oxygen form water, the most common liquid on Earth. Scientists have discovered a great deal about elements such as gold, hydrogen, and oxygen.

The smallest piece of an element that has properties of that element is an **atom**. An atom is very, very small. It would take billions of atoms placed side by side to equal the thickness of this page! The smallest possible piece of gold is a single gold atom.

Two or more different atoms can combine and form a new substance. When atoms do combine, the group of atoms is called a **molecule**. Most things in your daily experience are made of many, many molecules. The smallest piece of water is a single water molecule. A water molecule contains one atom of oxygen and two atoms of hydrogen. If a water molecule is broken down into the elements that make it up, the water molecule would disappear. In its place would be separated hydrogen and oxygen atoms.

Living organisms are made up of the same elements that make up Earth itself. It is an interesting discovery that every living organism is made up mainly of three elements: hydrogen, oxygen, and carbon.

Particles in an Atom

Every atom, whether an atom of gold, oxygen, or hydrogen, is made up of three types of particles—**protons**, **neutrons**, and **electrons**. The protons and neutrons are located in a central **nucleus**, the core of the atom. The electrons are outside and orbit the nucleus. The only way one element differs from another is in the number of protons, neutrons, and electrons.

- **Protons** are particles that have a positive electrical charge.
- **Neutrons** do not have a charge. They are electrically neutral.
- **Electrons** are particles that have a negative electrical charge.

proton   neutron   electron

Electric force holds electrons in orbit around a nucleus. The negatively charged electrons are attracted to the positively charged protons. Unless disturbed by an outside force, each orbiting electron is in a stable orbit. Electrons in an atom are in different orbits, each orbit representing a different energy level. The most energetic electrons are those in orbits farthest from the nucleus. The arrangement of electrons in each atom gives rise to the bonding property of elements—the way different elements combine to form molecules.

Nuclear particles (neutrons and protons) are held together in the nucleus by **nuclear force**. Nuclear force is much, much stronger than electric force. However, nuclear force acts only over very short nuclear distances. The weaker electric force acts over much longer atomic distances. Protons and neutrons are also exactly the same size. Each is more than 1,800 times as massive as an electron. Because of the size difference, almost all of the **mass** (amount of matter) of an atom is contained in the nucleus.

In their normal state, all atoms are electrically neutral—having neither a net negative nor positive charge. The number of electrons equals the number of protons. Although the exact orbital paths of electrons in an atom are not known, an atom is often illustrated as shown in the diagram of the neutral helium atom below.

THE HELIUM ATOM

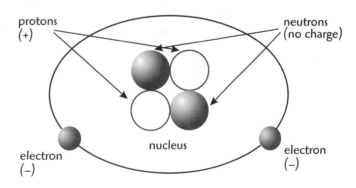

1. Oxygen and gold are examples of _____.

2. Water is an example of a _____.

3. Water is made of _____ and _____.

4. The three main elements in every living organism are _____,

   _____, and _____.

5. Three particles in an atom are _____,

   _____, and _____.

6. Electrons are held in orbit by _____.

Energy in an Atom

There are two sources of energy in an atom: the energy of orbiting electrons and the energy of nuclear particles.

- The energy we obtain from eating food comes from electrons changing energy levels as food molecules are broken down.
- The energy we obtain from nuclear power plants comes from the breaking down of heavy nuclei into lighter nuclei, giving up nuclear energy from the original nuclei.

More About Molecules

A molecule is made up of two or more atoms. When two or more atoms of different elements combine, a completely new substance is formed.

- A molecule of water is made up of one atom of oxygen (a gas) and two atoms of hydrogen (a gas).

THE WATER MOLECULE

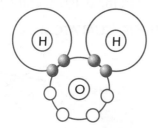

● = electrons shared by hydrogen and oxygen atoms

When combining to form a molecule, atoms often share electrons which then orbit both nuclei.

- A molecule of salt is made up of one atom of sodium (a solid) and one atom of chlorine (a gas).

THE SODIUM CHLORIDE MOLECULE

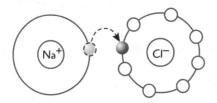

When sodium (Na) and chlorine (Cl) combine, one electron from sodium transfers to the chlorine atom.

- A molecule of propane (a gas) is made up of eight atoms of hydrogen (H), a gas, and three atoms of carbon (C), a solid.

PROPANE

The carbon atoms line up and are surrounded by the hydrogen atoms. (The electron orbits are not shown in this drawing.)

Chemical Formulas

A **chemical formula** is a shorthand way to show which elements are contained in a molecule. Symbols identify the elements, and small numbers (subscripts) tell the number of each type of atom.

- H_2O is the chemical formula for water. The subscript 2 indicates that there are two atoms of hydrogen (H) in one molecule of water. The symbol O, written without a subscript, indicates that one atom of oxygen (O) is in each molecule of water.
- C_3H_8 is the formula for propane gas. Each molecule of propane contains three atoms of carbon (C) and eight atoms of hydrogen (H).

Numbers before a formula tell that more than one molecule is present.

- $6H_2O$ represents 6 molecules of water. Each molecule contains 2 atoms of hydrogen and 1 atom of oxygen.
- $3Fe_2O_3$ represents 3 molecules of rust (iron oxide). Each molecule contains 2 atoms of iron (Fe) and 3 atoms of oxygen (O).

Chemical Reaction Equation

A chemical reaction equation represents how atoms combine to form molecules.

The equation for the formation of water is written as follows:

$$2H_2 + O_2 \longrightarrow 2H_2O$$

The substances on the left of the arrow combine to form the substance on the right side of the arrow.

- On the left, the equation says that 2 molecules of hydrogen (H_2) combine with 1 molecule of oxygen (O_2). Notice that each molecule of hydrogen (H_2) contains 2 atoms of hydrogen (H) and each molecule of oxygen (O_2) contains 2 atoms of oxygen (O).
- On the right, the substance that is formed is shown to be 2 molecules of H_2O. This is 2 molecules of water.

7 In 1 molecule of ammonia NH_3, how many atoms are there of

N (nitrogen)? _____ H (hydrogen)? _____

8 In $4C_3H_8$, how many molecules of C_3H_8 (propane gas) are there?

_____

9 In the chemical reaction equation $N_2 + 3H_2 \longrightarrow 2NH_3$, there is

_____ molecule of N_2 (nitrogen gas), and

_____ molecules of NH_3 (ammonia) are formed.

Cell Theory of Life

The invention of the microscope in the seventeenth century was a great help in the study of living organisms. For the first time, biologists could see beyond the limits of the human eye. Robert Hooke, a British scientist, looked at slices of cork with the new instrument. He was amazed at the tiny box-like cavities out of which the cork was made. Because these cavities reminded him of cells (rooms) in a monastery, he gave the name *cells* to these tiny units of cork.

Today, biologists know that **cells** are the basic building blocks of living organisms, both plants and animals. A cell is the smallest living unit that carries on the activities of an organism.

The **cell theory of life** is stated in three parts:

- The cell is the basic unit of life.
- All organisms are made of one or more cells.
- All cells come from existing cells.

Shown below are examples of plant and animal cells. Plant and animal cells have several common characteristics.

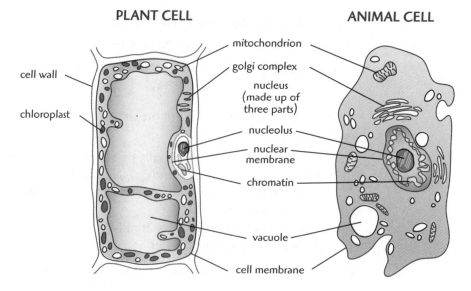

PLANT CELL   **ANIMAL CELL**

cell wall
chloroplast

mitochondrion
golgi complex
nucleus (made up of three parts)
nucleolus
nuclear membrane
chromatin
vacuole
cell membrane

Cell Membrane

Every cell has a **cell membrane**—a soft and flexible covering. The membrane holds the cell together and separates the cell from other cells. The cell membrane is permeable, allowing substances to enter and leave the cell. Food molecules, needed to provide energy and nutrients, enter the cell through the cell membrane. Waste products leave the cell through the cell membrane.

Nucleus

Plant and animal cells contain a single large oval (or round) body called a **nucleus**. The nucleus controls the activities of the cell. Also, the nucleus stores hereditary information in genetic material called **chromatin**. A small round body within the nucleus, called the **nucleolus**, is responsible for making protein that is used in new cell growth.

Cytoplasm

Outside the nucleus is the **cytoplasm**—a jellylike fluid of water, salt, minerals, and many types of organic (carbon-based) molecules that are essential to all life processes.

Organelles

Within the cytoplasm are **organelles**—specialized structures that carry on the work of the cell. Each organelle performs a special life activity of the cell. The nucleus is the most prominent organelle in most cells.

Special Structures of Plant Cells

A plant cell has two special structures not found in an animal cell.

- A **cell wall** surrounds the cell membrane of most plant cells. This wall both supports and protects the cell. In many plants the cell wall is tough but flexible. Cell walls make vegetables crunchy to bite and chew. In plants such as trees, cell walls are thick and rigid, providing the tree with great strength.
- **Chloroplasts** are organelles that contain **chlorophyll**—the green substance that is used to capture light energy. The plant uses light energy from the Sun to produce glucose—a simple sugar that the plant uses as its food.

❶ What are the three parts of the cell theory of life?

_____

_____

_____

❷ Complete each sentence by filling in each blank with the correct word.

① _____ is the organelle that controls the activities of a cell.

② The structure in the cells of a carrot that gives the carrot a crunchy texture

is called _____.

③ The soft flexible cover of a cell is called the _____.

④ The genetic material in a cell is called _____.

⑤ The substance _____ gives plants a green color.

Living Things

What Is a Living Thing?

Life science is the study of **organisms,** or living things. Living things, even **single-cell organisms,** are remarkably different things than substances formed from non-living chemicals, no matter how complicated. The simplest organisms consist of a single cell. **Complex organisms,** such as human beings, consist of hundreds of billions of cells working together to form a single individual. Understanding the remarkable workings of living things has been, and will continue to be, one of the greatest challenges facing scientists.

Living Things Have a Life Cycle of Five Stages

Living things, unlike non-living things, are characterized by a life cycle. This life cycle is generally divided into five separate stages.

- During the beginning stage, an organism takes shape. For complex organisms, the beginning stage is a single cell that begins dividing soon after being created, or soon after male and female sex cells combine.
- Growth is the period when an organism grows to its mature, or adult, size and develops the ability to reproduce, or create, another living thing. For some animals, such as a butterfly, growth is a time during which the animal may take on several distinct forms.
- During maturity, an organism uses energy mainly for the maintenance of life and for the raising of offspring.
- During decline, an organism is not able to keep itself in top shape. The organism generally is becoming less active.
- At death, an organism stops living. Following death, an organism goes through a natural decay process.

Living Things Are Composed of Cells

All living things are made up of cells. Cells carry out important life activities throughout each stage of an organism's life. Some tiny organisms, such as bacteria, consist of only one cell; other organisms, such as ourselves, consist of hundreds of billions of cells.

Living Things Are Active and Depend on a Source of Energy

Living things carry on many activities and need energy as they go through their life cycles. In your own life, hunger is your body's way of telling you that it needs energy. You satisfy this need by eating. Your body digests the food and releases energy and nutrients stored in the food. The nutrients are used to repair and build new cells, and the energy is used to keep all cellular activities going.

Living Things Reproduce

Living things reproduce—that is, they create another living organism that is very similar to themselves. **Reproduction** makes it possible for each type of organism to continue to exist by producing future generations of its own kind.

Living Things Respond to Stimuli

Living things respond to stimuli—anything in their environment that influences or causes a change in behavior. A **stimulus** may be something seen, heard, felt, smelled, or tasted. A living thing tends to respond to a stimulus in a way that helps the organism survive. For example, when a deer hears a mountain lion growl, the deer runs away. The big cat's growl is the stimulus. The deer's reaction—running away—is the **response**.

The Principle of Biogenesis

Even though the study of biology has been going on for hundreds of years, the important principle of **biogenesis** is only about 150 years old. According to this principle, life comes only from life. Each organism comes from the reproduction of other organisms. This principle may not surprise you, but before the mid-1800s, many people believed that insects and worms came from rotting soil. People also believed that frogs formed in clouds and fell to Earth during rainstorms.

Adaptation

Living things have adapted to conditions in their environment. A seagull, for example, is well suited for life along the coast. A seagull has long, angled wings that help it glide in coastal air currents as it hunts for food. These wings are well oiled in order to deflect ocean water as the gull picks its prey from the surf. The gull's webbed feet enable it to walk on sand and paddle on the water's surface.

❶ What five stages make up the life cycle of living things? _____,

_____, _____, _____, and

_____.

❷ Explain the principle of biogenesis. _____

_____

❸ In what ways is a polar bear adapted to its environment?

_____

_____

❹ Briefly describe how human beings differ from other complex organisms.

_____

_____

Cell Specialization in Living Things

A complex organism is a **multicellular organism**, one which consists of many, many cells. Multicellular organisms such as roses, trees, frogs, giraffes, and human beings all start life as a single cell. This single cell divides into two cells, and then each of these cells divides into two more cells, and so on and so on. This growth process continues and a recognizable individual soon develops.

From the first cell to the recognizable organism, a remarkable thing happens. Newly forming cells develop in ways different from the parent cells. Cells specialize in shape, structure, and function. This differentiation is called **cell specialization.** Cell specialization makes possible the complex life forms we see in the world today.

Tissue

As cells divide, groups of cells retain similar characteristics and functions. A group of similar cells working together is called **tissue.** Groups of similar cells in human beings form muscle tissue, nerve tissue, bone tissue, skin tissue, and so on.

Organs

A complex organism shows a high degree of organization not found in more simple organisms. Not only do cells work together to form tissue, but groups of different tissues may work together to form an **organ.** A human brain is an organ that is made of nerve tissue, fat tissue, and vascular (blood-carrying) tissue. Other examples of human organs are eyes, heart, stomach, and lungs.

Organ Systems

Several organs may work together to form an **organ system.** The digestive system is an organ system that provides a human being with a way of getting food energy from food sources. The digestive system includes the mouth, stomach, small intestine, large intestine, and other organs that aid in digestion. Other organ systems common to most animals are the respiratory system (used for breathing), the circulatory system (used for moving blood), the nervous system (used for transmitting messages to and from the spinal cord and brain), the reproductive system (used for reproduction), and the excretory system (used for the elimination of bodily wastes).

5 Unlike animals, most plants have a specialized structure that prevents them from moving around. Briefly describe this structure and its functions.

_____

6 What name is given to the protective tissue that covers the human body?

_____

7 Name the human organ that is responsible for each of the following:

pumping blood: _____ thinking: _____

breathing: _____

Relationships Among Living Things

A relationship occurs between many organisms in which the survival of one organism is closely linked to the survival of another organism. Here are some very interesting examples:

- *predator-prey relationship*—One organism kills and eats a second organism. An example is a lion that kills and eats a gazelle.
- *saprophytic relationship*—An organism takes nutrients from the remains of dead organisms. For example, a vulture eats a dead mouse.
- *parasitic relationship*—One organism takes nutrients from the living body of another organism and, in doing so, may harm but not kill the other organism. For example, fleas live on and take nutrients from the blood of a dog.
- *mutualistic relationship*—Organisms live together in a way that nutritionally benefits all the organisms. An example is a lichen, formed by a mutual relationship between a certain type of algae and fungus. Together, they can live and feed where neither could survive alone.
- *commensual relationship*—One organism nutritionally benefits from a second organism, while the second organism neither benefits nor is harmed. For example, barnacles attach themselves to the body of a whale and feed while moving through nutrient-rich water. The whale is not harmed by the barnacles.

Ecosystems

The most complex relationship among a variety of plants and animals occurs in an **ecosystem**. An ecosystem is a community of living things where the welfare of each population of like organisms is dependent upon the welfare of each other population of organisms.

An ecosystem is established to help each population of organisms stay alive, not to protect any individual member of each population. The emphasis is on the survival of the whole population of organisms, not on the survival of individuals.

8 As uninvited guests, small beetles often live in the nest of an ant colony, helping themselves to food. The portion of the food is usually not missed by the ants. How would you classify this relationship?

_____

9 Many tiny lice live on the body of a bird by slowly eating its feathers. The lice damage the feathers but do not kill the bird. What is this relationship?

_____

Molecular Basis of Heredity

After the publication of Darwin's theory of evolution, scientists became very interested in understanding biological inheritance. For example, how are physical and psychological traits passed from parents to offspring? Why, for example, do children so often look like their parents? Another interesting question is the following: When an organism grows from a single cell, how do the new cells know what special role to play? Why, for example, do some cells become muscle cells and other cells become bone cells or nerve cells?

Scientists realized each new cell must contain instructions that tell the cell what to do. Somewhere in that first cell of a developing organism is all the information that tells all newly-forming cells what type of cells to become. As an example, the single-cell first stage of a human being looks very much like the single-cell first stage of a fish. Each of these single cells must contain the instructions that lead one cell to grow into a human being and the other cell to grow into a fish.

Molecular Basis of Heredity

During the last two centuries, scientists began uncovering nature's secrets. They first discovered the laws of **heredity**—the passing on of traits from parents to offspring. Scientists concluded there was something that they named **genes** that played an important role in passing on traits from parents to offspring. It wasn't until the 1950s, though, that scientists discovered what genes actually are.

During the 1950s, scientists discovered that each organism does indeed have a set of coded instructions within each cell. This complete set of instructions is found in the nucleus of a cell, including the first cell the organism develops from. Genes are part of these coded instructions.

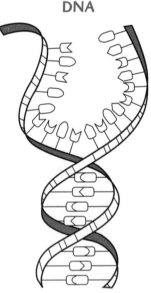

DNA

The nucleus of a cell contains a chemical substance called **DNA** (deoxyribonucleic acid). DNA controls everything the cell does, including reproducing to form more cells. Each strand of DNA is a large, complex molecule formed by chains of chemical compounds. DNA molecules form chromosomes that are each composed of a series of genes. The information for specific functions or traits are carried in these genes. Genes can be thought of as chemical carriers of information. The laws of heredity depend on the actions of molecular structures found within the nucleus of a cell.

One type of organism differs from another organism because of variations in DNA. Human DNA is different from frog DNA and monkey DNA. However, human DNA is more closely related to monkey DNA than to frog DNA.

DNA is a molecule organized in a double helix shape. When a cell divides, its DNA splits into two parts.

The theory of the molecular basis of heredity explains how both physical characteristics and behavior patterns are inherited. Information relating to both physical and behavioral characteristics is present in the genes found in DNA. Knowledge of DNA is also giving scientists a better understanding of how cells work. This understanding is showing great promise in the fight against inherited diseases such as sickle-cell anemia.

Reproduction and Genetics

As a result of mating, chromosomes from a male sex cell join with chromosomes from a female sex cell. Together, they form the chromosomes of the fertilized egg—the one-cell first stage of the offspring. This first cell begins to divide and duplicate itself.

The process of cell division is called **mitosis**. During the first step of mitosis, a cell makes a duplicate copy of the DNA in its nucleus. The **parent cell** splits into two new cells, called **daughter cells**. Each daughter cell contains a complete set of the parent cell's DNA and the chromosomes and genes that are part of the DNA. In this way, each daughter cell has the same set of genes as the original parent cell.

FIVE STEPS OF MITOSIS

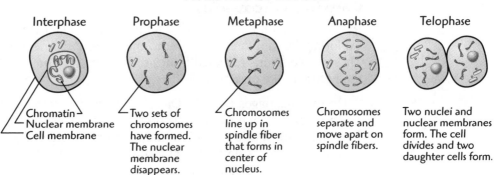

Interphase
- Chromatin
- Nuclear membrane
- Cell membrane

Prophase
Two sets of chromosomes have formed. The nuclear membrane disappears.

Metaphase
Chromosomes line up in spindle fiber that forms in center of nucleus.

Anaphase
Chromosomes separate and move apart on spindle fibers.

Telophase
Two nuclei and nuclear membranes form. The cell divides and two daughter cells form.

This is how an offspring receives chromosomes from each parent. Thus, an offspring has genes representing characteristics of both parents. Frequently, an offspring will receive genes with opposing characteristics (for example, a gene for brown eyes and a gene for blue eyes). In this case, one gene will keep the other characteristic from showing. The **dominant gene** for brown eyes will cause the offspring to have brown eyes. The **recessive gene** for blue eyes will still be present in the offspring's genes, but that characteristic will be hidden. The same genetic process occurs in plants as well as in animals.

- Examples of inheritable characteristics in humans are eye color, hair color, earlobe shape, and overall body structure.
- Examples of inheritable characteristics in roses are flower color, leaf shape, and plant height.

❶ Give a brief definition of DNA. _____

_____

❷ Name three of your own traits that are likely inherited.

_____

_____

Biological Evolution

To explain the wide varieties of organisms on Earth, scientists have proposed a theory of **biological evolution**. According to this theory, organisms evolve (change) over time. Each organism changes in a way that makes it better suited to live in its environment. The changes are known as **adaptations**.

The net result of biological evolution is that organisms today are suited for today's environment. A species alive today may look much different than the way it looked one million years ago. Scientists estimate that the variety of organisms today is the result of more than 3.5 billion years of evolutionary change. Speculations about biological evolution have been made since the early nineteenth century, but the modern theory of biological evolution began with the work of Charles Darwin.

Darwin's Discoveries

In 1832, a 24-year-old naturalist named Charles Darwin began a three-year study exploring the rain forests of South America and the nearby Galapagos Islands. These explorations revealed things to Darwin that forever changed his ideas about the nature of life on Earth.

On the Galapagos Islands, Darwin saw creatures that existed nowhere else on Earth. Darwin saw how animals on the islands were both similar to and different from the same species found on the nearby continent. Darwin concluded that each island species had originally come from the continent, perhaps thousands of years ago. At that distant time, each island species must have been exactly like its mainland relatives.

Darwin believed that, once on the islands, each species became isolated from the mainland. Then, because the island environment was much harsher than the mainland environment, the island species changed in both appearance and behavior from their South American relatives. These evolutionary changes (adaptations) took place over many generations, perhaps during thousands of years or longer. Darwin used the word *evolution* to refer to the process of gradual change undergone by the island species.

Darwin theorized that evolution occurs in all organisms. Over many generations, adaptations slowly occur. These adaptations may involve both structure and behavior. Darwin believed that evolution is a process that links millions of different species of plants, animals, and microorganisms on Earth today with those that lived in the past.

Darwin's Theory of Evolution

Darwin's theory can be summarized as follows:

There are differences (variations) among the members of every species. Many of these variations, called **favorable traits**, aid in the struggle for survival. For example, a hawk with long claws kills prey more easily than a hawk with short claws.

An **ecosystem** can support only a certain number of organisms of any one species. Competition for food and water, predators, and disease limit the population of each species. Only a certain number of hawks can live at one time in an ecosystem.

Members of a species with favorable traits are most likely to survive and pass on those traits to offspring. During a time of limited prey, hawks with long claws are more likely to survive than hawks with short claws. Eventually, hawks with short claws will become extinct.

Natural Selection

The principle that individuals with favorable traits are the most likely members of a species to survive, reproduce, and pass on those traits is known as **natural selection**. According to the principle of natural selection, only favorable traits are likely to be passed on to future generations. Darwin realized that natural selection, operating over thousands of years or more, could lead to the type of world he saw: a world in which organisms were superbly adapted to their environments.

Mutations

We now know something that Darwin did not. Evolution occurs because of **mutations**—unexpected changes in the coded instructions within the nucleus of a reproducing cell. These coded instructions are contained within an organism's DNA—genetic material within a cell's nucleus. Mutations occurring during cell division can cause cells to have new properties. Mutations can be caused by chemicals, X-rays, or nuclear radiation. Some genetic changes harm an organism, some have little impact, and some are beneficial. The result of a mutation is that an offspring can differ from its parents. A beneficial mutation, such as longer claws on a hawk, may be passed on to offspring.

Punctuated Equilibrium

Scientists today believe that evolution also occurs from catastrophic events such as an ice age. During an ice age, whole species of plants and animals become extinct, and other species then adapt to the new environment. This rapid change in the type of organisms on Earth is known as **punctuated equilibrium**. This may be what happened when dinosaurs became extinct 70 million years ago and the age of mammals began.

❶ Darwin's theory of evolution is referred to as "survival of the fittest." Do you think that this is a correct way to describe Darwin's ideas? Give a reason for your answer.

_____

_____

_____

Structure of Earth

During the fifteenth century, many people believed that Earth was flat, and that if you sailed off in a straight line you would sail forever. Other people believed you would come to an edge and simply drop off. Today we have a much better understanding of Earth.

- The shape of Earth is roughly spherical, shaped much like a basketball. Earth is known to be a little wider west-to-east than it is north-to-south.
- Earth's surface is about 71% water, divided into five large oceans.
- Earth's land portion, about 29%, is divided into seven continents and thousands of islands of various sizes.
- The oceans and land masses are the visible part of the crust, the outer skin of Earth. The crust varies in size, being about six miles thick below the oceans and as much as forty miles thick below high mountain ranges on the continents.
- The mantle, the supporting structure beneath the crust, is about 1,800 miles thick and is made up mainly of heavy rock and pockets of molten rock.
- The core is the central part of Earth and is divided into two parts: a solid inner core made of iron, and a liquid outer core that is composed mainly of melted iron. The inner core is shaped like a sphere with a radius of about 800 miles. The outer core is about 1,400 miles thick.

THE STRUCTURE OF EARTH

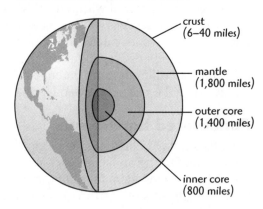

crust
(6–40 miles)

mantle
(1,800 miles)

outer core
(1,400 miles)

inner core
(800 miles)

❶ _____ percent of Earth's surface is covered by land, and

_____ percent is water.

❷ Earth's inner core is made of _____; the outer core

is _____.

❸ The radius of Earth (inner core + outer core + mantle) is about

_____ miles.

Plate Tectonics

In recent years scientists have discovered evidence suggesting that the continents on Earth sat side by side about 200 million years ago. According to the theory called **plate tectonics**, Earth's crust is made up of about twelve large plates and several small plates that slowly move around on the surface of the mantle. Although each crustal plate moves only about two inches each year, 200 million years is ample time for continents to have moved from their original locations to where we find them today. The movement of the plates is most likely caused by currents of molten rock within the mantle.

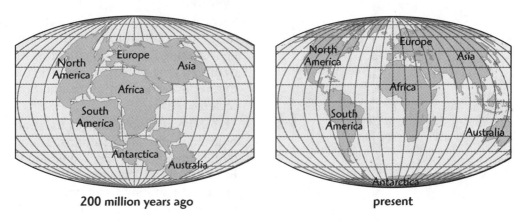

200 million years ago   present

The theory of plate tectonics does more than describe the movement of continents—often called **continental drift**. Plate tectonics also helps explain earthquakes, volcanic eruptions, mountain building, and the formation of continents and oceans.

- Earthquakes and volcanic eruptions occur between the boundary lines where two plates collide. When slippage occurs between two plates, an enormous amount of energy is released. This energy release may result in earthquakes near the boundary between the plates. California experiences thousands of small quakes each year along the plate boundary known as the San Andreas fault.

- Volcanoes can be caused by the tremendous pressure that develops as the edge of one plate tries to move under the edge of a second plate. Molten rock from a volcano comes from a sea of molten rock in Earth's mantle just below the crust.

- Changes in mountains, continents, and the ocean floor occur when two plates collide. During such collisions, the crust is raised by faulting, folding, or arching up layers of rock. When plates move apart, some parts of the crust sink, creating valleys with rock towering above. Volcanic eruptions themselves also give rise to new mountains. The country of Japan is an example of a string of volcanic mountain islands that formed near the boundary of two plates.

4️⃣ Briefly describe the theory of plate tectonics. _____

_____

Earth's Atmosphere

The **atmosphere** is the blanket of air that surrounds Earth. The atmosphere plays three roles in making life possible on Earth:

LEVEL OF
EARTH'S
ATMOSPHERE

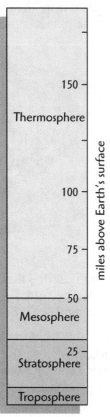

- First, the atmosphere provides the three gases necessary for life: oxygen, nitrogen, and carbon dioxide. All animals, including humans, breathe oxygen. Nitrogen and carbon dioxide are both needed for plant growth. Less important atmospheric gases include argon, neon, helium, and hydrogen.

- Second, the atmosphere protects us from most of the Sun's high-energy **ultraviolet light**. About 99% of all ultraviolet light striking Earth is absorbed by an atmospheric gas called **ozone**, a type of oxygen gas. The ozone layer is much thinner over the North Pole and South Pole than over other regions.

- Third, the atmosphere gives us weather—both clear blue skies and violent storms. The atmosphere acts as a huge energy machine, regulating the temperature of Earth's surface. The atmosphere controls both the amount of sunlight striking Earth and the amount of surface heat that escapes back into space. Through these two controlling processes, the atmosphere keeps Earth's surface temperature in a range that sustains life. The temperature at Earth's surface, together with Earth's rotation, gives us the wind and water movements that are responsible for our daily weather.

Scientists usually refer to four main layers of the atmosphere.

- The **troposphere** is the layer closest to the ground. Most of the gas in the atmosphere is in this layer within a height of about 3.5 miles. Almost all of Earth's weather occurs within the troposphere.

- The next layer up is the **stratosphere**. The stratosphere contains the ozone gas that protects us from harmful ultraviolet light.

- Above the stratosphere is the **mesosphere**, a layer of atmosphere in which air temperature drops with increasing altitude.

- The outermost layer of atmosphere is called the **thermosphere**, a region where the temperature rises with altitude. The thermosphere, together with the outer mesosphere, is often referred to as the **ionosphere**, a region that reflects radio waves toward the ground. The ionosphere makes it possible for radio stations to broadcast over hundreds or even thousands of miles.

5 The three gases necessary for life on Earth are _____,

_____, and _____.

Earth in Space

For thousands of years, humans have looked to the night sky in awe, marveling at the sight of an uncountable number of stars, a moon that goes through many phases, shooting stars, and comets. Prior to modern times, people had very little idea of what they were looking at. Just what were these things in the night sky?

Today we know much more than our ancestors even could have guessed. Some of these findings have had a deep impact on human thinking, from personal philosophy to religious teaching. The study of celestial (space) objects has traditionally been called **astronomy** and is one of the oldest sciences.

Astronomers have gained an understanding of planets, stars, and other objects in the universe that is absolutely amazing. With the further development of space vehicles, the international space station, and Earth-orbiting telescopes such as the Hubble Space Telescope, space science will likely play an ever-increasing part in all our lives.

Early Greek scientists believed that the objects in the night sky wandered around Earth in complicated loops. They named these strange objects *planets*, a Greek word meaning "wanderers." The belief that wanderers circled Earth in loops persisted until 1543 when Nicolaus Copernicus (1473–1543) suggested a bold new idea. Copernicus, a Polish astronomer, proposed that Earth and all other planets traveled in orbits around the Sun. This is the theory that space scientists believe today. The acceptance of the idea that the Sun is at the center of the solar system came to be known as the **Copernican theory**. We now call the Sun and the planets that revolve around it the **solar system**.

The Solar System

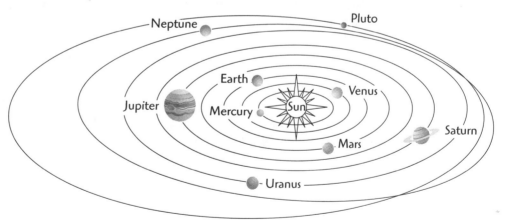

The solar system, as we know it today, consists of a central star we call the Sun, as well as nine major planets and their moons, the asteroids, and the comets that revolve around the Sun.

- The four largest planets are Jupiter, Saturn, Uranus, and Neptune.
- Four of the smallest planets—Mercury, Venus, Earth, and Mars—are those closest to the Sun.

- Pluto, the smallest, outermost planet has an eccentric orbit that sometimes crosses the orbit of Neptune. Very little is known about Pluto.
- In 2005, space scientists believe they may have discovered a tenth planet—a planet that is a little larger than Pluto but that is farther from the Sun than Pluto. Further experiments are planned in order to determine if this object is in fact a planet.

Asteroids

Asteroids are comparatively small objects that orbit the Sun. Most of these asteroids are found between the orbits of Mars and Jupiter. Many others, of all sizes, are in eccentric orbits around the Sun and may occasionally pass very close to Earth. Asteroids vary in size; large asteroids may be 600 miles across, while small asteroids may be as small as a grain of sand. No one knows how asteroids were formed, but one hypothesis is that asteroids are small pieces of planets destroyed long ago by collision with one another.

When small asteroids enter Earth's atmosphere, they burn up, appearing as streaks of light in the night sky. These streaks of light are called **meteors**. Fragments of meteors that reach the surface of Earth are known as **meteorites**. The surface of the Moon shows thousands of impact craters formed by asteroids striking the surface.

Comets

Comets are small objects that are made of dust and frozen gas. Most comets orbit the Sun in a predictable way. A comet can be seen from Earth only as it nears the Sun and part of its dust and frozen gas vaporizes to form a spectacular tail. The solid core of a comet may be small (three to nine miles in diameter), but the escaping gases seen in the tail can make a comet appear as large as the planet Jupiter. Many comets periodically pass close to Earth and are very visible in the night sky. One of the most famous is Halley's comet, which is visible about every 76 years. The first recorded sighting of Halley's comet occurred in 240 B.C. when Chinese astronomers reported seeing a "broom star."

Asteroid 243 IDA

Halley's Comet, 1986

Galaxies

Scientists have discovered that the universe consists of billions of star groupings called **galaxies.** On the average, each galaxy is believed to contain about 100 million stars. Our own Sun is in a large galaxy called the **Milky Way.** The Milky Way is believed to contain about 200 billion stars. The distance across the Milky Way is estimated to be about 100,000 **light-years.** Each light-year is the distance light travels in the time of one year—about 6 trillion miles. The distance between the Milky Way and the nearest similar galaxy is about 2 million light-years.

Facts About The Universe

The exact size of the universe is unknown, but it is incredibly large, taking light billions of years to get from the farthest known points to Earth. Scientists do, however, estimate the age of the universe as being somewhere between 10 and 20 billion years old. Also, scientists have long believed that the structure of the universe, including the Milky Way and our own solar system, results mainly from the force of **gravity.**

- Gravity holds stars together in galaxies.
- Gravity holds each planet in its orbit around the Sun.
- Gravity holds the Moon and artificial satellites in orbit around Earth.
- Gravity holds objects, including ourselves, on the surface of Earth.

In recent years, scientists have discovered that much of the matter of the universe is of a form called **dark matter.** No one knows what dark matter is, but scientists believe that dark matter has much to do with the fact that the universe is expanding—getting larger with each passing year. Investigation into the nature of dark matter is one of the most exciting areas of research in modern astronomy.

❶ Discuss what is meant by the solar system.

_____

_____

❷ Define each word below.

① asteroid _____

② meteor _____

③ meteorite _____

④ galaxy _____

❸ Briefly explain the Copernican theory. _____

_____

159

Answer Key

Pretest, pages 2–19

1 ⑤ Sentence 5 is the best summary: Atoms are so small that, for most experiments, scientists must be content with studying very large numbers of them at the same time.

2 ④ The author's attitude about robots can be best classified as supportive.

3 ③ Because they are like charges, two negatively-charged spheres will repel each other, pushing away from one another.

4 ② During hibernation, a squirrel's brain safely regulates its cells' levels of potassium and calcium.

5 ① A human can suffer a stroke when blood flow to the brain is restricted.

6 ② An unstated assumption is that either water or food-coloring molecules, or both, can pass through the membrane.

7 ③ A reasonable conclusion is that molecules of food coloring cannot easily, if at all, pass through the membrane. Water molecules have passed through but food coloring molecules have not.

8 ④ To determine whether owls and hawks can live side by side, you would need to know whether owls and hawks hunt the same prey.

9 ④ The discoveries made during the Renaissance brought religious values into conflict with science.

10 ③ The product $F_1 \times D_1 = 50 \times 10 = 500$; so, the product $F_2 \times D_2$ must also be equal to 500. $F_2 \times D_2 = 500$; $10 \times D_2 = 500$; $D_2 = 50$.

11 ⑤ A virus invades a cell in order to reproduce—to produce identical copies of itself.

12 ② A child has a one in four chance to inherit an SS gene combination when each parent has an NS gene combination.

13 ⑤ A major difference between a bird and a mammal is the method of birth. A bird lays an egg in which an embryo develops and later hatches. A mammal gives birth to a developed baby.

14 ③ The best example of convergent evolution is the legs of a spider and the legs of a cow. Spiders and cows are not related species: a spider is an insect and a cow is a mammal. All of the other choices have related species.

15 ⑤ The bird that is *least* dependent on keen eyesight is the bird such as a duck that obtains its food by sieving.

16 ③ The statement is a hypothesis because it is an proposed explanation of an experimental discovery.

17 ④ Between 1960 and 2050 the world's population is expected to triple (from 3 billion to 9 billion).

18 ② The main purpose of recycling is to convert waste into reusable products.

19 ① At time t_1, the growing hawk population is increasingly killing more mice.

20 ③ The Gaia hypothesis accounts for natural disasters that occur because of Earth's internal characteristics. Collision with an asteroid is beyond the scope of this hypothesis.

21 ② Excess cholesterol can lead to clogging of arteries, a common condition with a diseased and weakened heart.

22 ② The least helpful way of fighting the spread of AIDS is to tell children about AIDS only after they reach the age of 16.

23 ④ An earthquake on the ocean bottom can trigger a tsunami—a high sea wave with tremendous destructive energy.

24 ① At the time nuclear power plants were first developed, scientists believed that nuclear power plants were safe and that disasters such as a core meltdown could be prevented.

25 ③ Many people find the idea that humans may have evolved from a lower species very offensive—even though this is what scientific evidence strongly suggests.

26 ② The evidence of organisms that lived long ago is called a fossil.

27 ⑤ The modern treatment for cataracts is replacement of the affected lens.

28 ④ With the lens out of the line of vision, a patient would no longer have cloudy vision but also would not have the ability to clearly focus.

29 ③ The density of ice is less than the density of water. This means that ice is lighter than water. To be lighter, the molecules of H_2O must be farther apart in ice than they are in water.

30 ① The hypothesis is an unproven theory. The observed increase in atmospheric carbon dioxide may be directly related to the destruction of tropical rain forests.

31 ④ The process of photosynthesis involves chemical change because new substances are formed (sugar and oxygen).

32 ② The source of energy for respiration is chemical energy from food; the source of energy for photosynthesis is sunlight.

33 ⑤ Raising the temperature decreases the amount of carbon dioxide gas that a liquid can hold.

34 ③ The clue that would best indicate the possible existence of life on another planet would be the presence of carbon in a meteorite. Carbon is the basis of all life as we know it.

35 ① Pregnant women should not be allowed to work around dangerous chemicals.

36 ④ The likely origin of the phrase "mad as a hatter" is nineteenth century felt hatmakers. Because they were exposed to mercury, many suffered brain damage.

37 ⑤ The Moon orbiting Earth is an example of centripetal force, the force being provided by the gravitational attraction between Earth and the Moon.

38 ④ The source of energy that keeps a whirling ball moving in a circle is the person doing the whirling.

39 ② On the graph at the point where $d = 0$, the block's energy is all potential energy; this is true because the block is not yet moving at this point.

40 ④ The sum of the block's potential energy and kinetic energy remains constant as the block slides down the ramp. This is an example of the law of conservation of energy.

41 ⑤ The science needed for understanding how to send astronauts to Mars is already known. The technological goal of building the spacecraft to make the journey has not yet been accomplished. Each of the other listed goals depends on learning new information, not on achieving a technological result.

42 ④ The gravitational force is greatest between the two most massive objects that are closest together.

43 ① The molten liquid interior is not only below continents, it is also below oceans. In fact, the discovery of volcanoes on the ocean floor was a great surprise to many scientists.

44 ③ The continents to the left of the ridge are about the same distance from the ridge as the continents to the right.

45 ② The source of energy that is causing the sea floor to spread is heat energy from Earth's interior.

46 (5) The warming felt while sitting inside a car on a sunny day with the windows closed is very much like a greenhouse.

47 (3) The best visible evidence is the fact that the coastlines of the continents are like the edges of separated pieces of a jigsaw puzzle.

48 (1) The main source of energy in a star in the middle of its life cycle is the fusion of hydrogen to form helium.

49 (4) The change in shape of a constellation over time is proof that stars slowly move relative to one another over time.

50 (2) Pythagoras, even though many of his conclusions were incorrect, did recognize that mathematics is an important tool in the study of science.

Skill 1, pages 22–23

Reading Selection

1 Possible answer: During pollination, an important step in the reproductive cycle of seed plants, pollen from the stamen is transferred to the carpel. Some plants self-pollinate and others cross-pollinate.

2 self-pollinate: pollination from the stamen of a plant to the carpel of the same plant

cross-pollination: pollination from the stamen of one plant to the carpel of another plant

GED Practice

1 (5) The main idea of the passage is "The action of ocean waves can change the shape of an entire shoreline."

2 (4) Wing lift results from high pressure air on the bottom of the wing.

3 (2) Food nourishment takes place in three equally-important steps: digestion, absorption, and assimilation.

4 (3) Seawater consists of 10.6% sodium and 1.27% magnesium.

Skill 2, pages 24–25

Reading Selection

1 The author implies that bioremediation is very good for the environment.

2 Oil is an organic compound because bioremediation is used on organic compounds.

3 An inorganic compound does not contain carbon; an organic compound is carbon-based. Bioremediation works well on organic compounds but not on inorganic compounds.

GED Practice

1 (3) The passage says the population increased after DDT was banned. That implies that DDT caused the falcons' deaths.

2 (1) DDT may cause harm to many species of animals.

3 (1) According to the formula, light energy causes a silver bromide molecule to split.

4 (2) The writer implies that Orin's panels are the best-quality panels that money can buy.

5 (4) The writer wants you to infer that the panels are environmentally friendly.

6 (5) You can infer that exit doors are not locked during times the theater is open.

Skill 3, pages 26–27

Reading Selection

1 (1) nature; (2) nurture; (3) nurture; (4) nature; (5) both; (6) both; (7) nature; (8) both; (9) both; (10) nurture

GED Practice

1 (4) The chemical energy of the candle is changed to light and heat.

2 (5) The purpose of an oven is to provide heat for cooking. Therefore, an efficient oven provides heat but very little light.

❸ ② A wolf and a frog are least likely to compete because they eat different things.

❹ ③ You can measure how much volume the egg has by comparing the volume of water in both jars.

❺ ① The balance compares the weight of the two bricks.

Skill 4, pages 28–29

Reading Selection

❶ Possible answers: Similarity exists among many organisms at the embryonic stage. The DNA of humans is similar to the DNA of many other animals.

❷ Possible answers: Embryonic similarity may indicate common biological ancestry. Similarity in DNA may indicate common biological ancestors.

❸ Possible answer: Human beings do not share a common biological ancestor with other animals.

GED Practice

❶ ⑤ Explaining difference in jaw size as a result of difference in diet is a hypothesis, or tentative explanation. The first three statements can be agreed upon. The fourth statement is an opinion.

❷ ③ This statement is someone's opinion. Not everyone would agree that severe stress improves a person's work performance.

❸ ③ The asteroid idea is a hypothesis, a tentative explanation with insufficient evidence at this time.

❹ ② The date of extinction of dinosaurs is scientific fact based on evidence.

❺ ④ This is an opinion, the personal belief of some scientists.

❻ ③ This explanation for the change in weather patterns is a hypothesis, or tentative explanation, that needs to be proven.

Skill 5, pages 30–31

Reading Selection

❶ Possible answers: surprise, shocking news, seeing a snake, looking over a cliff

❷ As a result of stress or fright, the adrenal glands flood the bloodstream with two hormones: adrenaline and noradrenalin.

❸ Possible answers:
  ① The rate of absorbing oxygen increases.
  ③ You have an increase in muscle energy.
  ⑤ The bleeding of surface wounds is slowed down.

GED Practice

❶ ② Coal burning power plants produce atmosphere pollutants.

❷ ④ Building more fossil fuel power plants would increase global warming.

❸ ⑤ A lack of oil would cause mechanical breakdown of the engine.

❹ ② The drawing shows gas molecules in the air scattering blue light.

❺ ① The only reasonable cause is erosion from the impact of wind-blown sand.

Skill 6, pages 32–33

Reading Selection

❶ Manned flights are more valuable than unmanned flights.

❷ The author's assumption is that life exists, or has existed, on Mars.

GED Practice

❶ ① Cold water will freeze more quickly than warm water.

❷ ③ Some people think scientists will find a safe way to store or dispose of radioactive nuclear waste, so we can continue to build nuclear power plants.

❸ ① Weight loss is directly related to the calorie content of food. By limiting calorie intake, she will lose weight.

❹ ③ Readers will link the coffin with health danger by associating cigarette smoking with death.

❺ ⑤ The caption tells you that car buyers are impressed by a powerful engine.

Skill 7, pages 34–35

Reading Selection

❶ Possible answer: Human males take part in the life of the family and the raising of offspring.

❷ Possible answer: Human females usually have their own offspring and work to raise their own families.

GED Practice

❶ ④ A sealed jar contains a limited amount of oxygen.

❷ ① In a larger jar, the candle would burn for more than 24 seconds because it would have more oxygen.

❸ ⑤ Food particles left in the mouth can lead to tooth decay. Brushing will remove those food particles.

❹ ④ Rope C holds all the weight while rope A holds only half the weight. Therefore, rope C holds twice as much weight as rope A.

❺ ② Sunlight contains many colors. The raindrop separates the light into colors.

❻ ③ The arrow points to the southeast.

Skill 8, pages 36–37

Reading Selection

❶ You would need to know the time of the last high or low tide.

❷ You would need to know which type of tide preceded the tide expected at noon.

GED Practice

❶ ⑤ Many pollutants in food increase risks of cancer and other diseases. Fruits and vegetables have a lower level of pollutants.

❷ ② You see a lightning flash before you hear the thunder, so light travels faster than sound.

❸ ③ The driver's blood-alcohol level is above the legal limit. The other facts would not prove that he is drunk now.

❹ ④ You would need to know the risks and benefits of each of the three types of fat to determine which is most nutritious.

❺ ③ You would need to know the weight of each child. If their weights are equal, the teeter-totter would balance.

Skill 9, pages 38–39

Reading Selection

❶ Kimi's conflicts are between her religious values and her personal family values.

❷ Kimi should talk to her parents, family planning counselor, and/or the religious leader of her choice.

❸ Sean's conflict is between his work values and his moral values.

GED Practice

❶ ④ A person's health values will conflict with his or her use of commercially prepared foods.

❷ ⑤ Ellen would not want to use furnace oil energy because she wants to conserve natural resources.

❸ ② Genetic similarity between humans and chimpanzees causes conflicts with religious values of many people.

❹ ③ The author of the cartoon feels that cell phones can be annoying.

❺ ① The cartoonist believes that cell phone users do not show courtesy toward others.

❻ ③ This cartoon shows a person valuing the quality of the environment by recycling.

Skill 10, pages 40–41

Reading Selection

❶ Possible answer: Camouflage is a common adaptation of organisms found in the wild.

❷ A fish would be invisible to prey from below and invisible to predators from above.

❸ Because it is white colored, a polar bear is more easily able to sneak up on prey.

GED Practice

❶ ④ Homeostasis means maintaining constant internal conditions.

❷ ③ Heart rate increase during exercise would keep body organs and tissues supplied with the energy and oxygen needed for the exercise. The other examples do not maintain constant conditions.

❸ ⑤ Throwing a football is the only activity that would classify as work: force is applied and the object moves.

❹ ② Larger animals have a longer life expectancy than smaller animals.

❺ ④ The toad is an exception to the rule of larger animal–longer life.

❻ ① The squirrel is between the size of a mouse (5 yr) and a cat (13 yr), so you could estimate squirrel life at about 8 years.

Skill 11, pages 42–43

Reading Selection

❶ A zygote is a single fertilized egg cell.

❷ A blastocyst stem cell can differentiate into any cell contained in a human being.

❸ A neural stem cell is a cell that can become a spinal neuron cell.

❹ This process may be used to repair spinal cord injuries that cause paralysis.

GED Practice

❶ ② Messages travel from the axon of one neuron to the synapse with the dendrites of another neuron.

❷ ④ In the brain the majority of cells are neurons.

❸ ⑤ You cannot tell from the drawing that a virus can stay inactive for years.

Skill 12, pages 44–45

Reading Selection

❶ A dominant gene determines the effect of a gene pair.

❷ A blue-eyed child must be Bl Bl (two blue-eye genes).

❹ The family may have two children with brown eyes and two with blue eyes, or three with brown eyes and one with blue eyes, or three with blue eyes and one with brown eyes. However, all four could be brown-eyed or all four could be blue-eyed. Each time a child is conceived, he or she has all the gene combination possibilities available.

GED Practice

❶ ⑤ Gorillas and horses are the most different, so their genes are very different also.

❷ ④ The best summary is: Genes carry the hereditary messages that determine inherited traits.

❸ ③ The best evidence would be provided by identical twins separated at birth and raised in different families.

❹ ① Favorite sport is not an inheritable trait.

❺ ② Both parents are brown-eyed (Br Bl).

❻ ④ A blue-eyed child must have a Bl Bl gene pair.

❼ ⑤ If the parents have only brown-eye and blue-eye genes, it's not likely that their child will have green eyes.

Skill 13, pages 46–47

Reading Selection

❶ A carrot belongs to Kingdom Plantae.

❷ A mouse belongs to Kingdom Animalia.

❸ A bat would feed its young with mammary glands and protect its young from predators.

GED Practice

❶ ④ Scientists were making observations of animals in the wild.

❷ ② Chimpanzees have toolmaking skills once thought to belong only to humans.

❸ ② A monkey is a primate.

❹ ④ Lungs are not shown developing in these drawings. In fact, the fish will not have lungs.

❺ ① The drawings do not show that birds are closely related to fish. The third stage shows a great difference between fish and birds and a slight similarity between birds and humans.

Skill 14, pages 48–49

Reading Selection

❶ Nerve tissue provides the sensation of taste by carrying signals from the taste buds to the brain.

❷ Epithelial tissue, which covers the skin and lining of body organs, is the first defense against bacteria.

❸ The nose and ear are made of cartilage.

❹ Muscle tissue lets you raise your arm.

❺ Nerve tissue enables you to see.

❻ Nerve tissue is damaged in spinal cord injuries.

GED Practice

❶ ② Carrots are vegetable biennials that are harvested for the roots they produce in the first year.

❷ ① Pea plants are annuals because they die after one season.

❸ ③ A warbler would perch, or sit on a tree branch.

❹ ② A hawk would grasp, or pick up animals with its feet.

❺ ④ A and D (wading and swimming birds) would get their food from water.

❻ ⑤ The drawings would have the least relevance in a study dealing with the flying ability of birds.

Skill 15, pages 50–51

Reading Selection

❶ A monkey uses its tail for climbing; a crocodile uses its tail for swimming.

❷ Elephants' ears are used to regulate body temperature. It is also possible they are used to create noise for communication.

❸ The green tree frog's color enables it to hide in foliage.

GED Practice

❶ ⑤ A vestigial organ does not have a known use.

❷ ① Vestigial organs evolved from useful organs. This hypothesis is a possible explanation that cannot be proved at this time.

❸ ③ The tailbone is vestigial because we have no use for a tail.

❹ ① The incisors are used for biting off pieces.

❺ ④ The molars are used for chewing tough meat.

❻ ② The canines are very prominent in cats and dogs.

Skill 16, pages 52–53

Reading Selection

1 When a hyena screams at a lion, it is fighting back.

2 Quills provide a protective outer layer for the porcupine.

3 A blackbird is running away from the car horn.

GED Practice

1 ③ The mouse is showing self-preservation when it ran from the cat.

2 ② Building a nest is instinct.

3 ④ The parakeet has learned this behavior. This is conditioned response.

4 ② The dog is showing his instinct by chasing the cat.

5 ③ The cat is showing self-preservation.

6 ⑤ Learning to play checkers or any game is intelligent behavior.

7 ② Animals that live underground cannot use the sense of sight.

Skill 17, pages 54–55

Reading Selection

1 Thomas Malthus made the point that our food supply cannot keep up with uncontrolled population growth.

2 Malthus thought the best solution was limiting the population growth.

3 Malthus predicted widespread starvation, epidemic diseases, and war if population growth was not limited.

GED Practice

1 ② For population to increase, a country's birth rate must be greater than the death rate.

2 ④ The most sensible way of dealing with population is widespread family planning.

3 ③ If a country is dealing with overpopulation, it would not be concerned about increasing consumer product choices.

4 ⑤ The graph shows that life expectancies of women were greater than life expectancies of men.

5 ① Between 1900 and 2000, the life expectancy of women increased more than the life expectancy of men.

Skill 18, pages 56–57

Reading Selection

1 Renewable resources can be replaced in a short time; nonrenewable resources cannot.

2 Answers will vary.

3 Answers will vary.

GED Practice

1 ④ Savings in manufacturing costs is not a general advantage of recycling. In fact, it can be expensive to use recycled products.

2 ② Incineration, or the burning of waste products, would add to our air pollution.

3 ⑤ It would be pointless to recycle old wooden fence posts.

4 ① Paper is the largest component of our garbage (46 percent).

5 ③ Glass makes up 10 percent and metals make up 8 percent for a total of 18 percent.

6 ④ Food, wood, and grass make up 29 percent of solid waste.

Skill 19, pages 58–59

Reading Selection

1 An ecosystem is a community of organisms living together and dependent on one another.

2 A community of organisms lives in a habitat.

3 A food chain is the dietary interdependence of organisms in an ecosystem.

❹ The frog population will likely increase and that will result in a decrease in the insect population.

GED Practice

❶ ① "Competition for limited resources" means the scarcity of resources that many species need for survival.

❷ ③ A stable ecosystem is one in which the size of each population remains constant.

❸ ⑤ A hurricane cannot occur in the Rockies, so it cannot upset the ecosystem there.

❹ ④ The hawk is at the top of the food chain and is not eaten by any other organism.

❺ ① Chemical spraying would cause a decrease in grasshoppers, which would cause a decrease in frogs. The decrease in frogs would cause a decrease in snakes.

Skill 20, pages 60–61

Reading Selection

❶ Ecology is the study of the distribution of organisms on Earth and their relationships to their environment.

❷ Rain forests provide oxygen (the gas we breathe) into the atmosphere.

❸ At the present, the greatest threat to rain forests is logging and agricultural clearance.

GED Practice

❶ ④ "Endangered species" means a species in danger of extinction.

❷ ② The giant panda is most closely related to the black bear.

❸ ⑤ Land value does not provide environment for plants and animals. The value of the land for humans actually decreases the amount of land available for plants and animals.

❹ ④ Because of acid rain, tree growth is decreased.

❺ ① The sulfur in acid rain most likely comes from impurity contained in fossil fuels.

❻ ③ A volcanic eruption would naturally cause acid rain by putting pollutants into the air and clouds.

Skill 21, pages 62–63

Reading Selection

❶ Answers will vary.

❷ Answers will vary. Any of the actions mentioned in the bulleted list are correct.

❸ Child labor laws, better nutrition, vaccinations against disease, workplace safety, advances in medicine, and public awareness all contributed to increased life expectancy.

GED Practice

❶ ⑤ The mice who were not overfed lived longer and were healthier.

❷ ③ The mice with limited food lived longer, so the aging process was slowed down.

❸ ② Size of food trays makes no difference for the health or life expectancy of the mice.

❹ ① Having sufficient vitamins and minerals does not support the idea of overeating and poor health.

❺ ③ The human body needs a variety of vitamins. The chart does not explain which vitamin is most important or the difference between milligrams and micrograms.

Skill 22, pages 64–65

Reading Selection

❶ Answers will vary.

❷ Answers will vary.

GED Practice

❶ ④ A small number of people may get the disease for which they are vaccinated.

❷ ② The opinion that all vaccinations should be halted until vaccines can be made perfectly safe can be neither proved nor disproved.

❸ ⑤ If antibodies fight pathogens, then pathogens must be something that cause disease.

❹ ③ The immune system remembers an invading pathogen (from a vaccination or from a previous bout of the disease), so reaction to a second exposure is slight.

Skill 23, pages 66–67

Reading Selection

❶ Answers will vary.

❷ Possible answers include: have a ready supply of drinking water and food, have a battery-powered radio and flashlights.

GED Practice

❶ ② People need rescue and movement to a safe location before any of the other items listed.

❷ ④ Before a powerful hurricane, the safest thing to do is to move to a safe location. A category 5 hurricane can destroy everything.

❸ ③ The purpose of the Red Cross is to help victims of disaster.

❹ ① Officials must warn citizens and provide them with a safe haven or with a way to leave the danger zone.

❺ ⑤ This disaster was most likely caused by a tornado.

❻ ① Of the choices listed, the only one that is not a health or safety issue is lack of property insurance.

Skill 24, pages 68–69

Reading Selection

❶ Toxic chemicals may cause increased risk of cancer, reproductive problems, genetic damage, and birth defects.

❷ The Superfund Law holds polluters liable for health problems created by their pollution.

❸ Answers will vary.

GED Practice

❶ ⑤ The main danger from a nuclear power plant accident is lethal radiation poisoning.

❷ ② People who have been exposed to radiation my develop cancer many years later.

❸ ④ Workers involved in cleaning up the Chernobyl plant after the accident would be exposed to radiation over a long period of time.

❹ ③ The skull and crossbones show that the paint thinner is poisonous.

❺ ① Household products can create both health and safety risks.

Skill 25, pages 70–71

Reading Selection

❶ Answers will vary.

GED Practice

❶ ③ King said, "Science gives man knowledge."

❷ ② King said, "Religion gives man wisdom."

❸ ④ Scientists should not be secretive.

❹ ⑤ The polio vaccine was discovered in the early 1950s and inoculations were begun in 1955, so scientists would not be researching polio vaccines now.

❺ ① A scientist concerned about the effects of smoking is concerned about community health.

6 ② A tobacco company scientist could be concerned about his personal job security.

7 ⑤ Scientists have very little control over how scientific discoveries are used by society.

Skill 26, pages 72–73

Reading Selection

1 A fossil is the remains or traces of an ancient living thing.

2 Any two answers among those listed in the bulleted list are correct.

3 Half-life of carbon-14 is the time (5,730 years) it takes for half the remaining amount of carbon-14 in an organism to disappear.

GED Practice

1 ① According to the passage, life on Earth most likely started in a water environment.

2 ③ The passage says that early mammals were on Earth at the same time as dinosaurs.

3 ④ The statement is someone's opinion.

4 ⑤ The most likely age is 100,000,000 years because dinosaurs lived from 300 to 70 million years ago.

5 ② The backbone is the same as the spinal column.

6 ③ Of the pairs of animals in the list, only ducks and alligators lay eggs.

Skill 27, pages 74–75

Reading Selection

1 Dr. Christian Bernard performed the first heart transplant.

2 The number of heart transplants is limited by the number of available organ donors.

3 Answers will vary.

GED Practice

1 ③ IMRT is used to kill cancer cells.

2 ② IMRT targets specific cancer cells rather than all cells in the targeted area.

3 ⑤ Traditional radiation may damage non-cancerous cells and organs.

4 ② Blood pressure measures the pressure that blood exerts on the walls of arteries.

5 ④ The blood pressure reading is 125/75.

Skill 28, pages 76–77

Reading Selection

1 Insects and worms are most often seen in rotting soil.

2 It is surprising both that he knew as much as he did and that his ideas were considered correct for more than 1,400 years.

3 He would think the liver was diseased because he thought the liver was the main circulatory organ. He believed it moved blood to the outer skin where more skin was formed to replace the burned skin.

4 Harvey disproved some of Galen's theories, so he probably identified the heart as the main organ of the circulatory system.

GED Practice

1 ④ Lamarck believed giraffes grew long necks as a result of a lack of vegetation near the ground.

2 ③ The weight lifter worked to develop his muscle tone and cannot pass that on to his offspring.

3 ④ The cloth would keep flies away from the meat so that Redi could determine if the meat by itself would create maggots.

4 ① Maggots appear on rotting meat only after hatching from fly eggs.

Skill 29, pages 78–79

Reading Selection

1 Helium is a gas; hot tea is a liquid; a shell is a solid; a dinner plate is a solid; chicken broth is a liquid; milk is a liquid; a spoon is a solid; gasoline is a liquid; air is a gas; a newspaper is a solid.

GED Practice

1 ② At room temperature, toothpaste has the greatest viscosity of all the listed fluids.

2 ⑤ A liquid can have more or less viscosity depending on its temperature.

3 ② If two liquids are at the same temperature, their viscosity depends on the strength of chemical bonds.

4 ④ Dissolved salt changes pure water into a conductor of electricity. Electricity from the battery flows through the salt water to light the bulb.

5 ① When you are sweating, your skin will conduct electricity more easily because of the salt in your sweat.

Skill 30, pages 80–81

Reading Selection

1 Carbon is found in all organisms on Earth.

2 Organic chemistry is the study of molecules that contain carbon, also known as the chemistry of life.

3 Carbon and water are important for life on Earth. They have also been found on Mars.

4 Answers will vary.

GED Practice

1 ② All isomers have the same number of carbon atoms.

2 ④ The difference is in the arrangement of carbon atoms.

3 ⑤ Gasoline is the main petroleum product used in the U.S.

4 ③ 59 percent of petroleum is used in the production of diesel fuel, jet fuel, and gasoline for transportation.

Skill 31, pages 82–83

Reading Selection

1 Combustion is a chemical change.

2 Fuel, heat, and oxygen are necessary for combustion.

3 Heat and light energy are given off during a fire.

4 Water removes heat from the fire.

GED Practice

1 ② Neither chemical change can be reversed. The burned match and the toasted bread cannot be returned to their original forms.

2 ③ Eating the toast will produce additional changes as the body digests the toast.

3 ⑤ Place the nail in a cool, wet place. Water will initiate the chemical change.

4 ① Toasting the bread with sugar on it will make the sugar change chemically.

5 ④ Hydrogen and oxygen are the two gases present in water that are involved in electrolysis. H is hydrogen and O is oxygen.

6 ③ Electrolysis is a chemical reaction in which water is broken down into oxygen and hydrogen.

7 ② A higher voltage battery would cause more current to flow and increase the rate at which water is breaking down into hydrogen and oxygen gases.

Skill 32, pages 84–85

Reading Selection

❶ Fermentation of alcohol is an exothermic reaction. Heat is given off during fermentation.

❷ Photosynthesis is an endothermic reaction. Light energy is needed for photosynthesis to take place.

GED Practice

❶ ③ Activation energy is the energy needed to start a chemical reaction.

❷ ④ A lit fire in a fireplace requires activation energy to start the fire. Then it sustains itself and no more energy needs to be added.

❸ ② Heat starts the process of lighting a candle.

❹ ④ Without a needed activation energy, a reaction will not begin.

❺ ⑤ Cooking an egg is an endothermic reaction in which heat energy is supplied by the water.

❻ ① This is activation energy being used to start an exothermic reaction. Once the candle is lit, light and heat energy are released.

Skill 33, pages 86–87

Reading Selection

❶ A solution is a mixture of one or more substances dissolved in another substance.

❷ Solute is the substance that is dissolved; solvent is the substance that dissolves the solute.

❸ The sand does not remain in solution. Sand does not dissolve in water.

❹ A solution is saturated when no more solute can be dissolved.

GED Practice

❶ ④ A solid (the punch mix) is dissolved in a liquid (water).

❷ ③ A gas (carbon dioxide) is dissolved in a liquid (water).

❸ ① The water is saturated with sugar. There is so much sugar that no more will dissolve in the water.

❹ ⑤ The sweetness of the water will not change because no more sugar will dissolve in the water.

❺ ③ If more water is added, more sugar can be dissolved, resulting in less sugar on the bottom of the glass.

Skill 34, pages 88–89

Reading Selection

❶ Spontaneous generation is a theory that living organisms sometimes arise from nonliving matter.

❷ The Miller-Urey experiment showed that early Earth could have produced amino acids from a mixture of nonliving chemicals activated by an energy source.

GED Practice

❶ ③ Milk is pasteurized by boiling it to kill harmful bacteria. It was discovered that bacteria could be killed by boiling.

❷ ② Medical instruments are sterilized to kill microbes possibly present on the instruments before surgery.

❸ ⑤ The diagram does not mention nitrogen, so it was not important to Oparin.

❹ ④ An atmosphere containing methane comes first in this diagram of Oparin's theory.

❺ ④ Oparin hypothesized that the first cells formed in pools of water, which he called organic pools.

❻ ① Oparin's theory attempts to explain how the first living cells may have been created on primitive Earth.

Skill 35, pages 90–91

Reading Selection

❶ You should not swallow a household cleanser or get it on your skin.

❷ The juice will taste less acidic, less tart. The soda will neutralize the acid.

❸ Both water and baking soda can be used for safety. The water can wash off any acid spilled on your skin; the baking soda can be used to neutralize any spilled acid.

GED Practice

❶ ① Carbon monoxide gas is *not* smelly.

❷ ② Carbon monoxide gas is produced when fossil fuels such as coal, oil, or gasoline are burned.

❸ ③ Starting a car in a closed garage would keep the carbon monoxide gas enclosed in a small area.

❹ ④ Carbon monoxide keeps oxygen from being absorbed so it would cause death by lack of oxygen.

❺ ① Orange juice is acidic so its pH level might be 6. The other levels listed are all bases.

❻ ⑤ An antacid is a base so it must have a pH greater than 7.

❼ ② If it reacts with an acid to produce harmless byproducts, it is a base.

Skill 36, pages 92–93

Reading Selection

❶ Alchemists tried to turn different metals into gold; they also tried to find a way to stop aging.

❷ Democritus thought the size and arrangement of atoms made the difference between things such as taste.

GED Practice

❶ ③ Urea is an organic substance created by living organisms.

❷ ⑤ Wohler discovered that organic substances can be made from nonorganic substances.

❸ ① Other scientists were probably surprised because they had thought that organic substances could be made only from other organic substances.

❹ ③ Rutherford's model looks similar to the solar system.

❺ ④ Ancient Greeks imagined the atom as a solid sphere. Now we view it as an unusual mathematical system.

Skill 37, pages 94–95

Reading Selection

❶ The law of acceleration says a heavier object requires more force to throw than a lighter object.

❷ A wall socket provides electric current (120 volts alternating at 60 cycles per second).

❸ Lightning is an example of static electricity with positive and negative changes separated in the atmosphere.

GED Practice

❶ ③ The law of gravitation says nothing about the nature of light (colors of the rainbow).

❷ ④ The gravitational force between electrons is much weaker than the electrical force. The stronger electrical force causes the electrons to repel each other.

❸ ⑤ The flowing water pushes against the curving end of the sprinkler head, causing it to rotate.

❹ ② Increasing the rate at which water is flowing would cause more pressure to be placed on the rotating head.

⑤ ③ The sprinkler demonstrates the law of interaction: for every action there is an equal and opposite reaction.

Skill 38, pages 96–97

Reading Selection

① The Sun and Earth's hot interior are the two sources of energy for Earth.

② Energy is unlike a substance because energy is a property that cannot be touched.

GED Practice

① ④ Heat is the energy of movement of atoms and molecules.

② ② Heat will flow from the hot iron to the cold water until both are the same temperature.

③ ① Energy is carried in an electric circuit by a moving stream of electrons in the copper wire.

④ ⑤ All five of the listed forms of energy take part in the electric circuit. Chemical energy in the battery creates electrical energy which flows through the wires to create sound and heat energy in the ringer and light and heat energy in the lightbulb.

Skill 39, pages 98–99

Reading Selection

① The law of conservation of energy says that during an interaction, energy may change forms, but no energy is lost.

② Halfway to the floor, the book has an equal amount of kinetic energy and potential energy.

GED Practice

① ② During photosynthesis, light energy is changed to chemical energy—the energy stored in plant sugar.

② ② When you are sitting in the sunshine, sunlight is absorbed by your skin and changes to heat energy that warms you.

③ ⑤ The kinetic energy of the ball becomes energy used to break apart the building. Some of the energy becomes sound and heat.

④ ④ The girl's motion will be stopped by a combination of air friction and friction caused by metal swing parts rubbing.

⑤ ① Halfway, the girl has both kinetic and potential energy.

Skill 40, pages 100–101

Reading Selection

① Constancy is the tendency for certain things to remain unchanged. One example is the law of gravity.

② Cyclical change occurs over and over again. Evolutionary change occurs slowly and does not repeat.

GED Practice

① ③ In a state of equilibrium, change takes place in equal but opposite ways.

② ⑤ To maintain a constant human body temperature, the body continually adjusts to internal and external temperature variations.

③ ① Your weight would slowly increase to maintain the equilibrium between your body and the gravity.

④ ② The average energy of each gas molecule becomes equal. The energy of the molecules is shown in the diagram by the length of the arrows.

⑤ ④ The flow of heat made it possible for the average energy of each molecule to become equal.

Skill 41, pages 102–103

Reading Selection

① Technology is the production of products used to solve human problems and provide for human needs and wishes.

② Science is a search for understanding of the natural world.

③ The invention of computers has led to the reduced use of typewriters, both in the workplace and at home.

GED Practice

① ④ A major concern about rapid technological advance is the conflict between new knowledge and personal values.

② ① The main concern about the development of nuclear weapons is their possible use in war.

③ ③ The purpose of a photovoltaic cell is to change light energy into electrical energy.

④ ⑤ A solar-powered calculator uses a photovoltaic cell.

⑤ ① Increasing the number of solar panels would result in an increase in electric current. This will result in a more brightly glowing lightbulb.

Skill 42, pages 104–105

Reading Selection

① The invention of the telescope and the microscope helped start the Scientific Revolution.

② Newton believed that the Sun was at the center of all celestial objects.

③ Newton proved that sunlight is made up of a spectrum of colors.

GED Practice

① ④ Thales most likely based his theory on his observation of the surface of the sea near Greece.

② ③ Thales was not able to determine the distance of the Moon from Earth.

③ ⑤ Thales believed that water was the universal element.

④ ④ Archimedes' discovery is an important factor in both A and B: the design of a submarine and the anatomy of a fish. Both are immersed in liquid.

⑤ ① The weight of the displaced water is equal to the weight of the object.

⑥ ② Benjamin Franklin was trying to learn more about the nature of electricity.

Skill 43, pages 106–107

Reading Selection

① Earth is approximately 4.6 billion years old.

② Earth most likely developed from the collapse of a huge cloud of gas and dust called the solar nebula.

③ Most scientists think that the Moon was formed from part of Earth that was ejected during a collision with an asteroid.

GED Practice

① ④ The proposed model tries to explain why inner planets are made up of heavy elements and outer planets are gaseous.

② ② As the nebula was compressed, gravity overcame the pressure of hot gases.

③ ③ The outer planets were formed mainly from hydrogen, the lightest of all elements.

④ ③ The diagram shows the distribution of elements within Earth's core.

⑤ ⑤ The Moon was probably a molten sphere of liquid elements ejected from the surface of Earth during an asteroid collision.

6 ① The Moon is made of the same elements found on Earth's surface.

Skill 44, pages 108–109

Reading Selection

1 Earthquakes, volcanoes, tornadoes, and tsunamis bring about rapid, violent changes in Earth's surface features.

2 Soil is a mixture of tiny rock fragments and organic materials.

3 Weathering can cause both physical changes and chemical changes.

4 Possible answer: Erosion occurs along ocean beaches, in deserts, in river canyons, and on mountains or hillsides.

GED Practice

1 ④ Patterns in sand high on a beach are mainly caused by wind erosion, although water erosion may also play a lesser role.

2 ② When an acid breaks down a rock, chemical weathering is occurring.

3 ⑤ The Snake River Canyon was carved mainly by water erosion.

4 ⑤ Water erosion results from the waves at high and low tide. Physical weathering results in the crumbling of the cliff rocks.

5 ③ As the cliff is eroded, more beach is created.

6 ③ This illustration shows changes caused to ocean shorelines by the action of ocean tides.

Skill 45, pages 110–111

Reading Selection

1 A geochemical cycle is the movement of elements from one chemical storehouse to another.

2 Limestone, marble, and chalk all contain calcium carbonate.

GED Practice

1 ④ All phosphates contain phosphorous.

2 ③ Garden fertilizer is rich in phosphates because plants need phosphates for growth.

3 ① The death and decay of organisms enable the movement of phosphorous back to the ocean and back to the soil, which eventually may become rock.

4 ④ The source of energy that drives the water cycle is sunshine.

5 ⑤ Clouds form from water vapor in the air condensing into water droplets.

6 ② The oceans are Earth's greatest storehouse of water.

Skill 46, pages 112–113

Reading Selection

1 The greenhouse effect is the heating of Earth's atmosphere by sunlight together with insulating and warming effect of Earth's atmosphere.

2 Global warming is the slow increase in the temperature of Earth's atmosphere.

3 Scientists believe that air pollution is one cause of global warming.

4 Both Venus and Earth have a solid surface of minerals and an atmosphere.

GED Practice

1 ① Global warming could result in the slow melting of polar ice caps.

2 ③ A scientist studying global warming would not likely be studying any change in efforts to protect polar bears from extinction.

3 ⑤ Tropical rain forests play a role in maintaining Earth's normal temperature range by helping reduce excess carbon dioxide gas in the atmosphere.

❹ ② The cutting of tropical rain forests could lead to an increase in global warming because of extra carbon dioxide gas in the atmosphere.

Skill 47, pages 114–115

Reading Selection

❶ Fear led ancient peoples to believe in an assortment of gods, giants, and demons to help explain things they couldn't otherwise understand.

❷ Before accurate timepieces were invented, the measurement of time was limited by weather. (The Sun couldn't be seen on cloudy days.)

❸ Accurate timepieces enabled sailors to locate their ocean position.

GED Practice

❶ ⑤ Early Greek thinkers believed Earth has existed forever and has no beginning.

❷ ④ Leclerc used the cooling rate of a hot iron ball as a model for Earth when he determined Earth's age.

❸ ③ Earth's sea level reached its lowest level about 18,000 years ago.

❹ ① The ice age represented by the graph lasted about 35,000 years.

Skill 48, pages 116–117

Reading Selection

❶ In order from the Sun, the planets are Mercury, Venus, Earth, Mars, Jupiter, Saturn, Uranus, Neptune, and Pluto.

❷ The inner planets are the smallest planets; the outer planets are the largest planets.

❸ Stars are composed mainly of hydrogen gas.

❹ The energy in a star comes from hydrogen that converts to helium in a nuclear reaction.

GED Practice

❶ ④ The celestial object that traps light is known as a black hole.

❷ ① A supernova is a flash of light created when a massive star explodes.

❸ ② In a nuclear reaction in a star, two atoms of hydrogen combine to form one atom of helium.

❹ ⑤ The nuclear energy that is released is greater than the heat energy needed to start the reaction.

❺ ④ A star nears the end of its life as all of its hydrogen is converted to helium.

Skill 49, pages 118–119

Reading Selection

❶ The open universe model predicts that the universe will expand forever.

❷ The closed universe model predicts that the universe will eventually collapse.

❸ Evolution is the gradual change that takes place in the universe.

GED Practice

❶ ② According to the big bang theory, the age of the universe is about 14 billion years.

❷ ⑤ Within the first few seconds following the big bang, the elements that make up the universe were formed.

❸ ④ "The big crunch" jokingly refers to the closed universe theory.

❹ ③ As you fill the balloon with air, the dots move farther apart.

❺ ② The dots on the balloon represent galaxies.

❻ ① The balloon represents the universe.

Skill 50, pages 120–121

Reading Selection

❶ The invention of the telescope led to changing views of the universe.

❷ Galileo Galilei is thought to be the first scientist to use a telescope to study celestial objects.

❸ Galileo's discoveries resulted in conflicts between discoveries in science and long-held church teachings.

GED Practice

❶ ③ Mars has a gaseous atmosphere. Polar ice caps and wind are a result of an atmosphere.

❷ ⑤ The greatest jump in understanding Mars occurred as a result of spacecraft landing on Mars.

❸ ② When a planet has an atmosphere, the color of the planet seen through a telescope is the color of light reflected by the planet's atmosphere.

❹ ⑤ Both A and D give the impression to viewers on Earth that the Earth remains still while the Sun revolves around it.

❺ ③ Knowing that planets reflect sunlight, Galileo would have reasoned that this is the reason people on Earth are able to see planets in the night sky.

GED Posttest, pages 124–137

❶ ④ Identical twins are least likely to share favorite color because this is not a genetic trait.

❷ ⑤ The shape of earlobes is an inherited trait. If they have differently shaped earlobes, they must have originated as two separate eggs.

❸ ② Identical twins form when one fertilized egg cell separates into two cells that develop independently.

❹ ③ Newton concluded that the gravitational attraction of the Moon is what gives rise to tides on Earth. This fits with his law of universal gravitation.

❺ ② Spring tides occur two times each month, once at the time of the new moon and once at the time of the full moon.

❻ ③ Bacteria cells do not contain a nucleus, unlike most other plant cells.

❼ ④ Earth's northern regions point to a different part of the universe than do Earth's southern regions.

❽ ⑤ The major problem faced by relief workers in the Kashmir earthquake was getting aid to those who were injured.

❾ ① Oxygen gas is put in high-pressure metal containers because a lot of gas can be stored in relatively small containers.

❿ ② Birds are more closely related to dogs than dogs are to humans.

⓫ ④ The formation of life depends on each of the other listed items, but not on a source of hydrogen gas. This gas is not considered a critical building block of life.

⓬ ⑤ Volcanoes contributed gases to the developing atmosphere.

⓭ ② Material below Earth's crust moves through the crust onto Earth's surface.

⓮ ③ The source of energy that is responsible for volcanic eruptions is heat energy from Earth's core.

⓯ ① Feldspar is the only mineral listed that can scratch glass. It has a hardness rating of 6 or more.

⓰ ③ The statement "Diamonds are the prettiest of all minerals" is an opinion even though diamonds have that reputation.

⓱ ④ The Moon rotates once on its axis in the same length of time it takes the Moon to make one trip around Earth. One rotation means that the same side is always facing Earth.

18 (5) A couple may choose in vitro fertilization instead of adoption because of a desire to have a child that is genetically their own.

19 (2) A pandemic is different from other forms of community health problems because of the extent, seriousness, and speed of transmission of the illness.

20 (1) An unstated assumption is that the avian influenza virus can jump from an animal host (birds) to humans.

21 (4) The best way for humans to address the problem of global warming is to reduce our dependence on all types of fossil fuels. Each of the other choices would reduce global warming in one way, but (4) would reduce it in several ways.

22 (5) Global warming is a societal problem and addressing it is a societal need. Driving one's own car may give a sense of personal freedom, but it only adds to the global warming problem, especially when public transportation is available.

23 (4) A real missing-link fossil would show similarities between a human skull and an ape skull.

24 (1) Dawson most likely was responding to a need for professional recognition when he perpetrated the Piltdown Man hoax.

25 (3) The Piltdown Man hoax went undetected for years because of inadequate dating techniques. After the dating techniques were developed, the hoax was revealed.

26 (2) To determine the number of hydrogen atoms in a polymer, multiply the number of carbon atoms by 2 and add 2.

27 (3) When ice melts, no new substances are formed; melting is a physical change. All of the other reactions are chemical changes.

28 (5) In endothermic reactions, such as ice melting and ozone creation, energy is used up as the process continues.

29 (4) A sailor must assume that Polaris stays in the same position in the sky at all hours of the night—which it does.

30 (1) Sublimation is the name given to the process in which a solid evaporates directly to the gas phase without first becoming a liquid.

31 (2) The rate of dissolving increases with increasing temperature.

32 (3) In the *Exxon Valdez* oil spill, most birds died because of an inability to escape the polluted ocean surface and nearby beaches after their wings became soaked with oil.

33 (5) A goal of science, but not necessarily of technology, is to determine if life ever existed on Mars. The other goals are all technology related.

34 (3) A fresh orange is an excellent source of vitamin C.

35 (2) Widespread scurvy among sailors in ancient times was related to the difficulty of storing fresh fruit on board during a long sail.

36 (3) Specular reflection can occur on the surface of a lake, but only as long as that surface is smooth without ripples or waves.

37 (4) About 1.1 million species exist on Earth. (790,000 + 243,000 + 47,000 = 1,080,000)

38 (4) A black hole appears as a dark void in the sky. The presence of a black hole must be inferred from what isn't seen.

39 (5) The ducks respond to the cracker hitting the water by swimming toward it.

40 (3) The stimulus always occurs before the response. The purpose of the response is survival of the organism.

41 (2) The car stops; the driver keeps going, stopped only by impact with the steering wheel, dashboard, and windshield. The body stays in forward motion until it hits something that stops it.

42 ④ At impact, the driver's energy is transferred to the car through the seat belt and the airbag. That transfer of energy may save the driver's life.

43 ② Drinking alcohol can affect both normal body functions, such as walking and driving, and behavior, such as abnormal emotional reactions.

44 ⑤ The African savannah elephant lives in a much warmer habitat than the Asian elephant. You can infer this because the African elephant's ears are larger.

45 ③ Both species of elephants show the adaptive behavior of periodic flapping of ears—a behavior that helps elephants keep cool.

46 ① Human activity can help cause or can help prevent extinction of human beings. The writer implies that our care of the environment will determine whether or not we survive.

47 ④ The presence of many insect species along the shore of the lake is not likely to limit trout population in the lake. In fact, it might increase the population by providing more food.

48 ③ The long-term health of fish in the lake will be most directly affected by any water that flows into the lake that may bring pollution with it. The Long Tom River might bring pollution since it flows into the lake.

49 ⑤ Fern Lake will be an ecosystem where a stable average number of trout can coexist with stable average numbers of other organisms. When the trout capacity is reached, that number should remain nearly constant unless some disaster occurs.

50 ② Of the listed activities, waterskiing on the lake is most apt to be a source of water pollution. Water skiing is done with power boats, increasing the likelihood of oil and gasoline spills directly into lake water. Power boats would also create noise pollution which might decrease the number of fish.

Foundations of Science

Structure of Matter, pages 140–143

❶ Oxygen and gold are elements.

❷ Water is a molecule.

❸ Water is made of hydrogen and oxygen.

❹ The three main elements in every living organism are hydrogen, oxygen, and carbon.

❺ The three particles of an atom are proton, neutron, and electron.

❻ Electrons are held in orbit by an electrical force.

❼ In NH_3, there are 1 atom of N (nitrogen) and 3 atoms of H (hydrogen).

❽ There are 4 molecules of C_3H_8 (propane gas).

❾ $2 NH_3$ begins with 1 molecule of N_2 (nitrogen), and 2 molecules of NH_3 (ammonia) are formed.

Cell Theory of Life, pages 144–145

❶ The cell is the basic unit of life. All organisms are made of one or more cells. All cells come from existing cells.

❷ ① Nucleolus

② cell wall

③ cell membrane

④ chromatin

⑤ chlorophyll

Living Things, pages 146–149

❶ The five stages of the life cycle are the beginning stage, growth, maturity, decline, and death.

❷ The principle of biogenesis says that living things come only from the reproduction of other living things.

❸ A polar bear has long whitish fur to keep it warm and to provide camouflage.

4 Possible answer: Humans have a highly developed brain and can adapt to many different situations and environments.

5 The root system holds most plants firmly in the soil. The roots are also used to obtain water and nutrients from the soil.

6 Skin is the protective tissue covering the human body.

7 The heart pumps blood, the brain thinks, and the lungs breathe.

8 This is a commensual relationship.

9 This is a parasitic relationship.

Molecular Basis of Heredity, pages 150–151

1 DNA is the chemical substance within a cell that controls all cellular activity. DNA is a set of coded instructions made up of chemical compounds.

2 Answers may include eye color, hair color, body shape, or earlobe shape.

Biological Evolution, pages 152–153

1 Answers will vary.

Structure of Earth, pages 154–156

1 29 percent is land and 71 percent is water.

2 The inner core is solid iron; the outer core is melted iron.

3 The radius of the Earth is about 4,000 miles.

4 Plate tectonics is the theory that Earth's crust is made up of separate pieces that move on the surface of the mantle.

5 Oxygen, nitrogen, and carbon dioxide are the three gases necessary for life on Earth.

Earth in Space, pages 157–159

1 The solar system includes the Sun and the nine planets, their moons, the belt of asteroids, and other objects that orbit the Sun.

2 ① Asteroids are comparatively small rocky objects that orbit the Sun.

② Meteors are streaks of light in the night sky, caused by small asteroids burning in Earth's atmosphere.

③ Meteorites are fragments of asteroids that reach the ground.

④ A galaxy is a large grouping of stars.

3 The Copernican theory says that the Sun is at the center of the solar system with Earth and other planets in orbit around it.

Glossary

activation energy the energy needed to enable a chemical reaction to take place

adaptation a physical or behavioral characteristic particularly suited for survival in an organism's environment

air resistance friction caused by air on a body moving through the air

asexual reproduction a method of reproduction in which an organism is produced from a single egg

asteroid any of the very small celestial bodies that orbit the Sun, mainly between Mars and Jupiter

astronomy the study of all celestial bodies in the universe

atmosphere the blanket of air that surrounds Earth

atom the smallest part of an element that can exist on its own

axis an imaginary line running through Earth's center from the North Pole to the South Pole around which the Earth rotates

behavior an organism's actions or reactions to its environment

big bang theory the idea that the universe began with an explosion of a dense, hot, compact mass under extreme pressure

binary fission a method of reproduction in which a cell simply divides into two new cells

biodegradable organic materials that naturally decay

biodiversity a healthy variety of plant and animal species that coexist in an environment and make the environment more stable

biogenesis the principle that living things only come from other living things

biology the study of all living things

bioremediation the removal of polluting substances by the action of microorganisms

black hole the collapsed leftover of a supernova; a black hole is believed to be the most massive (dense) object in the universe

botany the study of plants

calorie a measure of food energy

camouflage a coloring pattern that enables an animal to blend into its surroundings and not be seen by predators

carbohydrate the main source of food energy, made up of starches and sugars

cell the basic unit of life

cell membrane the soft, flexible covering that holds a cell together and separates it from other cells

cell specialization the process in which the cells of an organism develop in different shapes, structures, and functions

cell wall a tough, flexible covering that surrounds the cell membrane of a plant cell

chemical change a change that produces a new substance

chemical equation a shorthand way of describing what happens in a chemical reaction

chemical weathering the softening and crumbling of rock brought about by chemical change

chlorophyll the green substance in a plant cell that is used to capture light energy

chloroplast an organelle in a plant cell that contains chlorophyll

chromosome a group of genes that carries genetic information for various traits

cloning the process of creating a genetically identical replica of an organism

cold-blooded a classification of an organism that cannot control its own internal body temperature

comet a small object made of dust and frozen gas that orbits in a predictable path around the Sun

compound a group of molecules that each contain the atoms of two or more elements

conductor a material in which electrons can be made to flow

conservation the controlled use and preservation of natural resources

continental drift the movement of continents

convection currents currents of molten rock within the mantle, some carrying heat to Earth's surface

convergent evolution the process whereby unrelated organisms develop similar structures

Copernican theory the idea that the Sun is at the center of the solar system

crustal plates the exterior layer of Earth's crust (surface); also called tectonic plates

cytoplasm a jellylike fluid of water, salt, minerals, and many types of organic molecules that are essential to all life processes

density the amount of matter per unit of volume

digestion the breaking down of food into nutrients that an organism's cells can use

DNA a large, complex molecule formed by chains of chemical compounds

dominant gene one gene in a gene pair that determines the effect of the gene pair

ecology the study of the relationship of organisms to their environment

ecosystem a community of populations of organisms and the habitats and natural resources that affect the community

egg the female sex cell

electric current the flow of electrons in a material

electric force the force that holds electrons in orbit around the nucleus of an atom

electromagnetic wave a wave that can travel through a vacuum

electron a particle with a negative electric charge that orbits the nucleus of an atom

element a pure substance composed of identical atoms

embryo an organism in its early stage of development

environment all the living and nonliving things that affect an organism's life in some way

epidemic the rapid spread of an infectious disease through an entire population

erosion the natural movement of rock fragments over the surface of Earth

evolution a series of changes that occur over time

extinction the dying off of an entire plant or animal species

fetus the pre-birth stage of some animals

fission the splitting of the nucleus of an atom

flower the part of a plant in which reproduction occurs

food chain the interdependence of organisms for food

force any push or pull that can affect an object either in motion or at rest

fossil trace remains of an organism of a past geological age

fossil fuels fuels, such as petroleum, coal, and natural gas, that are used to produce energy for industrialized societies

fraternal twins two children who develop from two eggs fertilized by two sperm during the same reproductive cycle

friction a force that slows a moving object

galaxy a large group of stars

gas the phase of matter in which the molecular structure of a substance is relatively loose, allowing atoms to move apart independently of each other

gas cloud a vast cloud of gas and dust out of which a star may form

gene a strand of DNA that carries the information for a specific trait

genetics the study of how characteristics are passed from one organism to another

geothermal energy energy that comes from Earth's hot interior

global warming the overheating of Earth's atmosphere

glucose a simple sugar that is used to produce energy in plants

gravity a force of attraction between every two objects, being greater for objects of greater mass and decreasing with distance between objects

greenhouse effect the natural heating of a planet by the process of atmospheric gases trapping heat energy

habitat a home for community of organisms

heat the energy of moving atoms

homeostasis an organism's tendency to maintain constant internal conditions

humidity the measure of water vapor in the air

hydrocarbon a compound composed of only carbon and hydrogen

hydroelectric power electrical energy formed by the conversion of the energy of flowing water

immune system molecules, cells, and organs that defend an organism against pathogens

inertia the natural resistance of matter to change its state of either motion or rest

insulator material that protects against electric shock

invertebrate an animal without a backbone or skull

ionosphere the region of Earth's atmosphere that reflects radio waves toward the ground

isomers molecules that have the same number of atoms, but whose atoms are arranged in different ways

kinetic energy the energy of motion

landfill a place where solid wastes are buried

law of conservation of energy During any interaction, energy may change from one form to another, but no energy is lost.

laws of motion laws formulated by Isaac Newton that describe the motion of objects under the action of one or more forces

law of nature a property of nature that does not change

law of universal gravitation Every two bodies in the universe attract because of gravitational force, the force depending directly on mass and indirectly on distance.

lever a simple machine in which a small force applied through a large distance at one end results in a large force applied through a small distance at the other end

life cycle the stages of life that all living things go through: beginning, growth, maturity, decline, and death

light the range of electromagnetic wavelengths that humans can visually detect

light-year the distance that light travels in one year; about 6 trillion miles

magnetism a property by which an object may attract and also repel another object

matter anything that has weight and takes up space

metamorphosis the process in which insects and amphibians go through stages of life

meteor a bright streak of light in the night sky caused by a meteoroid burning up as it enters Earth's atmosphere

meteorite a fragment of a meteor that is found on the surface of Earth

migrate to move from one place to another

mitosis the process of cell division

molecule a combination of two or more atoms

multicellular organism an organism that consists of more than one cell

mutation a change in the genetic information within a cell

natural resources resources provided by nature that are available to support life

natural selection the idea that individuals with favorable traits are the most likely members of a species to survive, reproduce, and pass on these traits

nerve impulse electrical signals that travel to and from nerve cells throughout the body

neuron a nerve cell; brain tissue is mostly neurons

nonconductor a material in which electrons cannot be made to flow

nonrenewable resources resources that cannot be replaced or that take hundreds or thousands of years to replace

nuclear force the force that holds neutrons and protons together in the nucleus of an atom

nucleus an organelle that controls the activities of a cell and stores heredity information; the core of an atom

nutrient a food substance an organism can use for tissue growth and repair, as well as for energy

nutrition the study of the health value of food

orbit the path in which a planet travels around the Sun

organ a group of different types of tissue that work together

organ system a group of organs that work together

organelle a specialized structure within the cytoplasm of a cell that performs a special life activity

organism a living thing, plant or animal

osmosis the movement of atoms or molecules across a semi-permeable membrane

ozone a type of oxygen gas that surrounds Earth and absorbs ultraviolet rays

pathogen a harmful bacterium, virus, or fungus that invades the human body

phases of matter the three main forms of a substance: solid, liquid, gas

photosynthesis the process by which a plant changes sunlight, carbon dioxide gas, and water into glucose

physical change a change that does not produce a new substance

planet a celestial body that revolves around the Sun

plate tectonics the theory about the movement of Earth's crustal plates

pollen a grain that contains the male sex cell of a flowering plant

pollination the process by which flowering plants reproduce

pollution any form of contamination that affects the quality of life

population all organisms of one type

potential energy stored energy

polymer a hydrocarbon that contains a large number of carbon atoms

predator an animal that hunts other animals

prey an animal that is hunted by another animal

protein a molecule that is necessary for cell growth and repair and sometimes energy

proton a particle in the nucleus of an atom that has a positive electric charge

punctuated equilibrium a form of rapid evolution in which species suddenly appear or disappear on Earth

radioactivity the property of some types of atoms in which the nuclei are unstable and break apart, releasing particles and high-energy light waves

radioactive waste toxic radioactive elements that are a byproduct of nuclear power plants

reaction rate the speed at which a chemical reaction takes place

recessive gene a gene that has no effect if a dominate gene is present

recycling the breaking down of trash into its component substances and reusing them in new products

reflection the process by which a light, water, or sound wave bounces off a smooth surface

renewable resources resources that can be used and then replaced over a relatively short period of time

reproduction the process by which an organism produces future generations of its own kind

respiration the process in which food sugar is broken down and energy and carbon dioxide gas are released

revolution a planet's complete trip around the Sun; the Moon's complete trip around Earth

scientific method a logical way to perform experiments and to draw conclusions that are supported by all available evidence

sexual reproduction a method of reproduction in which two different sex cells join and produce offspring

social behavior the behavior of animals of the same species as they live together

soil a mixture of tiny rock fragments and organic materials produced by living things

solar cell a device that produces electricity when sunlight strikes it

solar energy energy from sunlight

solar nebula a cloud of interstellar gas and dust from which the solar system is thought to have formed

solar system the system comprised of the Sun and the nine (or more) planets that revolve around it

species a group of organisms that have the same number of chromosomes and display similar traits

sperm the male sex cell

spore a tiny reproductive cell of a plant

static electricity electricity in which electrons are transferred from one object to another, and an electric force is formed without further electron motion

stamen the male reproductive structure in a flowering plant

stem the part of a plant that holds the leaves up toward sunlight and transports water and minerals from the roots to the leaves

stem cells special cells in the early stage of embryonic development that are able to differentiate into different types of cells

stimulus something that causes a change in an organism's behavior

supernova a flash of light caused by the explosion of a massive blue star that has become too hot to be stable

synapse the point of contact between two nerve cells

technology the use of knowledge, materials, and tools to solve human problems and to provide for human needs and wishes

temperature the measure of heat energy; the measure of the warmth of the air in Earth's atmosphere

tissue a collection of similar cells working together

ultraviolet light high-energy light from the Sun that is harmful to life

unicellular organism an organism that consists of a single cell

vacuole a large compartment in a plant cell that stores water and other liquids

vacuum a space that contains no matter

vertebrate an animal with a backbone and a skull

vestigial organ a small or imperfectly developed organ that seems to have no use

virus an infectious agent that can be found in all living organisms

vitamin a chemical necessary for proper body growth, body activity, and the prevention of certain diseases

weathering the breaking down of rock into smaller pieces by natural processes

warm-blooded a classification of animals who can control their own internal body temperature

wave a periodic disturbance that carries energy

wavelength the distance between the highest or lowest points of two adjacent waves

Index